William Bence Jones

The Life's Work in Ireland of a Landlord

who tried to do his duty

William Bence Jones

The Life's Work in Ireland of a Landlord
who tried to do his duty

ISBN/EAN: 9783337324452

Printed in Europe, USA, Canada, Australia, Japan

Cover: Foto ©Suzi / pixelio.de

More available books at **www.hansebooks.com**

THE

LIFE'S WORK IN IRELAND

OF A LANDLORD

WHO TRIED TO DO HIS DUTY

By W. BENCE JONES

OF LISSELAN

London

MACMILLAN AND CO.

1880

PREFACE.

IN reading the following papers I must ask attention to the dates at which they were written, else it may be thought there are differences between them at some points. The subject-matter of all being the same, the same facts are now and then mentioned in different papers in a somewhat different point of view, suggested by the circumstances. Such repetitions could of course have been omitted, but the small differences seemed to give a reality to the whole, and besides, the points repeated are generally the turning-points of the subject.

In order to form a sound judgment, there are several matters that must be borne clearly in mind.

FICTION 1. That all Ireland is alike and in the same hopeless and distressful state. The real difficulty to be met is only in part of Connaught and some other remote and mountainous places, perhaps one-fourth of Ireland. In the rest there is no real difficulty, though the agitation has of course been carried everywhere to try what can be got from it.

FICTION 2. That no landlord has done anything to improve the land or the people, or spent any money for that end.

Many landlords, like myself, have spent very large sums for that end, and with thoroughly satisfactory results in all ways. More expenditure is no doubt wanted.

FICTION 3. That evictions are cruel and equivalent to signing the death-warrant of tenants, who have no choice but the workhouse, there to remain till they die.

Broken tenants are to be met with in every sort of occupation. I have had some who have done thoroughly well, much better than they could have done as farmers. Others are labourers, well off as such. Their children grow up as good as any others. There is not one word of truth in this complaint.

FICTION 4. That tenants in Ireland are too poor to contract freely.

They are the keenest and best bargainers in Europe, and more often get the best of the bargain than the other side does. Jews cannot live in Ireland. They have no chance. Not to hold contracts binding at once opens the door to a flood of mischief. Forty years ago this practice was common in regard to all public contracts. Any one who wished to get a contract took it at any price, and then trusted by the help of his friends to fight through it to advantage by scamping the conditions, or getting increased payment. Till we conquered and routed this system, many of us (all who were honest) lived in a state of declared war with a large part of our neighbours. Since we won the battle, nobody thinks of taking a contract who does not mean to fulfil it.

Lastly, I venture to remind all that there are three such evils in the world as lying, drink, and debt. Unhappily not only have these vices penetrated to the Holy Isle of Ireland, but there is sad reason to believe they took up their permanent abode there and have thriven ever since.

Any tenants who are subject to such bad habits are on the sure road to ruin. Are they to be protected from the effects of their own faults ? or, like the rest of mankind suffering from the same vices, left to the ordinary consequences of these ?

W. BENCE JONES.

December 1, 1880.

THAT which has happened in the few days since the above was written throws so much light on the whole question, that I think it is right to tell it. My rent-day, as usual, was December 7. This was well known to all. It was thought, if I could be driven to accept Griffiths' valuation instead of the rent due, it would be a great triumph, as all knew how well off my tenants are, and the punctuality and ease with which they pay their rent, especially in a thoroughly good season like this.

If I had to give way, others might be more easily coerced.

So a systematic attempt was made. For a week or two before reports were common that my tenants would only pay Griffiths' valuation, and meant to come in a body on the rent-day, to say so.

But as it was known so many were very friendly with me and my family that they were sure to pay, the first step taken by the Land League was to send a notice to the tenants by post, ordering them not to pay more than Griffiths' valuation. On the morning of Friday, December 3, market-day, a threatening notice was found stuck on my hall door, and a hole dug in the grass near, fully three inches deep, as an emblematical grave, in which, the notice said, I and my son were to be buried. Threatening notices were also stuck up about the town of Clonakilty, denouncing all sorts of injuries to any of my tenants who paid more than Griffiths' valuation.

On Saturday morning the Cork *Examiner* and *Herald* had reports of a speech made at Clonakilty the day before at the Land League by the Rev. Father O'Leary, a young priest of the parish; most part of it was mere coarse abuse of me, the sweepings of all the vulgar dislikes for twenty years past in a small town, arising from everything besides land—*e.g.* that as a magistrate I fined a publican, for selling porter on Sunday, more than some approved of, which, as there are more than forty public-houses in the town, is very likely. He luckily condescended to particulars in what he said was oppression of a few tenants, which I will answer farther on. Some one was so ashamed of this speech as wholly discreditable to the Roman Catholic Clergy and Church, that in both papers the speaker was called Mr. O'Leary, instead of Father O'Leary.

Those who take any active part in the Land League in Clonakilty are, in addition to the Priest, only inferior townspeople, or a chance farmer or two, none of whom enjoy any respect from the inhabitants of the neighbourhood.

These threatening notices, I am told, are all written by a shoemaker.

Monday, 6th, there was a Fair, and our tenants at it were again threatened worse than ever, especially those friendly to us. One very old man, who is very rich though paying near three times Griffiths' valuation, and who has long been an actual friend of me and my children, was stopped in the dusk and had some water thrown in his face to make believe it was vitriol, and was urgently threatened.

The 7th was my rent-day. Some men posted themselves in the ruins of an old house, a mile off (not on my land), and, as any tenant came near, ran out and thrust before his eyes a threatening notice.

The tenants assented at the gate. A few, from one reason or other, paid about £100 : about £1300 should have been paid.

In time about six came into my room and offered Griffiths' valuation. The rent of four of them was £100 a year each, or more. Two of them had leases freely taken from me. The other two were yearly tenants, who had held at the same rents for thirty or forty years. The two leaseholders grumbled about high rent. Their rent is £1 per acre for really good land. The other two had nothing to say. They knew, and I knew, they had done capitally out of their land, and that it was worth more than they pay for it.

They begged earnestly I would not think the worse of them for not paying. It was all fear they said. To the whole of them I said, they could go their own way, and I would go mine. They were all civil beyond description, all inquiring affectionately for one of my sons who was ill.

When these went out no more would come in to me. The great object of the rest was to keep out of sight of the window of the room where I was, for fear I should see them. They were dodging out of sight round corners, and, in fact, I did not see half of them.

I heard afterwards that before they separated one or two schemers proposed all should lodge Griffiths' valuation in the Bank in the names of two or three. But they were much too cunning for that. It would have suited the two or three too well. Anything so sheepish as the whole affair I never imagined. It was beyond laughable, except for the miserable moral state it showed. I had many messages before the rent-day telling me to have no fear of the rent; it would be paid directly the law was again in force. I still get such messages, and I hear

of tenants paying money into the Bank to keep for
paying it.   It was quite clear our tenants were all,
or nearly all, more than ready to pay their rent as
usual ; and as there is not at this moment one shilling
of arrears due in the rent-book, there can be no doubt,
in such a year as this, that there were very few or
none unable to do so.   From first to last the whole
thing was intimidation practised by the Land League,
and fear on the part of the tenants. Of course, besides
the emblematical grave, I have constant threats of
being shot.   It is only in Ireland that in the nineteenth century any one can really enter into the
meaning of Job's comforters.   From a certain vein
of the Old Woman, that is very common here, everybody comes with a kindness it is impossible not to
value, to condole with one in one's troubles, and
everybody repeats all the rumours that are afloat
with different exaggerations and circumstances, real
or imagined ; so that, if one did not know the country, one's life would be a bad one.

But, further, I am threatened that I shall be Boy-
cotted.   As I have a large number of sheep and
cattle fattening, it is known it would bother me much
if they could frighten away my labourers.   My
bailiff sent three carts of oats to be sold in Bandon
market in ordinary course.   The carts were followed

about by a mob howling that no one dared to buy the oats. I beg those Englishmen who are so tender over constitutional rights in Ireland to consider what these facts mean. On the morning of the 11th the Land League sent threatening notices by post to all my men to try to frighten them away, which they will probably succeed in doing. The Government of England surely never in civilised times so abandoned its peaceable subjects to lawlessness and misrule. It is a scandal and wrong such as was never known among us in the worst times. I told the tenants on the rent-day that I meant to shut up my house and place, put all the land into grass, and give no more employment. The land will pay much better at present in grass, and the saving in wages and outlay will leave me much more money to spend than I have ever had. The loss of wages to the labourers would be very great, as they sensibly feel, and they begin to ask, Who will pay us our wages? The good wages that I pay are of course a help, and I have let them know that if they will stand by me they need have no fear that I shall not stand by them. What will be the result of course I cannot tell. I have got some police brought near to encourage them, but I fear the reign of terror is too strong for them.

Father O'Leary said in his speech, which I have

mentioned, that I oppressed my tenants with rent, and he named two cases, besides some tenants of land near the town of Clonakilty.

One of the cases was a Mrs. Welsh, who died last September. Her farm was hired from my grandfather, her father-in-law, more than fifty years ago, and has been held since at the same rent. Forty years ago I arranged with her husband he should have it for his life at the same rent. He died ten years after, when, as the rent was very low, 14s. 3d. per acre, and prices had risen much, I was at full liberty to increase the rent. As Mrs. Welsh was a widow with children, I let her go on on the same terms till her death last September, more than thirty years. She married her eldest daughter to a wealthy match, and gave her £140 fortune. To her second daughter she gave £130 on marriage. The same to her third daughter. The fourth daughter is still unmarried, and she bought a farm for her and stocked it last autumn, that must have cost as much. She took a farm of 200 acres for her eldest son,—getting it by a recommendation to the landlord that I gave her,—which must have cost her £200 to stock, and she left £90 in cash and my farm fully stocked at her death. I asked her son £1 per acre for the farm for thirty-one years, most of it being good land. I clear nearly £2 per acre off adjoining land, which I farm myself, and which is less good. This is what the Tenant League calls rack-renting. The second case is still stronger. A tenant named Lucey held 118 acres of a farm I bought, at £84 rent. Much of the farm is the very best land in the parish, really first-rate land. I offered him the farm at £1 per acre. He refused it again and again, sowed flax in the most of it, and did all the injury he could. The excellence of the land made me hold it myself with a dairy. The first year I cleared £151 net as rent. Five years after, 1870, the farm cleared £223. In 1875 it cleared £283. In 1880 it cleared £288. This is clear of all deductions except the interest on the value of the cows,—perhaps £30,—and about £10 interest on money laid out in draining, etc. I asked the tenant £120 rent for the farm, which Father O'Leary and the Land League declare was a rack-rent. All the others complained of are on some land I have, that is very near the town. Fields near the town let at £3 per acre. Three acres feed a cow. The milk sells for 1½d. to 2d. per quart in the town, and the cows thus pay £14 to £18 each, from which £9 deducted for rent of three acres leaves a good profit.

As the land is farther off from the town it lets for

£2 per acre. It is very good land, with town
manure near, and letting freely to townspeople for
£4 per acre up to £6 per acre. It runs towards the
sea, where a bank of calcareous sand is very advantageous for manure.

Hayes, who is mentioned as oppressed, was a
butter-dealer on a large scale. His mother was so
before him, and made money by it. She built a large
store for butter, and for working it, and raised the
old clay-mortar walls of the dwelling-house, and
slated it. Hayes did the same for a cow-house. The
old walls built with clay-mortar can still be seen.
Hayes's brother also dealt in butter, and had a farm
from me on the same land. He died of smallpox,
leaving his widow £3000, made wholly whilst my
tenant from the business. Hayes's land would let for
much more rent than he pays to persons in Clonakilty
as accommodation land.

White, who is also complained of, has very good
land with southern aspect, adjoining Hayes's. It, too,
has much advantage from seaweed and calcareous
sand as manure. The farm next White's, which does
not belong to me, let last year to a well-off shopkeeper
at 45s. 6d. per acre. It is not as good land as White's.
I believe White's land is well worth the rent of £2
per acre, and assert that land near a town has a fair

accommodation value which it returns to the occupier quite different from land in the country.

Father O'Leary knew these facts and others, and by suppressing them he made that appear true which he knew was false. I think his conduct will not be approved by his Church.

I have never raised any man's rent except at long intervals of thirty-one years or his life. I fix the rent carefully on my own judgment, taking fully into account the tenant's backwardness and want of skill. If after two or three years I think him still over-weighted, I do some improvement on a barn or cow-house that adds to the value of his farm. There is, of course, endless talk; but I have never known an industrious man to fail on my valuation.

W. B. J.

DECEMBER 12, 1880.

CONTENTS.

CHAPTER I.

CHAPTER II.

CHAPTER III.

CHAPTER IV.

CHAPTER V.

CHAPTER VI.

b

CHAPTER XV.

CHAPTER XVI.

APPENDIX.

CHAPTER I.

IT may perhaps be useful to give some account of twenty-five years' work in the management and improvement of an estate in Ireland.

Five years ago much was heard of the greatly improved state of all classes in that country, and their general prosperity. During the past two or three years, however, statements very much the reverse have been common. The gloomiest pictures have been drawn by some, and it has been doubted whether any substantial improvement in the condition of the people, especially the tenants, has taken place. It has been said the land is not paying even for outlay on drainage, that the settlers from England and Scotland are not thriving, and in short that hopelessness is as much the fate of Ireland as ever.

A plain narrative of what has actually been done on one estate may throw some light on these opposing accounts, and enable a judgment to be

B

formed,—What degree of truth there is in either or both of them?

The estate is in the South of Ireland. It originally consisted of about 2000 acres, but has gradually been increased by purchase to near 4000. It had been left wholly to agents, and thoroughly neglected. One hasty visit in two generations of owners was all the personal care known to have been given to it. It need hardly be said no money had been laid out on it. From accidental causes the farms were less subdivided than on many estates. They averaged about 25 acres. Some contained 50 acres or more, and many were from 10 to 15 acres.

It is on the Carboniferous slate formation. The surface is undulating, with somewhat rounded hills, 300 or 400 feet high. The soil on the hills is generally rather thin, *i.e.* the rock not far from the surface and often breaking out, but in quality a fair turnip loam. The bottoms, and sometimes sides of the hills were wet with springs, and peaty, often cut-out peat-bog, but occasionally deep good land. On the whole it is land of fair quality, but very little could be called thoroughly good land. The climate is one of the wettest in Europe, cool in summer and mild in winter.

The course of treatment (farming it can hardly be called) pursued formerly was paring and burning for potatoes, with such manure as there was applied to the same crop. This manure was chiefly earth drawn the previous autumn to the yard, and mixed with the small quantity of dung a starved horse or two, and the few cattle kept, made, and sometimes with calcareous sea-sand besides. The potatoes were followed by wheat, and if the land would bear it, this again by oats once or twice, and then left to rest, as it was called, three or four years, *i.e.* to grow weeds (no grass seeds or clover whatever being usually sown) till some sort of skin was formed, enough to burn again. It may easily be judged what was the result of such a course. Very little stock could be kept; 20 bushels of wheat per acre were thought a capital crop—12 bushels were more frequent; green crops were almost unknown; draining hardly thought of. Rents were very irregularly paid, and tenants were little better than paupers. A reduction of rents on the estate had been tried, but arrears still accumulated. There never was any certainty what money would be received, and it was a source of constant vexation and difficulty to the landlord, whilst the tenants were most of them always in trouble. All this was before the potato failure was thought of.

It was at last resolved to try a system of improvement that had succeeded elsewhere.

An agent was altogether dispensed with. All former arrears of rent, with trifling exceptions, were wiped off, and it was announced that all future

rent would be rigorously insisted on about three
months after it fell due, on regular half-yearly days,
fixed conveniently to suit local fairs. Two or three
of the worst tenants, believed to be incorrigible,
were ejected *in terrorem*, and their farms divided
among the better sort. The growth of small quantities of clover and turnips was made compulsory,
and a Scotchman set to work to teach how to do it.
Prizes of improved ploughs were offered for the best
crops, and a small model farm was started.

It was uphill work for some time, and only
carried out by personal influence and superintend-
ence ; but at the end of five years the stock on the
estate had doubled, and the rent was regularly paid
on a single day in each half-year without trouble,
whilst not more than six or eight tenants, including
the first victims, had been turned out. It need
hardly be added that the rest were better off than
they had ever been before.

All this had been done by two or three visits in
the year from England, but at this time circumstances led me to reside on the estate. Things went
on thus improving for two or three more years, then
the potato failure and famine came, with the complete upset of the social state previously existing.
By that time we had got into such a condition that
the first failure of 1845 seemed hardly to affect
the tenants. Even in the great failure of 1846
there was nothing like distress among them. The

larger dependence upon stock, and the larger experience in the growth and use of clover and turnips, enabled them to face the troubles of the times much better than their neighbours ; but when the summer of 1847 came, with the great emigration, and prospect of still further failure, it became clear that the system that had formerly answered could no longer do so.

I think the direct effect of the break-down of the social system in Ireland, depending on the potato crop, has never been sufficiently observed in England. It was not merely a famine, where, as soon as it was over, people had only to go on again in the old ruts, but a great social upset, where, after it was over, quite new ways had to be entered on, which very few knew anything about, and in which no one could feel any confidence whether he would succeed or fail. The difficulties to be got over were really immense.

In the district of which I am writing, a complete truck system prevailed. The tenant provided the labourer with. cabin, potato land (the labourer manuring it himself), grass for two or three sheep, the wool of which was spun into frieze for coats, etc., by the labourer's wife, a small patch of flax, spun in the same way for linen, and he drew home the turf which the labourer and his family had dried themselves. All this was paid for by work at so much per day, the man himself being fed on potatoes by

the farmer whilst at work besides. The farmer thus
got his labour and a manured field for corn the
following year without money out of pocket, whilst
the labourer got all the chief necessaries of his life
in exchange for his labour, also without money.

It is easy to see the effect of the potato failure
upon such a system. Money wages at once became
indispensable. This was just what the farmer had
not to give, whilst the labourer could not otherwise
live. He therefore could not stay where he was,
and so the farmer lost his labour and his manured
field, whilst the cabin became roofless. And hence
an entirely different social state was forced in;
farming became more of a business, requiring outlay
of money at least to some extent, and so dairy and
stock farming have increased, because needing less
of such outlay than tillage. This again has caused
less employment for the labourer, whilst from the
day his labour was paid for in money, the attraction
of the higher money price of such labour in America
operated with double force, and hence increased
emigration. To the smaller and poorer farmers,
who had little or no stock, the change was doubly
severe. In addition to other troubles, they were
forced to buy meal on credit for themselves and
their families for many months of the year. Doubtful if any new plans would succeed, and without
means to carry such out, they were indeed between
the upper and nether millstones.

But to return from this digression. In the summer of 1847 several of the worst-off tenants on the estate proposed to give up their farms and emigrate, although a reduction of rent had been made, to continue whilst the bad times lasted. They were given some help to enable them to emigrate, and many of them went off.

But a general discouragement and unsettlement throughout the country now set in. No one, either landlord or tenant, felt any confidence in the future, or in fact could see what was the best course to follow. Throughout the country numbers of tenants were giving up their farms and going away. Often all the tenants of a plough-land would run off by night to a distance with stock and crops, leaving the landlord to recover the possession of the land as he could by ejectment, perhaps twelve months afterwards, and with a heavy arrear of rates upon it. It was a common saying among the tenants that "the landlords and labourers would soon have the land all to themselves." It was a terribly anxious time. No one could tell from half-year to half-year what course things would take, and that he might not have every acre he owned thrown on his hands. To lay out capital at such a time on improvements and doubtful farming was felt to be nothing less than spending what might be wanted before long for actual subsistence. Few who went through that time of wretchedness will ever forget it.

Of course, under these circumstances, it was impossible to relet any land thus given up at the former rent. Yet if relet for less, it would have caused still more trouble among the remaining tenants, who would have resorted to all means in order to get a like reduction on their own farms. It was therefore resolved to keep in hand any land that could not be relet at the former rent. Four to five hundred acres were thus taken up. This was done simply to avoid worse evils. The land, in spite of the improved condition of the tenants, was still miserably poor, and of course it was the worst who failed. All the objections to "gentlemen's farming" were strongly felt, and no instance was known in the district of such farming having paid. The opinion of those best able to judge was, that tenants could make such land pay best, and there were many instances of gentlemen taking up considerable farms, and after spending largely on them for a few years, being glad to get out of them again. Of course, there was the general consideration the other way : that improved farming, with reasonable skill and judgment and capital, ought to pay better than the wretched system prevailing. But no one was known to have done it, and the almost universal opinion of the country found loud expression in the saying, "He will soon be tired of that." No one who has not tried it can tell what is required to face the discouragement of having to work out a plan

against the universal opinion of everybody about
him. Still it had to be done. It was partly
smoothed over by the idea that at the worst it would
answer to improve somewhat the very poorest of the
land, and perhaps in a year or two times would
mend, and it might be relet at the former rent.
During the famine years a good deal of draining
and reclamation of waste land had been carried on,
for the sake of giving employment. It was intended
that the tenants should pay the interest on this, but
they were generally unable or unwilling to do so.
So a good deal of this sort of land had also to be
held.

Thus another new system was started. The
buildings of the former model farm of 50 acres were
enlarged, and partially adapted for 500 acres now in
hand; and it was resolved to try sheep largely, as
not requiring outlay for buildings. The land was
greatly scattered, just as it happened to be given up
by the tenants. Some of it was three miles from
the buildings, but it was well placed for roads. It
has since been constantly changing to some extent,
parts being let to adjoining tenants when it could be
done to advantage, and other farms of tenants who
failed added instead. One advantage there was.
Much tillage was clearly unsuitable both to the soil
and climate. The rainfall and constantly mild
moist atmosphere, so unsuited to corn, were the very
conditions needed for grass. There was no trouble

in getting a close sole of grass in three years, such
as an English farmer might easily suppose was old
pasture; and most good farmers agreed that dairy
and stock farming paid better than anything else in
this district, even before the famine.

The course of farming followed was to break up
the land for oats, where it would give a crop; then
turnips manured, half of them fed on the land by
sheep with hay, and the rest given to cows and
young stock in the yard, only a few head being
fattened. The turnips were followed by oats again
and grass-seeds, and the land was then left in grass
for four or five years, or till it was convenient again
to go over it. The poorest fields were first attacked,
because it was thought if the land was let again in a
few years, an improved face on these parts would
help to let it, and ensure a better rent. But in truth
they looked such utter starve-alls, that for the sake
of one's own feelings it was needful to improve them.
The effect of the turnips fed off with sheep was little
short of magical. Even on the worst land it never
failed at once to give a good crop of oats and seeds
after, and to put the land thenceforth in a state to
pay something.

On parts of the land that were suitable, and
where the old buildings answered, small dairies were
started; the cows being let to some of the best of the
labourers, whose wives understood butter-making.
Any tenants who were turned out and did not

emigrate, were, if they liked, employed with their
families, but treated merely as other labourers.
Some of these have proved our very best men, and
are still with us. It has for years been their pride
to go to mass better dressed than the small farmers
around.

Yet the results of the first three or four years, as
shown in the balance-sheets, were far from encourag-
ing: 7s. or 8s. per acre for rent and interest was the
best that could be made, after charging all that
could be fairly charged to capital as permanent
improvements. And for this a large outlay was
needful. The land that had been gone over, no
doubt had a very improved appearance, but the
whole required the same process. The lea oats
seldom returned the seed and labour, and 50 or 60
acres manured in a year made slow progress over
500.

But in spite of discouragement it was resolved
to go on. The former rent of the land thus taken
up varied from 9s. 6d. to 20s. per acre. It averaged
on the whole about 17s. At length in 1851 the
return for rent and interest rose to 12s. per acre;
1852 was no better; but in 1853, a year of high
prices for everything, the balance suddenly started
to 27s. The next year, however, it went back to
22s. In 1855 it was 23s. 6d., and in 1856 it fell
off again to 21s. 6d. In 1857, however, another
great step was gained, and 31s. was reached, though

in 1858, from accidental causes, it again went back
to 22s. 6d.   1859 was somewhat better, but only
25s.   At last in 1860 and 1861 it again exceeded
30s.; then came 1862, the first of our series of wet
years, only producing 20s.; and 1863, still worse,
18s. These deficiencies were, however, partly caused
by 80 acres of poor land having been thrown in,
and by a change of bailiff, and throughout it must
be remembered that additions of poor land and other
accidental causes partly account for the fluctua-
tions.

May 1864, again, however, brought the profit up
to 28s. 6d.   It is believed we have not yet nearly
reached the highest profit to be made.   It is certain
all the land is capable of far higher condition.
These results have been *bona fide* balances, after
charging bailiff's salary and all expenses; not landlord's improvements, as buildings, drains, and fences.
They have been made up always to May 1, because
corn and stock had then been mostly sold, and so
little was left for valuation, except permanent stock
which has been kept at a nearly uniform and rather
low price.   A good deal of guano and bones is
used yearly, and all charged to the year, but not
much cake or corn was used for feeding, though
we are now beginning to do so largely.   It need
not be said the crops have improved, especially
where the land has come a second time under
manuring.   Nor that the land itself is in a different

condition. Its whole appearance is changed. It would be hard for any one who had not seen the process to believe it is the same land.

Now as to the effect on the rest of the estate. After the famine years were over, the same course as before was pursued with the tenants. Whatever rents they had promised were punctually enforced, unless for very definite causes, and any tenant that could not pay was considered unfit to remain on the land. On the other hand, they were allowed to understand, that no one paying his rent would have it raised or be dispossessed during his life, unless for gross misconduct. The objections to so long a tenure were not overlooked, but on the whole it was considered an advisable concession to the feelings and prejudices prevailing in the country. Of course where a tenant died or gave up, his successor had to make a new bargain, and in this way a steady rise in the rental has gone on. No sale of his interest (as it is called) by a tenant to a successor was ever allowed, directly or indirectly. The tenants saw before I did that the farm was paying. And the first result was to put an end to all scheming. The talk "He will soon be tired of that," gave place to, "No wonder he can make it pay, with capital and no rent to pay." It was useless to pretend poverty and neglect their farms in hope of getting a reduction of rent, or throw them up in order to spite the landlord. They saw that the more land was surrendered, the better profit would be made.

The rent being strictly enforced, and yet never raised during a tenant's life, there was one clear way of success left open, and only one, viz.—industry and manuring the land. All saw that if they did not take this way they would lose their farms, from which a better profit would be made, whilst if they did succeed, they were safe to reap the fruits themselves for a reasonable time. In bad years the utmost exertion and economy were no doubt necessary in order to pay the rent, but then, when good years came, nothing was hanging over them, and all the profit was their own. Anything like habitual neglect or extravagance thus very soon felt the pinch. It made constant steady exertion and self-reliance almost compulsory, and thus tended to correct a weakness of national character. It is a remarkable fact, that from beginning to end there has not been a single instance of a really industrious tenant ever failing. However bad the times, every honest hard-working man has got through. Something also was due to the tenants seeing a determination that somehow the estate should be thoroughly improved. Building, draining, fencing, reclamation of waste, were all steadily carried on. The opinion of the labourers, who found themselves better off than their neighbours, with constant work for themselves and their families, was also not without influence.

As soon as it was found practically that tenants
could make money under such a strict system (as it
was thought), a considerable moral effect was produced.   One must live in Ireland fully to appreciate
the difference between " a warm" or even " snug "
Irish farmer, and the same man out at elbows.   It
is hard to believe they are of the same race.
Nothing has been done for many years to urge or
encourage particular crops, even turnips.   The one
only exhortation has been " Manure your land
better."   It was very early seen that more manure
is all that is wanted to make the land pay, and
that nothing else will do it.   Whatever the causes,
however, it is certain the tenants have thriven
wonderfully, and are thriving more and more every
year.   They have every appearance of prosperity
about them.   The arrears on the estate at the
present time amount to £3.   The rent day, instead
of a day of long faces and complaints on one side,
and sharp words on the other, is got over by three
or four hours' work with pleasant greetings and
cheerful words.   I do not think it is possible there
should be a better feeling between landlord and
tenant than exists.   No driver (or under-agent as
such men now call themselves, the vilest class in
the country) has been kept at all for many years.
I believe there are very few on the estate who do
not feel that though the management is strict, yet
it is considerate, and that they are regarded with

sincere goodwill and personal liking. I know that they show similar goodwill in return. Many of them have actually come to understand that it is better for them their landlord should know they are well off, than they should keep up the time-honoured practice of protesting their poverty on all occasions.

I have said that in the past ten years near 2000 acres have been added to the estate by purchase. This has been done by separate purchases of 300 or 400 acres each. The same plan has been followed with these, except in one important point, which perhaps, more than anything else, proves how thorough the success has been. Any really idle or bad tenants have been at once got rid of (there were, however, very few of these). With the rest, whenever there were no leases, the rents were considerably raised. I was under no engagement, express or implied, with these tenants, and therefore felt at liberty to make my own terms with them. I accordingly let them the land at the highest rent in my opinion it was worth to them. This was often a very considerable advance on the former rent, but was still less than in my judgment the land was intrinsically worth, and than I believed I could make of it by farming it myself. It could not have been carried through, unless the men had known I should take up the land myself if my offer was not accepted ; but nevertheless there was terrible grumbling in every case, and vehement predictions of certain ruin under such a rent. Three or four years in every case have, however, altered the story. Every single man has thriven. They had no choice but industry and manuring the land, and these soon made a much greater difference to them than the higher rent, and both the tenants and farms are now in quite other condition than they were in when the purchases were made. I need not add the purchases pay a good deal better interest than that at which they were bought. Two unfortunates were so unwise as to refuse the offers made to them ; many and bitter have been their lamentations since.

So plain has the whole thing become, that having lately taken an old tenant, in whose judgment I had confidence, to help me in valuing land I wished to buy, I had to discuss with him how much the rents might be raised. In giving his opinion that a much higher rent might be charged, he added, " Of course they will grumble, and maybe at first have hard work to pay, but in five years they will be as well off as the rest of us." I was met not long ago with the following speech :—" I cannot understand how it is. Your property is let one-third higher than many others in the neighbourhood, and yet your tenants are twice as independent and well to do as those who are paying so much lower rents."

The answer, I believe, is in the facts stated above.

C

And this is the result of twenty-five years' work. I need not point out what a rise of five shillings per acre in the rent means to the landlord, if at the same time his land is in as good or better condition. I believe, besides this, that if raising the condition of the tenants and labourers had been the one object aimed at (and in truth it was in great part the original object, as a matter of duty), it could not have been more successfully reached in the time.

To conclude. I believe deliberately, that there is a mine of wealth for both landlords and tenants in the land of Ireland. Both classes are nearly equally to blame for not working it. The capital required is sufficiently within the reach of both. The proportion of the rent that the repairs of an English estate cost, would do the landlord's part quite as fast as is desirable; while on every estate there are tenants enough with sufficient capital to farm the whole of it well, if the idle drones were gradually got rid of. Many landlords are greatly to blame for ignorant neglect of their estates. All that is wanting on their parts is that they should make the most of their land, with fair dealing towards the tenants, as men do elsewhere, and with the clear recognition of the fact that the interests of landlord and tenant are really inseparable. On the other hand, the tenants are to be blamed for very unreasonable expectations. They look on a farm literally as a possession of an inheritance, not as a business, subject to similar risks and conditions as any other business, and from which if a man can make a living whilst in it, and when he leaves it can carry away something more than he began with, he may be well satisfied. They think that any improvement in their farms gives them a claim to indefinite consideration. It may have repaid them ten times over, but that goes for nothing, and they lose far greater profits to themselves, for fear their landlords might gain by a higher rent even years after. Nothing can better show their feeling than the fact that a twenty-one years' lease is thought hardly worth having. The instances of landlords unduly taking advantage of a tenant's improvements are at least as rare as in England or Scotland, and there is nothing but these silly expectations and the suggestions of tenant-right agitators to hinder any prudent tenant from farming well.

Good tenants are just as valuable to Irish as to English or Scotch landlords, and their value is at least equally felt. Such tenants have no difficulty in making fair agreements both as to rents and improvements. Among the bad tenants there are some as thorough rogues and schemers as can be found in the three kingdoms; yet when one of these is got rid of, just the same outcry is raised by tenant-right advocates as if Virtue herself was suffering.

In judging of the state of Ireland, I think very

few realise how utterly low the condition of the
country was in the year 1800, or any time in the
previous century that may be taken as a starting
point.   It was a state of excessive backwardness,
not to call it by the harsher name of barbarism;
and if this is lost sight of, no one can judge fairly
of the progress that has been made.   I believe for-
getfulness of this fact is the key to half the con-
tradictory views of the condition of Ireland; that,
in truth, great progress has been made, though the
state of things is still far short of what is to be
wished for.   In some districts the progress has been
much greater than in others.   In the district I have
been writing of, I am certain it has been immense.
We are in a wholly different state in all respects
from that we were in twenty-five years ago.   Men's
ideas are quite changed.   I can remember when the
improvement of an estate and its tenantry was
always spoken of as an impossibility, the dream of
an inexperienced enthusiast.   It is very different
now.   Twenty-five years ago, except on the farms
of gentlemen and townspeople holding land, a plough
was not to be seen.   I do not think there was one
on my estate.   There were things called ploughs
that would scratch the surface, but all the art of
man could never turn a furrow with them—*i.e.* with
a log of wood sharpened and shod with iron, and
the other parts of a form like the pictures of the
implements used by the ancient Romans.   Ten or

fifteen years before that time, the carts had solid discs of wood by way of wheels. A clergyman, still living, told me that when he got a large parish in the neighbourhood there were three carts in it that had spoke wheels. When one of these went along the road people used to run down from their work two or three fields off to look at the wonder. I doubt whether in the same time greater progress was ever made in any country; but bad years of course check progress, and we are apt to forget how long it takes to remove the recollection of past evils and abuses, and to break clear of their effects. There are many men still alive who can tell all the incidents of the rebellion of 1798 in their own neighbourhood from what they saw as boys. It is only a few years since men were alive who could tell what they had themselves suffered from the penal laws. Numberless other facts could be mentioned, showing the utter backwardness of the country fifty years ago.

Finally, it must always be remembered there is still plenty to do, and will be for many a long year, and those who only look at what is wanting will have no trouble in making a strong case.

CHAPTER II.

IRISH RENTS.

JANUARY 16, 1868.

IT is often said in England that rents in Ireland are unduly high from over-competition for land.

I farm between 600 and 700 acres. The rent when I took it in hand averaged 17s. per acre, and I only began to farm it because no one, in spite of competition, would give me that rent for it.

The clear net profit for rent and interest over all expenses, bailiff and everything for the past fifteen years—*i.e.* since 1852 to May 1867—has steadily increased from 21s. 6d. to 35s. 6d. The past two years have cleared 35s. 6d., and the land is steadily getting into higher condition, and will pay still more.

This farm has been well farmed in all ways. Besides, I have had in hand two outlying farms of 80 and 120 acres, not large enough to support a separate farming staff of horses, etc., and too far off to be well worked with the large farm.

These have been worked much as a common

Irish farmer of fair means would have farmed them, —the land, as it was, put in grass without any special efforts to improve it, and then stocked. They have made a still larger profit after the first year or two—very seldom under 40s. per acre. This has arisen from less outlay in working them, but, of course, they are not improving like the large farm.

The accounts have been kept simply as a matter of business for my own guidance, and everything I know of charged against each year, sometimes even in excess, lest I should be deceiving myself; because, strange as it may seem after the talk that often goes on about Irish landlords, most of them are quite aware that land cannot pay more in their own hands or a tenant's than it can be made to produce—that you cannot have more from a cat than its skin.

I have tried once or twice to let farms, with proper house, buildings, etc., and in good condition, at a fair proportion below the rent I was making. It was still a good deal above the former rent. So no good tenant with means and character would give me the rent, and I go on farming them myself. My object was, having proved I could do the thing myself, to show a working tenant doing it also nearly as well. But in this, so far, I have not succeeded. The land is a rather light turnip loam, useful, but very far from high quality land, with a very damp climate that makes oats the only corn that will succeed, but perfect for roots and grass. The acres are English acres.

Now, as to tenants. I have about 3000 acres let to tenants. The rent for the past twenty years has been paid on two fixed days in the year, without agent or under agent. I begin at 10 A.M., and before 3 the half-year's rent has been paid and lodged in the bank, three miles off. Of the whole number of tenants, there are only five or six who are not thriving according to my wish, though I charge as smart rents as I think the land can pay well.

Two years ago the sister of one tenant married with a fortune of £500, and the tenant got nearly as much with his wife in return. Fortunes of £100 and over are common, and less than £50 would be thought very low. I mention these, because at no time is the true wealth or poverty of tenants in Ireland so surely shown as in their marriages.

One part of the estate runs up to a small town, and the land is held by shopkeepers and others who are well off. Having other means of living, they have no motive for giving more rent than will leave them a fair profit, yet nowhere else is there anything like such competition for the land nor such improvement on it. The rents are rising accordingly. But the reason is plain. New milk that used to sell for 1d. per quart in the town has for some years sold for 1½d., butter having risen in the same proportion. Land for potatoes lets to artisans in the town, and labourers earning much higher wages, at £4 to £5 per acre, instead of £2 or £3. Curiously, too, carpenters, masons, shoemakers, etc., though earning much higher wages themselves, especially grudge paying the higher wages of labourers for cultivating their potato gardens, so they put the same manure on half the former quantity of land to save labour and raise a better crop. Of course, the land gains by this. In fact, these town tenants cram the land with manure. The farming is still very bad, but they have learnt the one lesson of manure, and thus are making a better profit at high rents than they used to make at low.

Is this undue competition or exorbitant rents? Or the fair profit of good management and judgment paying both landlord and tenant? As to ill-will on the estate, there is none of it. Of the few tenants who are not thriving, two are good sort of fellows, but careless and lazy, of the "raal ould sort;" two are old men past work, without families (one has a son, a scamp now in gaol, who, when loose, will not work, but spend all he can wring out); three are being eaten up alive by relatives they have got as helpers and labourers on the farms; one is a pet of a neighbouring gentleman, and loses pounds in picking up half-crowns; and the last is a small shopkeeper whose business has failed. In twenty-five years that I have lived in Ireland, and all through the famine, I have never had a single instance among my own tenants, or among my neighbours', of an industrious, honest tenant who has failed or lost his land. I have seen honest, idle fellows fail, and one or two industrious scamps from their own scheming. Wonderful as it may seem, a good tenant is as valuable to a middling or bad Irish landlord as to another, and he knows it. And there are very many Irish landlords who are neither bad nor middling.

I have omitted to say that all sheep and cattle produce, including dairy, has been for years from 50 to 100 per cent higher than it was fifteen years ago in Ireland, partly from improved markets, partly from improved communications, partly from improved quality.

My books and land are open to any one who thinks well to look into the above statements.

CHAPTER III.

IRELAND AS IT WAS AND AS IT IS.

JANUARY 22, 1868.

IN judging of the state of Ireland there is one main
point that time is yearly making more obscure. No
one in England, and very few in Ireland, realise what
was the state of that country fifty or seventy years
ago. Everything was low and excessively backward,
socially and physically, to an extent that is now very
hard to conceive. If I call it by the harsh name of
utter barbarism, it will be only the truth. It is plain
that without a clear view of the state of things at the
starting-point from which improvement began, it is
impossible to judge what has been the degree of progress. My opinion is clear that, however much is
wanting, the improvement has been immense, but is
overlooked because the starting-point is not properly
observed.

Read any accounts of the rebellion of 1798.
Consider the horrible savagery on both sides. It
suits each party now to talk of the misdeeds of its
opponents. The truth is that no savages ever per-

petrated more cruel outrages on humanity than both sides committed. One was on the side of the rebellion, the other on the side of Government—that was the only difference. I allude to 1798, because many memoirs and journals of that time enable an opinion to be formed by those who do not know Ireland.

Does any one think that the character of those who thus acted on both sides ceased to be the same when the rebellion was over; or that the same temper and vices did not go on in them and their children?

There are men still alive who can tell every incident of the rebellion in their own neighbourhood from what their own eyes saw as boys. I have had such details related to me by an eye-witness, with his notes on the persons engaged, as Jack ——'s or Pat ——'s (men whom I knew) father, or uncle, or other relative. Everybody can tell the story, from hearsay, of numerous and fearful murders, often of unoffending persons, and even women and children, and no less cruel retaliation on rebels—*i.e.* any one suspected as rebels. So clear are these traditions, that half the fears of Fenian outrages the two last winters were from the recollection of that time. And, on the other side, I had many instances myself of farmers and labourers among my neighbours in downright fear of "the army" (as they called even a company of soldiers) from the opposite recollections of that time, and begging me for protection.

Now, compare the Fenian outrages in the outbreak

last March with 1798. One policeman in Kerry dangerously wounded; one in Cork killed. I forget if there was a third. Then outrages on private persons. One bank manager at Kilmallock, of inquisitive disposition, standing outside his door to see the fun while the police barrack was besieged, got a bullet in his jaw; and that was all with armed bands going about for days.

It may give some idea of the physical state of the country if I give some facts about the district I know best—*i.e.* the large district extending seventy or eighty miles to the west of Cork. Seventy years ago the post went into it once a fortnight, but then only as far as Bandon—twenty miles. There was no post any farther, and the district fifty or sixty miles off did without. The roads, little better than rocky paths, went up and down hills as steep as it was possible for a horse to travel. A gentleman living thirty-five miles from Cork told me it used to take him in summer from early in the morning till dark to get home, with four horses. If he did not start till breakfast time, it was a good journey to be home by midnight. He usually walked himself, beating his carriage by hours. His next neighbour, twelve miles farther, had to make two days of it. When he got near home there was a part of the road that it was impossible for horses to drag a carriage up—a sort of stairs of rock—so word was sent before that the master was coming, and tenants and labourers turned out to meet him, and dragged the carriage up this rock by main force, while the horses had enough to do to get up themselves.

This place was called "The Leap." The king's writ was considered useless beyond that place, and to this day a saying remains in the country, "Beyond the Leap beyond the law." Great tracts were inaccessible to wheels, and all horse-work was done by panniers on the horses' backs. Illicit stills flourished everywhere, because kegs of whisky were carried so much easier than corn in bulk. A friend who undertook the improvement of an estate of 11,000 acres, in 1822, told me no wheeled vehicle had then ever entered it; and once, at first, having lost himself on the estate snipe-shooting, they had to send two miles for the man who could speak English to tell him the way home.

In a previous chapter I have spoken of the carts with discs of wood instead of wheels, and the wretched apologies for ploughs that alone were used in the country. In 1788 Arthur Young saw horses drawing such ploughs by their tails. At that time turnips or clover were nearly unknown in the district. Turnips were never grown except by gentlemen, and clover or grass seeds of any kind were only sown in small patches. Corn crops were taken year after year, as long as the land would grow any, and then it was left to rest, as it was called—*i.e.* to grow weeds and nothing else, till a skin formed that could be pared and burnt for potatoes and corn again. All this is now wholly changed.

When I first knew the country, thirty or thirty-five years ago, any idea of improving an estate or its tenants was scouted by every one as an impossibility, the dream of an enthusiast. It did seem a very hope-less task, with the country overrun with population, in this district not tenants but labourers. Very seldom the old potatoes held out till the new crop was fit to dig, and begging and starvation for a month or two, and sometimes longer, were the consequence. Fever was regular every summer more or less. The first charity I took part in was getting a fever hospital built, and direly was it wanted. Now it is never used unless for cholera.

If I said overnight I wanted 50 men for a job of work, there would be 100 waiting next morning begging for employment; and the wages 6d. per day. I paid 8d., and was thought a model of liberality. It was a great mass of poverty that you seemed to make no impression on, do what you would to relieve it. It appeared just to close in upon you again on all sides as if nothing had been done.

It was the most hopeless, dispiriting work con-ceivable, and, looking back on it, I do not know how one faced it, and can wonder at no one who gave it up in despair. And this went on until the famine twenty years ago.

I cannot stop without one more illustration. More

than twenty years ago, walking with a friend who had
been at work in the country for many years, he drew
my attention to a very fine old man we met, above
the class of farmers. "There is an instance of the
change in this country," said my friend. "I remember old B. the greatest faction-fighter and leader of a
faction in the country." Faction fights went on then
at every large fair, unless magistrates and troops were
there to stop them (it was before the new police), and
often they were not stopped without bloodshed. "At
that time on Colonel ——'s estate they could get no
rent whatever paid, and the agent gave up. One
morning old B. walked in to the Colonel and said, "If
I get a year's rent paid in a week, will you make me
your agent?' 'If you get me half-a-year's rent,' was
the answer, 'you shall be agent and welcome.' So
B. gathered his faction and went down with a strong
band to the estate, and announced his intention of
living with his band at free quarters on the tenants
till the year's rent was paid, and on the day week
after the first interview the Colonel found the year's
rent on his breakfast table."

At and after this time, to keep up his prestige, at
the principal fair in the district, B., arrayed in a
cocked hat, and with a broadsword at his side, used
to march the fair—*i.e.* walk round it when thickest
with his greatcoat held by one sleeve over his shoulder
behind him as a challenge to all the world to dare
to tread on it. Just think of the state of society in

which such things were possible. " Yet," added my friend, " a week or two ago old B. caught a boy in his garden, probably after his gooseberries, and gave him two or three cuts with his switch, and the next day, when the boy threatened to summon him for the assault, paid a pound rather than be taken before the magistrate."

In truth, the change to the present time is very great. Land, houses, everything, have another face, however much is still wanting. Compare any small town with what it was. I remember, a few years ago, a middle-aged man at a public dinner saying, in reference to this improvement, " When I was a boy, for a bet I undertook to throw a heavy sledge hammer over the highest house in the town. Now, no man could throw it half the height of many houses. We had bogs then close to the town on all sides where now are fine pastures."

In appearance and dress neither men nor women are the same people they were before the famine. Wages are double and steadily rising. If a bad time comes, fair exertion can grapple with and substantially relieve it. The very complaint that the tenant class have millions in the banks they would like to invest in improvements (though only very partially true) is proof how the farmers have thriven. The cattle and sheep compared with their forefathers, would form very fit illustrations for a new edition of Mr. Darwin's book. Good roads everywhere. On the main lines

of communication great roads, that I can remember
being called military roads, and such they really were,
made after 1798, open the country.

Read any engineer's report within the last seven
years of any bridges or river drainage or waterworks.
There is sure to be a statement that special provision
is necessary because the floods come down now so
much quicker in consequence of the improved land-
drainage on the upper streams and feeders. Some
one must have done this drainage. If the landlords,
it proves that they are at work for good. If the
tenants, it proves there must be many tenants who,
somehow or other, are not afraid of their improvements being taken advantage of by landlords.

Consider, also, what is proved by the character
and conduct of the police. All Irishmen, mostly
Roman Catholics, but by the union of firm discipline
and fair dealing perfectly efficient and trustworthy.

Look, on the other hand, at the drawbacks there
have been to the progress of the country. Agitation
for emancipation till 1829. Then tithe war till 1835.
Then O'Connell's rent and repeal agitation till 1844.
Then Smith O'Brien's foolery till 1848; and, lastly,
the still greater foolery of Fenianism in the past
three years.

The fifteen years from 1850 till 1865 was the only
period of moderate quiet Ireland has had since 1798,
and that was just the period of greatest improvement
of all classes. Men forget that it takes generations,

and not years, to improve all classes in a country, and it is emphatically all classes in Ireland that need improvement.

The greatest difficulty in bringing about improvement in Ireland is that all classes, in nearly equal degree, though perhaps in different ways, require to be raised.   Time and patience are essential for that.

CHAPTER IV.

FEBRUARY 1868.

I HAVE stated in previous chapters the common-sense views of a resident on rents in Ireland, and the great improvement in that country since the beginning of the century. I wish to do so once more on what is called "the land question." It should never be lost sight of that the farmers are only half the agricultural population. The labourers are the other half.[1] The interest of the labourers is not at all identical with that of the farmers. Their treatment by the farmers is of the very closest and hardest kind. Such cases come before any one living in Ireland continually. I cannot tell how often in the year the words of Solomon in the Proverbs rise in my mind about "the poor man that oppresseth the poor," etc. If the farmers were treated by the landlords with one-half the hardness they show the labourers, there would be plenty heard about it. One

[1] The number of labourers has greatly lessened since this was written.

or two landowners in a district giving employment
in draining or farming largely affect all the labourers
in it for good. Not only do wages rise, but more
than one member of a family being often employed,
ideas of comfort and prosperity in their condition of
life are spread that are very valuable. Several of
my labourers' families draw 20s. to 25s. per week
wages. I need not add with what effect!

May heaven forgive those who represent the Irish
tenant as an innocent, simple being, unable to take
care of his own interests or make a bargain for himself. A more barefaced fiction was never put forward. If any one in England has a doubt on the
subject, let him try a dealing with the first Irishman
he can catch (who is sure to be a cousin, at least, of
some tenant at home), and he will soon find out if he
has not met his match.

Of course, as in every class everywhere, some are
sharper and some softer; but as a body Irish tenants
are as sharp and shrewd and as well able to hold
their own as any class in the country. Like others
of the lower orders, they have a strong love of law,
and are much better up to it than English tenants.
They resort to it with entire freedom, and are re-
strained by no scruples from taking advantage of
every quirk, honest or dishonest, that the very ingenious body of attorneys who now abound in every
corner of the land can suggest for the moderate fee
of 5s.

They are neither worse nor better than any other class. They have all the faults of the country and the good qualities. There are the same good and bad qualities among them in the very same proportions and degrees as in the Irish M.P.'s, for example, whom every one knows and can judge of. Personally, I have much more good than bad to say of those I have to deal with or am acquainted with. I know them to be improving much in all respects, especially in knowledge, though they have still much to learn. In every district there are a number of thriving, well-to-do, strong farmers (as they are called here), whose numbers are steadily increasing. There are many good fellows among them, and many also backward and lazy, and some as thorough schemers as can be found in the three kingdoms.

One chief reason why few leases are now granted is the impossibility of enforcing covenants against tenants who have small means of payment. One party is, therefore, bound by the lease, while the other is not bound. As to covenants for good farming, they would be just laughed at; and what is the use of other covenants when damages for their breach cannot be realised? To the more substantial tenants who are growing up very few would refuse a lease for twenty-one years. I have no leases, but every good tenant (all mine, but a few) knows he may have a lease for twenty-one years for asking. Tenants would prefer thirty-one years very naturally; but

considering the chances of change in prices and the
value of gold, is there anything unreasonable in
thinking twenty-one long enough ?

When it is said that a tenant on leaving a farm
should be paid the unexhausted value of any permanent improvement he has made in it, I do not
believe there is one landlord in a hundred that
objects to such a proposition. The only conditions
desired are that the improvements shall be *bonâ fide*
improvements, properly done and recorded, so as to
avoid after disputes and the setting up of indefinite
and fraudulent claims.

The want of such provisions was the great defect
in Mr. Fortescue's Bill of 1866. There was nothing
to secure that the improvement was *bonâ fide* made
at all or was properly done. It was not even
registered. All was left to be ascertained years after,
when, perhaps, most of those were dead who knew
the facts, and litigation and numerous frauds would
have been the sure result.

Much has been made of the question whether the
landlord's assent to the improvement shall first be
required. Except as a question of principle, I have
always thought this was of little practical importance to either party, provided only the improvements are *bonâ fide* made and well done and recorded.
The number of landlords who are such idiots as to
refuse their assent to real improvements that would
better secure their rent, and at some after time add

to it, is so small as to make no practical difference
to the country; and, on the other hand, so long as the
improvements are real and well done and recorded,
to pay the fair unexhausted value can be no loss to
any landlord, whether he assented beforehand or not.

It is a mere delusion that farmers in Ireland are
burning to carry out useful improvements, and are
kept back by the landlords. It is earnestly to be
wished the fact was so, for the remedy would then be
easy. There is one test of the anxiety of the farmers
to improve that always seems to me conclusive.
How do they carry out those parts of their work that
will repay them in a single year, such as cleaning the
land of weeds, and sowing and gathering the crops in
proper time? Cleaning of weeds pays on the one
crop. The sowing and reaping in proper time costs
no more than when done too late, and often less.
Every one with the most superficial knowledge
of Ireland knows that the cleaning of the land is
simply execrable, and that one-fourth to one-half the
crop is often lost by its being sown too late or
gathered too late. Not an autumn passes that hay
nearly black may not be seen in cocks for months;
and I have often observed that fine weather early in
harvest is sure to do fatal harm, because so many
presume on it, and leave the crops for bad weather.
Every year I see crops manured well enough to give
a full return reduced to one-half by being sown late
and half-cleaned. What is the use of talking about

a desire to spend money or labour in permanent improvements by men of this sort? Very few farmers
have the knowledge, or skill, or energy needful for
carrying out the draining of half-a-dozen acres. They
do not rightly know how to go about it, even with
the money in their pockets. The money or trouble
it will cost is the one thing thought of; the effect of
the work and result are overlooked. One of my
labourers does far more work than a farmer's labourer.
When tenants do attempt a job, nine times out of ten,
unless it is a shopkeeper from a town or person above
the farmer class, the drains are made two feet deep,
or a little over. They do not half dry the land, and
choke in a few years. It is much the same with
buildings. Unless the landlord helps and insists on
their being well done, they are scamped to save a few
shillings, so as to lessen their value by half.

It is the fear of having to pay for such half-done
improvements, and of claims with even less foundation, that has caused dislike of Tenants' Compensation
Bills? It is for the true interests of the tenants
themselves that such improvements as they make
should be done effectively and well. It is only their
ignorance that makes them content with inferior or
bad work. Litigation or fraud can never do good to
either tenant or landlord.

Lord Mayo's Bill of last Session was the greatest
boon that was ever offered to the tenant-farmer of
any country. It gave as full compensation for *bonâ*

fide works as the Bill of 1866, and by registration prevented after-fraud and litigation. Its system of loans was of great value to the tenant. It was, of course, received with a howl in the House of Commons by the extreme Irish party; but the people at home were wiser than their M.P.'s, and have seen how great the gain would be. Everybody now wishes for it—as a *pis aller* at least.

But it is said fixity of tenure and peasant proprietors are the true remedy. Besides other objections to fixity of tenure, it would just stereotype the evils of all estates now badly managed. There are many estates still divided into farms too small to support a family, or with farms carved out by the tenants themselves on the principle of a good field and a bad one to each, so that a man's share is situated in half a dozen different spots. (I had lately such a case, a purchase, with one thriving tenant on it out of many at very low rent, and he had nineteen acres in seven separate bits.) Neglect, and not bad intention, is the main fault of Irish landlords, and on no estates are the tenants so ill off as on those where they have been left to arrange for themselves, and allowed to get in arrear from indulgence. Fixity of tenure would cruelly injure those who have spent life and money in improving the condition of their estates and tenants, in the expectation that they or their children would profit by it; while it would do little hurt to the neglectful landowner, who cares only

for his rent. Those who had screwed their rents up
to the utmost would be least hurt, while whoever let
lowest would lose most. It would also at once
deprive all the more intelligent and improving
owners of every motive for improving their estates.
It is these men who have been and are now the
pioneers and leaders in all agricultural improvements,
—the very improvements the country most needs.
To throw them overboard can produce but one
effect.

But fixity of tenure has been tried. There are
many long leases everywhere. There are three such
cases in this neighbourhood. One adjoins my land.
The owner, living at a distance, thought he would
secure his rent and be satisfied, so he offered leases
for 1000 years. The tenants said it was not long
enough, and, thinking it did not make much odds to
him, he made it 2000. The tenants are of the average
sort; they have much improvable land. In the
famine they very nearly failed. One small field of
one and a quarter acre reclaimed is the whole improvement done in the twenty-five years that I have
known the land. My tenants are richer men. In
the other cases the leases are for 200 and 100 years.
The tenants are neither worse nor better off than the
average. One lately sold out to go to America.
On being asked why, he said his landlord was good
and fair (as is the case—a Roman Catholic and a
Liberal); but the farm was not large enough to

support him and his family in comfort, and so he thought it best to go.

If it is thought Mr. Bright's plan of small proprietors would answer, it can be tried with no risk or loss. Very simple machinery—the same, indeed, that now makes loans for draining, etc.— would make loans to two-thirds of the value to occupiers buying the fee of their farms in the Estates Court. Both interest and principal would be secure, so that the cost would be nothing to the country, and the plan could be extended if it succeeded.

I do not believe it would go far, glad as I should be if it did so. There has for many years been a company at Manchester, called "The Irish Land Company," for this very purpose—buying land in the Estates Court and selling it again to the tenants. It has bought a great deal of land, but has sold very little, if any, and very naturally complains much of the apathy of the occupiers.

· It is said by some that "political economy" will not do for Ireland. I believe, on the contrary, the direct opposite is the truth. The one thing to be avoided is doing anything that cannot be justified by sound principle. Ignorance and neglect and general backwardness are the main causes of the troubles of both landlords and tenants. So far as my knowledge goes, whenever an estate is managed on strict business principles, as an enlightened man alive to his own interest, and looking closely to it, but acting fairly

and uprightly, as he would in any other sort of
business, the tenants as a body are prospering and
contented. The great fault of the landlords has been
and is that they do not spend money in developing
their estates as they ought to do, and might do, to the
advantage of themselves and all classes in the country.
But there are some who do it, and example in success
is contagious. The younger ones are doing it more
than the older, and much the larger part of the
draining done is done by the owners. It is surely
self-evident that in a purely agricultural country the
development of the resources of the land is the one
source of increased prosperity to all classes. Any
honest and sound mode of forcing on that development is justifiable, but quackery and partisanship can
do no good. Relying on a class more backward and
ignorant, and at this moment doing less than that
whose defects it is wanted to supply, is only leaning
on a broken reed. Improved public opinion is probably the greatest remedy.

Ireland is the very land of enormous exaggerations
and want of common sense. The art of making
capital out of a little by-talk both tall and soft is
here understood to perfection, while the scheming,
both personal and political, is wholly without bounds
or conscience, the reverse of all that is independent
and manly. Only those living in it can realise the
extent of these evils. Yet all the time the great
majority of the people, of all ranks, both Roman

Catholic and Protestant, go on quietly their own way, and are very little and but indirectly influenced by the talk around them, desiring quiet above all things. If 1 may sum up in one sentence the experience of twenty-five years in the country, it would be that resolutely doing what is right, with fair consideration towards others and complete disregard of talk, is the surest way of improving Ireland.

CHAPTER V.

LEASES.

SEPTEMBER 1869.

I THINK Lord Portsmouth is wrong in attributing the fact of leases not often being given in Ireland to political motives.

Any one who considers that nearly all the M.P.'s in Roman Catholic parts of Ireland are of one party, and nearly all in Protestant parts of the other party, will see that tenants' votes really are not of sufficient value to make any one sacrifice his pecuniary interests for their sake. It does not pay. The end is not attained. On both sides the game is too hollow to make it worth while. Here and there a grandee with political ends to gain may, perhaps, act on such motives. But a very great majority of landlords care far too much for their pecuniary interests. In spite of tall talk, not one-tenth of the sacrifices are made for politics in Ireland that are made in England or Scotland.

I have watched the matter for thirty years, and am convinced this idea of political motives being an obstacle to leases is mainly a tradition for the state

of things a generation or two back, when political
influence meant very substantial gains. A few
modern instances have been taken hold of, and exaggerated for opposite political ends, and thus the
idea has become current.

I believe the true reason more leases have not
been granted in Ireland is a commonplace one.
Practically, it is not possible to enforce against the
tenant any covenant in a lease, except that of paying
the rent, and this can be just as well enforced when
there is no lease.

The effect of a lease is, therefore, altogether one-
sided. Practically, the landlord is bound by it, while
the tenant is not. This is especially the case when
the tenant, from any cause, fails to dwell on his
farm. I suppose no one doubts that idleness, drink,
family quarrels, folly and ignorance of all sorts, do
break tenants in Ireland as often as elsewhere. My
experience is, that these faults are more common
here than elsewhere. When a tenant with a lease
begins to fail, the land is cropped and scourged without either manure or mercy. The stock is gradually
sold, unavoidably causing more cropping, buildings
are neglected, and often wrecked, ruinous bargains in
advance for even two or three years made, selling the
right of cropping the fields for a little ready money,
and thus payment of the rent is kept up sufficiently to
prevent an ejectment till the land is reduced to a state
that is inconceivable by any one who has not seen it.

I am describing real instances that have happened to myself under a lease. I have had the land reduced till it would not even grow weeds.

When there is no lease, this process is very much shortened. A couple of years of waste is the most that can occur.

It is forgotten that Irish tenants not usually having substantial means, when the landlord comes to look for his covenants, be they ever so reasonable, he finds it a case of suing a beggar and catching a ——, and when the tenant has means, as tenants are naturally and rightly put on juries, it must be an extraordinarily clear case indeed in which a landlord can get a verdict for breach of covenant.

All those covenants that are universal on well-managed estates in England and Scotland for treatment of the land, especially in the last years of the term, against repeated corn crops, the sale of hay and straw off the farm, ploughing up valuable grass lands, upholding buildings even when built by the landlord, wholly or in part, or allowed for (which is far more common than the advocates of one side represent), are of no use at all in Ireland. A lease is literally on the part of the tenant, "Heads I win, tails you lose." Can anybody wonder with such a state of things that leases are not common. Surely, these common motives of self-interest are enough to account for the facts ?

The one motive in favour of giving leases is, that

E

the security may induce the tenant to farm better, and a higher rent be the result at the end of his term.

And, as if to cut away this one motive, a higher rent at the end of the term is the very thing tenant-right agitators most object to.

The truth, however, is, that the improvement of an estate, so far as it depends on the tenant, is not the result of a lease or no lease ; but of the character of the landlord, and those who represent him.

I can show an estate with very few leases, I will venture to say, though I do not know Lord Portsmouth's estate, just as highly improved as it, and with the great majority of the tenants flourishing in all ways ; and, which is the surest test, yearly producing sums of money for the marriage of their sons and daughters that astonish me, well as I know their circumstances.

After more than twenty years' work, I shall in two or three years more have finished the drainage of the whole, which I and not the tenants have done. There is hardly a good building I have not helped to build ; and as soon as the outlay for draining is over, I mean to take the buildings in hand, and do all of them wholly myself, instead of leaving them to the tenants to do partly. It is the simple matter of fact that, every year that passes, the treatment of the land in Ireland is improving, and the tenants as a class are making more money. Many of those who talk loudest about tenant-right are men in the neighbourhood of large towns, with good capital, and in the same position as tenants in England or Scotland hiring farms; and instances can be given of some among them who have hired farms for short terms at very favourable rents for themselves, and very naturally desire fixity of tenure at the same rate.

Nowhere in the world do questions so much require to be looked at from both sides as in Ireland; if for nothing else, because of the wretched want of truth that is the prevailing sin of the country. The Church has been overturned in order to conciliate the Roman Catholics, and at once demands are put forward by them on education, that all other parties agree cannot be conceded; but which will give ten times more active trouble than the Church question ever gave. Both sides ought to have been looked to from the first.

It is the same with the land. There are, no doubt, bad landlords to be found in Ireland, and there are also good landlords, to whose example and exertions a very large part of the present improved state of things is due. There are also good tenants deserving every fair encouragement, and there are a large number of tenants as hopelessly and incorrigibly bad as can be, some from faults of character, some from ignorance, some from circumstances; such as holding a small plot of land that no human skill in such a climate could enable to support with comfort the mouths upon it, or having such a holding scattered about in six or eight different patches of an acre or two each. (Not seven years ago I bought 400 acres, the farms of which were all thus in hotch-pot. They did not remain so many months. In another case, on a friend's estate, one such patch was three miles apart from another.)

Nothing is easier than to look only at the bad landlords and the good tenants, and to shut your eyes to the existence of good landlords and bad tenants, and a result will then be arrived at that landlords ought to be eliminated, and the present tenants stereotyped.

Common sense, in looking at both sides of the question, is all that is needed to form a sound judgment. If any one doubts, let him seek out the Irish who are in his neighbourhood. He will find very few who are not the brothers and relatives of tenants here. He will find a fair proportion of good ones, and the rest will give him some idea of the difficulties to be faced.

CHAPTER VI.

THE "TIMES" IRISH SPECIAL CORRESPONDENT ON THE LAND QUESTION.

SEPTEMBER 1869.

IRISH landlords have a clear injustice at the present time of which to complain—the extent to which mere hearsay is being used as evidence against them.

A number of men, M.P.'s, newspaper correspondents, and others, have been travelling about Ireland this autumn. They hear much and they see whatever a short time allows, but the value of what they hear or see mainly depends upon whose hands they chance to fall into. Not to insist on the fact that the moral habits of the country are thoroughly untruthful, and that the inquirers, being total strangers, have no means of judging in what degree their informants can be relied on, and who out of all question are undeserving of credit, it is plain that the truth as to every story of landlord's misdoings depends upon all the facts being known. If the question, "When it happened?" is asked, it may turn out to have been thirty years ago, under a state of things that has wholly or nearly passed away. If "where?" be asked, it may turn out to have been in a district very unlike most of the country. If "how often?" it may turn out to have happened very seldom, or even that such a thing was never heard of before; as in the case of Mr. Scully's monstrous proceedings, which caused the Ballycohey outrage. If it is asked " whether all the facts are told?" it may prove to be like the *Times'* correspondent's blunder about Clonmel. He was told of land on a mountain that had been wholly reclaimed by poor men, who were settled on it by the late Sir W. Osborne, and he wrote very strongly and properly on the hardship of turning out such men without compensation for what they had done and the equitable rights such improvements give. Of course, he was not told that the men who reclaimed this mountain had so multiplied and got into such misery, that when the famine occurred, the owner had to buy them out and help them to emigrate, and that their land was relet to the present occupiers, who had nothing to do with its reclamation. In truth, every reason that makes hearsay evidence inadmissible in a court of justice is still stronger against its being believed on such a subject as this. Many informants from whom the hearsay is got have the strongest motives for misrepresenting the facts, and, as their names are not given, know well they can do so with impunity. It is a fact that some of those the *Times'* correspondent (*e.g.*) allows

it to appear were his informants are notoriously
among the very worst landlords in the country; and
some of his aggrieved tenants are not peasants at all,
but half-sir holders of large farms; men in all respects
perfectly able to take care of themselves, and much
more likely to wrong a landlord than any landlord is
likely to wrong them—the very class who used to be
middlemen, the hardest and sharpest in the country.

In truth, the grossest sinner in this matter of hearsay is the *Times'* special correspondent. Time and
place and name are in most cases withheld, and
often the case is told so vaguely that it is impossible to
identify it, and it cannot be contradicted because no
one is sure what is referred to. Over and over again
grave charges begin with—" I have been told," " I
have heard," " It is said." Sometimes he cannot
help seeing that the statement, as made to him, is
either untrue or exaggerated. But instead of therefore rejecting it, because he is not sure as to what is
true and what is false—a mild qualification in part
is added, and a belief in the substance expressed, so
as to give a colour to the story more unjust and injurious towards those charged than if it had been
asserted to be true. In that case the statement would
perhaps have been seen to carry its own confutation
on its face.

Of no county from which he has yet written has
the *Times'* correspondent given so black a character
as of the county of Cork. Now I have lived there as

an Englishman for twenty-six years, and I knew it
for some years before. During that time there have
been hardly any serious agrarian crimes of any sort.
Landlords and their families have gone in and out by
day and by night with the most absolute fearless-
ness, and without precautions of any kind. Roman
Catholic judges, consistent Liberals, who, besides long
experience of all Ireland as judges, having been previously law officers of the Crown, have had specially
to attend to such subjects, have repeatedly compli-
mented the county on its state, and attributed it to
the way the resident proprietors discharge their
duties. Since the famine the whole state of the rural
population, both farmers and labourers, has completely changed. They are so improved, they are not
like the same people. There are few estates on which
there are not now ten well-to-do farmers for one
there was before the famine. The fortunes these
peasant farmers give their daughters are increasing
year by year. £100, £150, £200 are common. I
actually saw a settlement on a marriage two years
ago, where £300 was paid; and such fortunes are
given when there are three or four children to be
provided for on the same scale. I do not know of
there having been even a suspicion of a proposed
clearance in the county for twenty years past. The
main products of the county (those its soil best
suits), butter, pigs, stock of all sorts, fat and store,
cattle and sheep, have doubled in price and greatly

improved in quality in the past fifteen years; yet it is very rare to find rents raised more than 20 or 25 per cent, and on a majority of farms they have not been raised at all. Finally, the complaint most often heard from farmers is that there are no farms to let; a pretty sure proof that, somehow, tenants are seldom turned out. It is admitted that in this county the practice of tenants selling the goodwill of their farms does not exist. This means that County Cork landlords have not been in the habit of making in-coming tenants pay up the arrears of those who failed. They have had the sense to see that to clean out an incoming tenant of his capital is the worst thing possible both for him and themselves, because it necessarily cripples him in stocking and manuring and doing well in his farm, and often ties a log of debt about his neck that is his ruin. It is believed that this is one cause of the peaceableness of the county. It is hard for an honest man who hires a farm from the owner, paying only the rent he agreed for, to fancy it is in any sense his own. And if a rogue hires it, he knows at bottom, as well as the other, that he has no right in it but what he agreed for. Thus indefinite ideas of right have been pre-vented. I think these facts, for they are facts, show that the *Times'* correspondent has not given the whole case, even when he is not otherwise incorrect.

But in truth he is often far from correct. He is wholly wanting in that which is the best part of a lawyer's training, the instinct of getting at the real facts. Take his account of a wrong he says he found out himself—a tenant who had built a house costing £100, ejected for non-payment of a year's rent—£28. A few questions by any one who knows the country would show that this story cannot be accurate. What was the actual cost of the house or near it? It is plain £100 is only a round guess. Over three and a half years' rent spent on a dwelling-house would be an unusual outlay by a wealthy landlord in England. It is quite beyond the habits and ideas of an Irish tenant. It is a safe rule in Ireland to divide all figures by 2, but even £50 would be much more than the usual cost of a house for such a farm. Then, when was the house built? Did the landlord pay for the timber (as is most common), or for timber and slates? If the house was built fifteen years ago, before the great rise in the cost of building, it is certain the cost was very moderate. If the landlord did not help, it is equally certain everything was done (naturally) in the most inferior and cheap way. Clay for mortar (stone abounds everywhere), the worst sort of timber, excessively slight, a flat roof with common small slates (the county abounds in inferior slate), earth floors, small windows, not meant to open; no one who has not seen it could believe the cheapness with which inferior buildings were and are put up. If the facts were investigated, I believe it would be found the cost was not nearly half the sum

stated. Then as to the rent due. Whether holding
by lease or by the year, a year's rent must have been
due *before* an ejectment for non-payment of rent could
be begun, and it is very unlikely a decree could be
got till a large part of another half-year had passed.
Then if the year fell due at Michaelmas, it is certain
the tenant got his crops. They would be threshed
and gone long before a decree was executed, and besides it is almost the universal custom to give a leaving tenant his crops and stock, besides forgiving him
the arrears and any law costs. If the year's rent fell
due at Lady Day, by the time a decree was executed
it would be too late in the spring for the landlord to
sow any crops in the land that year. It is clear,
therefore, that more than a year's rent was owing, or
spoilt as they say here, and the story is not all told
at that end either.

CHAPTER VII.

IRISH DISAFFECTION.

SEPTEMBER 1871.

I AM convinced that a great majority of the Irish people desire quiet and order before all things.

It is the fact, that never before was there such prosperity of all classes in Ireland. Farmers are especially thriving. Shopkeepers in every small town are carrying on a trade such as was undreamt of twenty years ago. The goods shown to-day in their shop windows include numbers of articles of comfort and even luxury, such as then it would have been thought silly to ask for. Artisans and labourers are getting wages unknown before.

No doubt it is a natural consequence that when Jeshurun waxes fat, he should kick, yet such kicking partakes more of the nature of capering than of vice. Any way, it is quite different from the kicking caused by want and dire misery.

Further, there was never a time in the memory of any one living when disaffection and discontent did not prevail among large classes in Ireland. The farther you go back in the present century, the greater and more widespread was such disaffection. Even thirty years ago, in O'Connell's Repeal agitation, the movement was out of all measure greater than it is now. Less than twenty years before that, there was positive insurrection in many parts. In truth, peaceful progress has been steadily advancing and bearing its sure fruit, only men cannot learn that generations, not years, are needed for a people to emerge from the state of abject barbarism in which Ireland was sunk in the eighteenth century.

Lately we have had Fenianism. It was really a reflex product of American social and political ideas. It did not deserve anything like the importance that was given to it. It never touched the true industrial classes in Ireland, except town artisans and some of the labourers. But no sooner had it exploded than it was worked for their own ends by Irish politicians.

It should never be overlooked that Irish politicians live by using every sort of disaffection and discontent that may exist in the country for their own purposes, even though they may not have sympathised and may not still sympathise with the particular disaffection itself. Home Rule has now been started. It is nothing but Repeal under another name. If it did not mean that, nobody would care for it. If it was not Repeal, it would be only a bigger Grand Jury with more power of jobbing for a few. But being what it is, Repeal, it absorbs

Fenianism and all Fenian sympathies on the one side and the politicians who have capital to make out of agitation on the other.

The stronghold of Fenianism was in the large towns. It had no strength at all anywhere else, except in one or two of the very worst districts of the country. The town of Limerick and much of the county (the Kilmallock fight will not have been forgotten), with Dublin and Cork towns, were the most infected places.

No one can have watched the late Limerick election without seeing that sympathy with Fenianism, and nothing else, was its true characteristic. The Attorney-General had prosecuted the Fenians, Mr. Butt had defended them : the release of the Fenian soldiers still undergoing their sentences was a constant and main topic. Mr. Smyth, the Home Rule M.P. for Westmeath, had just played the same card in the Phœnix Park. The Limerick Roman Catholic priests were not allowed to take any part in the election. Many of Mr. Butt's chief committee men declared they would not act if any Roman Catholic priests were on the committee. This has from the first been a leading principle of Fenianism, not to suffer the Roman Catholic clergy to interfere. It is quite well known to be the true feeling of those who call themselves the leaders. It is thoroughly American, and is destined, directly or indirectly, to have a larger result than anything else about

Fenianism. It is no doubt true that if there had been a contest, the savage violence of the Fenian partisans was such that bloodshed would surely have occurred. Every threat of violence, every word of Repeal, was loudly applauded. All else was ignored.

I think it is therefore quite clear what is the issue now before the country. It is simply Fenianism and Repeal. I shall surely be asked, What are its prospects and what is the danger from it? I am convinced there is no danger, provided the law be firmly enforced. Without that, all other remedies will be useless, or worse than useless.

I have already said the great majority of the people desire above all things peace and quiet. Every day there is less doubt what view the Irish Protestants take of Home Rule. They have no sympathy with Fenianism or Repeal. The Census has made clear how great is the strength of the Protestants. It is certain that by next year, 1872, their numbers will be one to two and a half, and the two and a half steadily diminishing each year by emigration.[1] Such a minority, independently of its greater education, intelligence, wealth, and habits of energy, is conclusive of such a question as this. The majority, even if of one mind, cannot put down such a minority and dare not try. It is not half big enough for the purpose.

But the majority is not all of one mind, nor any-

[1] The Census proved to be very slightly above this proportion. ;

thing like it. I am not one of those who think ill of
Roman Catholics as such; a large proportion of them
are fully to be relied upon. They know well enough
what awaits them at the hands of such as Mr. Butt
and his friends in a Fenian or Repeal Government.
Nothing is more astonishing to us here than the way
in which Mr. Butt's character and conduct seem to
have been forgotten in England. Some Roman
Catholics may no doubt be influenced in voting at an
election and may flirt with Home Rule for personal
ends, just as a few Protestants may do, but a very
large proportion of them will not help it.

It is the fashion to say the Roman Catholic
priests will have to follow their people into disaffection. I believe the priests have never before had so
hard a game to play. The interests, or supposed
interests, of the Roman Catholic Church have hitherto
been bound up with their own personal power. This
power has been very great, and is prized by them
above everything. On the other hand, it is certain
that the Fenians positively hate priestly interference
of any sort. Their leaders love power as much as
the priests do, and they are eaten up by an insatiable
vanity of self that never will submit to the rule of
the priests or any one else. If they ever had the
upper hand, there would be an end of the power of
the priests, and the priests know it.

For a time, and in some places, especially large
towns, where hitherto the power of the priests has

not been so unlimited as elsewhere, there will be attempts at compromise, just as there were at Limerick—the open management in the hands of the Fenian Repealers and secret conditions with the priests. But this will not do generally. It would soon issue in the loss of most of their personal power by the priests. They will not give up this power.

What the result will be no one can foretell; but it is clear this Fenian principle of non-submission to the priests will bring about a state of parties in Ireland such as has never before existed. The priests cannot follow into Fenian Repeal such of their people as join it, except by giving up most of their power. They have never been placed in such a dilemma before.

F

CHAPTER VIII.

1873.

FENIANISM was the greatest imposture of modern times. It was an exhibition of the worst side of Irish character. Its origin was in the United States, and it depended, for such life as it had, on the subscriptions of the Irish of the States, raised systematically by persons who were paid a percentage on the sums they collected, and who probably stole as much more as they liked, any real audit being plainly impossible. A desire somehow to help the old home, and that anxious fear of each other, which is so marked a feature in Irish character, and is such a contrast to English independence, were the motives for giving. Without doubt the credulity of the givers was frightfully imposed upon.

In Ireland the movement had a certain hold in the large cities of Dublin, Cork, and Limerick, and in one or two of the most turbulent country districts, notably in parts of Tipperary and Limerick. In the smaller towns there were a few members of the

brotherhood, but very few; a dozen or twenty in
most towns was a full allowance, scarcely more than
the number of the police stationed in the same place.
Every man among them was known to the police,
and they were carefully watched. In the cities they
were the merest rabble of shop-boys, and such like.
In the smaller towns some were rather above this
class, the sons of traders, and persons in better
circumstances, but still none had any force of character or influence. Of course the foremost were exalted
into A's and B's and the other mysterious ranks of the
society, thus tickling the small vanity that is such
a misfortune in Ireland. Some of these men used to
go out on Sundays and holidays to the out-of-the-way
parishes in their neighbourhood, and with their own
money, or money supplied from America, give unlimited
drink to any young fellows they could collect, which,
with such an inducement, it was not hard to do, and
then they would go through the farce of measuring
with a tape to see if the youths were tall enough for
the Fenian army, and similar rubbish.

The movement, such as it was, drew into itself all
the disaffection and half-disaffection that existed in
the country, all the remnants of O'Connell's Repealers,
Smith O'Brien's cabbage garden rebels, the personal
jealousy towards England and Englishmen, that temper and discontent which go to form extreme opinions
in other countries, even in England and Scotland.

The thoroughly understood tactics in Ireland are,

that even though you may not be disloyal or wish
for separation from England, yet if you have any
cause for discontent, or think you have, or desire any
change political or religious, you should join and further
any agitation that is on foot for the chance of what
may be got.   In this way Fenianism had a sort of
shadow of strength, though really without substance.
Throughout nearly all the country districts it was
without even this small pretence to strength; but
then another Irish device came into play—the en-
deavour to cause fear.   When an Irishman gets into
a dispute or quarrel, his first remedy is always to
boast and to threaten, and, strange to say, these boast-
ings and threatenings have an effect on the enemy,
though he knows how empty they are.

Every kind of report was circulated to add to the
importance of the Fenians, their drillings and inten-
tions.   Drilling was the favourite tale, with time
and place particularised.   No doubt near Dublin and
Cork there was some drilling, though not much,
but in the country neither the drillers could be found
nor any one who saw the drilling, or even any one who
could say he heard it from a man who saw it.   When
any one came to me to tell of drilling, I always asked
" Did you see them drilling?"   "No."   "How do you
know they were drilling?" Jack —— told me!" "Did
Jack see them?" "No, but Pat —— told him." I could
never get nearer than that.   Magistrates and police
were all alive for information, but none could be had.

Alarmists took this dearth of evidence as another cause for fear, arguing that the organisation was so perfect that no one could find out what was doing. In truth there was no real organisation in the country parts, and therefore nothing to find out. But every chance advantage was taken to cause fear, and the timidity of the peaceable part of the community, and their credulity, made them swallow anything, however absurd. Each small town believed that the next town, fifteen and twenty miles off, was "a hot-bed of Fenianism" (that was the favourite expression), though its own local knowledge obliged it to confess that it was not bad itself. Amongst the overwhelming majority of loyal and innocent, there was thus great terror, and every ridiculous story was at once believed and exaggerated. Cool-headed men, to whom abundant opportunities of knowledge both private and public were open, and who had the strongest personal motives for forming a sound judgment, since wives, children, and all that they had were at stake,—said from first to last that the movement was unmixed imposture, and acted accordingly.

It is a matter of history that an outbreak was attempted near Dublin and in Tipperary, and that an effort was made from Cork to join the "Tipperary boys." The story of Fenianism at Cork and its neighbourhood, is a good illustration of what the movement really was. It had considerable hold there, Cork being a city of 80,000 souls and a sink of all that was worst in Munster, whilst as the place for embarkation for America it had conveniences of its own for such a purpose.

When the outbreak occurred, 2000 or 3000 of the lowest rabble of Cork started for Tipperary to assist. They were physically worse than inferior. A stipendiary magistrate, a man of much police experience, who saw them returning, and also many of them in gaol, described them as not even sturdy roughs, but the most wretched assemblage of shop-boys and butchers' and bakers' boys he had ever met with—a thoroughly useless class, without one quality to fit them for their enterprise. About fifteen miles from Cork this mob came to a country police barrack in a lonely place, with its five policemen. This they resolved to attack. The house was a bad one for defence, and the police had to withdraw to the upper storey as the best way of defending themselves. The Fenians got in below, and fearing, though so many, to storm the five men above, they set fire to the house. But as the fire grew serious they became frightened lest the policemen should be burnt, so they entreated them to come out, declaring that their victims would be committing suicide if they stayed there, and they brought a ladder and put it to a window to help them to come down, which accordingly they did, as soon as the fire made it necessary. All this had taken time, and it was known that there were troops at Mallow, six or

seven miles off, between them and Tipperary, so
somehow the report arose that these troops were
coming to attack them. Whereupon a panic ensued,
and they dispersed in every direction across the
country, leaving the five policemen they had captured
to go where they pleased, every man of the mob only
thinking how to get safe back to Cork by some
roundabout or bye-way. Most succeeded in this,
but the weather was unusually severe, and, not daring
to go by the direct roads, many had to lie out for a
night or two with little or no food, and arrived back
in Cork the most pitiable objects imaginable. Many
were taken, but were so absurdly harmless that they
were not thought worth prosecuting. A magistrate,
whose country place is a few miles from Cork in an
unfrequented direction, walking about his grounds,
captured three or four lying hid in his shrubbery.
When he had got them he did not know what to do
with them, for all the police of the next station were
away on special service elsewhere, so finally he resolved to let them go, as in no way dangerous to any
one, and so he did. They went down on their knees
and blessed him as their greatest benefactor.

When the shock of the failure of the outbreak
had passed off, it was thought needful to do something for the revival of the Fenian spirits in Cork.

There was an old Martello tower on Cork Harbour,
under the care of two superannuated artillerymen,
with their wives and families. On an evening when

it was known that one of the defenders was absent in Cork, and whilst the other was at tea with the two wives, the Fenians invaded the tower, and captured it without resistance. They retired in due course, carrying off a very few old muskets.

It was known that the Cork police had a sort of parade every morning at half-past nine, at their chief barrack, when all the men were present before going on duty for the day. So one morning, as a gunmaker was opening his shop and arranging his window, very few people being in the street at that hour, some men walked in, fastened the door, put a pistol to the shopman's head, threatening to kill him if he resisted; swept into bags such arms, revolvers, etc., as suited their purpose; walked off, and dived into low back streets in the neighbourhood, where all traces of them were lost.

The Corporation had a little store in a lonely place outside the town, where the shopkeepers kept their gunpowder, for fear of explosions, bringing it into the town in small quantities for sale. This was broken into at night, and some powder stolen.

A gentleman who had been in the army, and lived a mile or two from Cork, was known to be paralysed, and to keep arms, so it was thought both safe and glorious to attack him. He was in his sitting-room, unable to move from his chair, but hearing the noise, and being suspicious, he told his wife to give him his pistols, and on the men coming

in, he fired at one, and hit him in the groin. Upon
this they all ran away. Having only women in the
house besides himself, it was some hours before they
ventured out for help. The unlucky man shot was
found not far from the door, near a wall, dying of his
wound. He was an underkeeper from a private
lunatic asylum a mile off. His comrades were so
frightened that they dared not stay to help him in
any way, or attempt to carry him off with them.

Another gentleman's house was attacked when
he was alone in it with his servants. He managed
to get upstairs where he had arms, and began to
shout out his intention of shooting them all from a
window commanding the door by which they had got
in, enforcing his threats with a shot or two. Not
knowing the house well, they soon got frightened,
and ended by entreating the housekeeper to beg the
master not to shoot them, and they would go away
peaceably. So a treaty was made on these terms
between a single man on one side and a large party
on the other, and they left the house without doing
any damage.

Another night, a militia regiment being quartered
at Mallow, and the arms deposited in a store joining the outer wall of the barrack, a hole was broken
through from the outside by a party from Cork, and
a few of the arms were stolen.

It will be observed that in all these cases, there
is not the least sign of resolution, but an attempt to

cause fear and keep up excitement, sometimes quite
melodramatic. This was the object intended, and
nothing else.

If any one wishes to see what the movement was
worth, let him read the narrative in *Fraser's Magazine* for July 1872, of the man calling himself
General Cluseret. He had been mixed up in the
American war, and in divers revolutionary out-
breaks in Europe, and was supposed to have some
military skill. The Fenians had proposed to him to
take the command in Ireland, and he came to London for that purpose. But first, he asked to be
satisfied that 10,000 men were armed and in some
degree organised. Afterwards he reduced his demand
to 5000 men. There were neither one nor the other,
nor any number of men, either armed or ready to
take arms. His contempt expressed for the whole
affair is the best comment on it.

The true cause of the weakness of Fenianism and
all such movements in Ireland, and indeed of many
other mischiefs of very different kinds, is the want
of truth in the Irish character. Of course, there are
exceptions, but speaking generally there is no truth
amongst them, hardly more in one class than in
another. It is a main cause of the troubles of the
country, but it also draws the teeth of seditious
movements. The very quickness and cleverness of
the Irish, which is most striking and admirable, adds
to the effect of this want of truth. Every one at

bottom understands his neighbour's motives and his game. No one places undue weight on his words, or thinks the worse of him for acting differently from the way he had said he would act, or ought to act, should interest lead in that direction. Every one would do the same himself if he had the chance. For example, when a swindler, whom every one knows to be a swindler, and would not trust with five shillings, is a leader of a movement like Home Rule, that is no objection at all even in the eyes of men of fair character. They will join the movement all the same, and think they can use it for their own ends. The whole machinery of agitation, the newspapers, meetings, speeches, lies, are so thoroughly understood and worked, that any one might be deceived by it.

It is because men living in the country have the same battle with untruth to fight every day of their lives, that they often take so much less serious a view of Irish agitation than those who know Ireland less well. The great fact that no one really trusts another, and the weakness this causes in any seditious movement, is simply fatal to it. It is an old moral that some truth is needed even for successful wickedness.

One of the most remarkable results of Fenianism was how, directly it was over, everybody sprang upon it to make political capital out of it. The murder of the police officer at Manchester and the

Clerkenwell outrage, though both plainly the work of a few, caused an undue excitement in England. This added to the value of the opportunity, and it was worked accordingly.

But the worst mischief of all was the way Mr. Gladstone and some of his supporters, though none to the same extent as Mr. Gladstone himself, used Fenianism to justify the Irish measures of his Government. No opinion either for or against those measures is needed here, whether as affecting the Church or the Land. Any one who likes may take for granted that they were right and fit. But the way in which Fenianism was used as a justification for them was unmixedly mischievous and bad. It made the acts appear like concessions to violence and rebellion, and lessened any chance of their doing good. The demands from the disaffected party in Ireland have grown more and more unreasonable ever since. They feel that it is impossible to say now what may not be granted by Parliament, and that fear is the most effectual of motives for reaching their ends.

No doubt thorough justice should be the principle of dealing with Ireland, but besides this, and before all things else, it is needful that the law, whatever it may be, shall be enforced on all.

It is a great mistake to think that blarney will succeed with those who are the most perfect masters of blarney in the whole world, and sentimental blarneying talk in high places has of late been a curse to Ireland.

P.S.—Much of the above account of Fenianism applies, *mutatis mutandis*, to the agitation of the Land League. The Land Leaguers have taken a social end to aim at, which would profit every man of one class if it could succeed to ever so small an extent. It is natural and innocent that every tenant should prefer to pay less rent than more. The desire to do this, and so to benefit himself at the cost of his landlord, is the whole strength of the agitation. Add to this the belief that Messrs. Gladstone and Bright and a majority of the present Government are hostile to the landlords and glad of a reason for injuring them, and still more, and before all else, that though life and property are unsafe in a large part of Ireland, no effective step is taken to enforce law and order. It is this last fact that gives its strength to the agitation and causes it to differ from all other agitations that have gone before it.—*November* 1880.

CHAPTER IX.

I DO not want to express any opinion for or against the Land Act. There it is, as a fact, and landlords and tenants alike have to make the best of it.

Here is one bad effect of it, however, that was not intended or foreseen—the exaggerated and unscrupulous opinion of their own claims that the Act has raised in the minds of many of the tenant party and their advocates, and of which the bitter tone that many newspaper correspondents write in is a symptom.

The Courts are really as favourable to the tenants as it is possible for any courts to be. Such leaning as they have is in favour of the tenants and against the landlords; and whenever there is a fair doubt the tenant gets the benefit of it. Yet these men will speak of the Courts as some have done, because the Courts have felt themselves obliged by justice to give decisions against the claims of tenants. The truth is that many of the claims of tenants have been grossly extortionate. What is to be thought of a tenant who, having bought the fag end of a lease from a previous tenant, and failing in agreeing with the landlord for a new one, at its expiration thinks himself justified in putting in a claim for the cost of all the labour and horse-work used in the ordinary cultivation of the farm during all the years he held the old lease, as an unexhausted improvement? Can there be any wonder that one of the judges, Mr. Justice Fitzgerald, in hearing an appeal at the present summer assizes, 1873, on one of these exaggerated claims by a tenant, remonstrated strongly against the practice, and said it had become one main duty of the Courts to protect landlords against such exorbitant claims?

The very name of contract is hateful to many, because these exaggerated claims rest on undefined ideas of rights, which break down before definite facts. It is absolutely certain that the principle of the Land Act was to take the actual usages of each district or estate as constituting an implied contract on both sides. Where there was an express contract or lease, that held good. Where there was no express contract, the implied contract from usage was made binding, as the custom of the country is in England. No doubt this rule caused hardship in individual cases both to some landlords and some tenants, but in the great majority of cases it was fair enough. No rule could possibly have met with fairness all the numerous diversities of individual circumstances. The

Land Act never professed to lay down a new abstract
system of the rights of landlords and tenants. On
the contrary, it took the rights as it found them in
fact, from usage, and as they were acted on by good
landlords. But as to permanent improvements, it
shifted the presumption from being in favour of the
landlord to being in favour of the tenant. The com-
monest justice required that the present tenants
should only have the benefit of what they had done
themselves, or some one belonging to them had done.
What other tenants, strangers to them, had done, did
not concern them, whoever else it concerned. Again,
many improvements, as draining, pay thoroughly for
themselves in a certain number of years. A tenant
was not to be paid twice over for such improvements;
hence the limitations of the Act in these respects.
The decision that tenant-right in Ulster, though sale-
able when the tenant is dispossessed by the act of the
landlord, cannot be sold at the mere will of the
tenant without the consent of the landlord, which so
much excites the anger of some, only means that
such was the usage before the Act, and therefore
the Court so held. It will be found that what I
have said explains any apparent anomalies. There
may have been individual cases of the exercise of
the coveted rights, but no such general usage.

Consider how great was the gain to Irish tenants
from the Land Act—all existing usages of the Ulster
tenant-right legalised elsewhere, four, five, seven

years' compensation for capricious eviction, or else the security of a thirty-one years' lease; compensation for all permanent improvements, and for unexhausted manures. The truth is, the facts are proving, what many asserted before the Land Act, that the faults of the Irish tenants themselves, and not the circumstances in which they are placed, are the cause of their being what they are. There are some good tenants, no doubt, but they are comparatively few, and the number of those who have made considerable permanent improvements is very few indeed. The reason the Courts cannot give, in many cases, larger compensation is, that when it comes to the proof, the permanent improvements are not there. These exaggerated claims are put in in the hope of raising a prejudice on behalf of the tenant, on the principle that where there is so much cry there must be some wool. After the Land Act passed I went to every tenant on an estate of 4000 acres, and took down in writing his statement of what permanent improvements he had made, and their cost. I wrote down strictly his own statement, even when I knew it was untrue, in that case adding my own comment separately. It is a greatly improved estate, much before its neighbours, and the tenants are nearly all well-to-do, and do not owe a shilling of arrears. Yet there were only two or three cases in which the cost of the improvements, as stated by the tenant himself, exceeded one year's rent, and these two or three were little over it. No one ever gets rid of a tenant for the most justifiable cause without losing far more than a year's rent. I believe my experience will hold good in most other parts of Ireland—with exceptions, no doubt, but exceptions are not the rule to be acted upon. The statement that the improvements of tenants have made half the value of the land, has not a shadow of proof to support it. It is very significant that on this subject an advocate of the tenants expressly excludes the decisions of the Courts, which hear both sides of the question, and confines himself to the evidence on his own side. *Valeat quantum.* It is easy to make out a case in that way.

In conclusion, I have only to protest against the whine (so often a last resort in this subject) that Irish tenants were not free agents in hiring land. So long as the world lasts, if one man wishes to hire what another man is not obliged to let, but can make money of by holding himself, the latter will have the best of the bargain—that is all. It is just the same in all buying and selling. The Irish tenant class are the shrewdest, the keenest, and most cunning bargainers in Europe. Even the lazy and useless, who would let any amount of money slip through their fingers for want of a little self-exertion, are unmatched in a bargain. If there is only one soft or weak spot in a landlord's position or character, it is absolutely certain to be taken advantage of, and is taken advantage of to the utmost. If a landlord is at any time so unwise as to insist on a higher rent for his land than it is worth, it may be taken, but it is taken by men of no means, trusting to the chapter of accidents to running in arrear, getting remissions, etc. There is no fear that such men ever make permanent improvements. Any one who has had to do with land management in Ireland knows that when times are good and prices of produce high there is a much better demand for land, and higher rents are freely offered by solvent tenants for any land to let. When times are bad and prices low, much lower rents have to be accepted. I have seen this variation many times in my experience, both before and since the famine. There cannot be a more healthy sign of the market. But then in Ireland, when bad times come, those who hired land in good times at a higher rent suitable to the times, set to work to howl in hope of getting a reduction of rent. Tenants in Ireland, like tenants elsewhere, have hired land for their own profit, and (putting aside exceptional times, like the famine, which no prudence could meet) a large majority of tenants have made a profit by the land they have hired, in spite of want of capital, ignorance and idleness, that would have ensured failure in any other business on earth but farming. That some have failed is no wonder. The wonder is that with such habits so many succeeded. In thirty-five years' experience I have never known one honest industrious tenant to fail.

I have no personal interest in Ulster tenant-right one way or other, but having watched it closely all my life, I am convinced the gain of it is only to the tenant who first gets it, having got his land without having had to pay for it, or who is able to stretch it, and so get a higher price than he paid for the same value. In all other respects it is a loss to both the tenant and landlord. There is the same objection to it that there is to letting land with a fine, with the further evil that the fine is fixed by a keen competition. The principle of tenant-right never was compensation for permanent improvements made by tenants, but sale of the right of occupation. This is proved by the right having been as strongly claimed and allowed where no improvements whatever had been made by the tenant on the farm, or very small improvements, as when there were considerable improvements.

CHAPTER X.

IRELAND, 1840–1880.

APRIL 1880 (*Macmillan's Magazine*).

HAVING been at work for over forty years improving
an estate in Ireland, on the old-fashioned, downright
way common sense suggests, it has been urged upon
me that it might do good at the present time to give
an account of what has been done. I have had no
new plans of improvement, but began simply with a
very neglected estate in the extreme South, having one
advantage only, that the subdivision of farms had not
yet gone so far as elsewhere (most being still twenty
or thirty acres in extent). I have nothing to boast
of, except that the work has succeeded. The plan
pursued has been gradually, with some reasonable
consideration, to get rid of the bad tenants, and give
their land to the good ones who remained, thus
enabling them to do better still. It was nothing
else but a process of Natural Selection, in which the
tenant's own qualities, good or bad, were made the
cause of the Survival of the Fittest.

It was clearly seen from the first that the Irish

difficulty was a moral difficulty and nothing else—
in the true sense of the word *mores*—as I think no
one could doubt who saw the typical Irish tenant as
I saw him forty years ago, dirty and ragged, his
breeches without a button at the knees, and his
worsted stockings about his heels, hopelessly unim-
provable for any useful end involving continued hard
work or steady purpose. I had no thought either for
or against clearing the estate, as it is called. I wanted
it in the hands of good tenants.

The hindrances to any man's prosperity in Ireland,
of whatever class, are simply his own faults. A few
may have met with hardships and drawbacks, as some
will do in every country under the sun, I suppose, so
long as this world is not Heaven. But every honest
industrious man in any walk of life in Ireland has
chances of prospering better than he would have elsewhere, so far as my knowledge extends. And the
best proof is that honest, industrious men invariably
prosper. I am constantly asked by men of different
classes, What they shall do with their sons? I have
the same answer for all. If honest and true, their
chances in Ireland are far better than any others I
know of anywhere.

There has been no difficulty in the way of any
man in Ireland that ordinary industry and energy
could not get over. The true hindrances have been
his own faults. Drink, indolence, debt, and scheming, with ignorance and want of self-reliance as

consequences. 1. *Drink* is much the most common and ruinous fault, not alone drunkenness, but taking a drop whenever he has a chance. The enormous multitude of public-houses lately mentioned in the House of Lords, and of which I could give grievous proofs, shows clearly the drinking habits of the people. I know of nothing that might do so much good as lessening the number of public-houses by one-half, by permitting only one renewal for every two vacancies that happen. 2. *Idleness*. Let any one look at the armies of docks and thistles enough to seed a parish in every field he passes—even in the beloved potato gardens—and the matting of couch besides, which farmer and wife and children look at with idle hands because such weeds are supposed to keep the crop warm. Milk unskimmed till a green fungus shows on it, and all chance of good butter is gone, though so small an improvement in the quality of the butter as would make it worth 2d. per lb. extra, would put a million a year into Irish pockets. Haycocks left in the field and the rain until near winter, and their value so reduced by half. I name these things because their profit or loss is all in the same year, and to do them rightly would pay many fold, even if the farm were given up at the year's end. 3. *Debt* I need not speak of. It is universal. Nor 4, *Scheming*, which has been the very life-blood of agitation (since the time of O'Connell downward), and of almost everything else that is done in Ireland, being, as it is, the

natural outcome of the universal want of truth. 5.
Ignorance. Not the want of the three R's, but of
common-sense principles and facts, the knowledge of
which seems like an inheritance of light when one
has lived long in Ireland. The ignorance is equally
great whether it relates to farming or any other kind
of work or duty, either Magistrates', or Poor Law
business, or any other, for the right performance of
which a knowledge of sound social principles is
wanted.

There are a few points I had perhaps better begin
by disposing of.

The Land Act made little difference to me. My
work was done long before it was dreamed of. I had
very few bad tenants left. Most of the land was in
the hands of the good tenants, with farms of sufficient
size to employ a pair of horses thoroughly, the minimum size with which it is possible for any one to
farm economically. The chief effect of the Land Act
on me has been, that when a tenant from any cause
has gone to the bad—I am obliged to wait for some
years longer until he hangs himself completely, before
I can get rid of him. It is mainly a matter of time,
and that he is thus able to reduce his farm more than
it otherwise would have been reduced. Once a tenant
has reduced his farm, he is sure to fail sooner or later,
whatever help he may get, or lucky seasons may happen to him. It is never a single fault that, in my

experience, sinks a tenant. Even drink takes a long time by itself. But the man who drinks is generally indolent too, and often quarrelsome with his family and neighbours. And as he finds himself doing badly, he gets in debt to banks and usurers, and so his end is hastened.

All through the bad famine times, and the many years I have been in Ireland, I never knew a single case of an honest, industrious tenant, either my own or my neighbours', having failed. At the rate land is usually let, if the farm has not been run out, and no big leak like drink exists, it is sure to pull its occupier through till better times come. Again and again I have seen tenants under great drawbacks, as widows with young children, do better than their neighbours who had far more chances, only because they worked on quietly and steadily even on a bad system. Once a tenant's faults have brought him low, I never knew an instance of his recovery. His impoverished land was the stone round his neck that drowned him.

It would be much better for all concerned, land-lord and tenant and labourer, as well as for the country, that when a tenant has run out his farm he should give it up quickly, instead of struggling on for years in deepening debt, under the operation of the Land Act. He would have more left if he gave up quickly, because he would be less in debt, and his land, because less reduced, would yield more produce

afterwards. In this way the Land Act is a real
hindrance to improvement, a grievous one to those
who had not got their estates in order before it
passed. Instead of its being possible to improve a
neglected estate in ten or twelve years (as it was when
my work was done), a much longer time and greater
loss of money are unavoidable. Fewer landlords,
therefore, are willing or able to undertake its improvement. In this respect the Act is wholly hurtful, with no gain to set against the loss, except that
of enabling bad tenants to hang on some years longer,
whilst more thoroughly ruining themselves. The
Act was a makeshift resting on no sound principle.
It has stopped a small evil at the cost of hindering
all improving landlords from doing good, and retard-
ing the improvement of the country.

But the most curious evil the Act has caused has
been by the greater facilities for debt it has given the
tenants. As by the Act a tenant *cannot* now be
turned out of his farm without large compensation,
except for non-payment of rent, he is by so much a
safer debtor to banks and usurers and shopkeepers.
One of the most discouraging features of Irish
character is indifference to debt. It is almost as bad
in one class as in another. So long as money can be
borrowed anyhow to go on with, everybody seems to
think all is right. Whatever the cause, it is certain
that the extent to which people of all sorts, from the
labourer upwards, go in debt, is ruinous. Debt of

course at last produces its certain fruit. And whilst being ruined, the debtor and his family are kept in chronic misery. Some of us, for many years past, have protested that this almost universal state of debt is one great evil to the country. The banks are greatly to blame for lending to men they know to be insolvent, provided they can get security. The pinch of the past year has revealed what neither friends nor opponents of the Land Act foresaw—numbers of tenants have borrowed on the strength of the better security the Act gave them, and as in a tight year banks and all lenders have to draw in for their own safety, these men are in trouble in consequence. The money has been spent unproductively. I need not say what is the result.

By the Land Act Parliament tried to give protection to tenants against the landlords, and it has produced ill effects in another direction worse than those it was meant to cure. To prevent a very few capricious evictions it has greatly increased the facilities for debt, and will surely ruin great numbers for one it saves from capricious eviction. Debt slips on, little felt in better years except by the renewal of bills, a tight year like the present comes, and the man is ruined. Some of our wise M.P.'s have talked of a bill to hinder ejectments for non-payment of rent for twelve months. But what good is it possible for a ruined man to do in a farm? I ejected one tenant last winter; and between the time I got the decree

and its execution a fortnight afterwards, no less than
five or six decrees for debts were executed upon the
stock he had, and it is known there are more still to
come.   The occupation of a farm by a ruined tenant
is a loss to all, especially to himself and the public.
Stopping ejectments could cure nothing.   It would
leave the evil and its cause untouched.   When will
men learn that a pauper is a pauper and nothing else,
whether he is a tenant or not? and so long as he is
a pauper, he can only act as such.   It would make a
change above words in Ireland, if men could only
learn to know a fact when they see it before their
eyes.

The Home Rule party have come to think it the
most hopeful plan that tenants, with the help of loans
from the Government, should buy the fee-simple of
their own farms whenever the estate is for sale, and
so become peasant proprietors.

If moderation and judgment are used in the number and quality of such peasant purchasers, no objection can be made to this plan.   A good tenant will
make a good peasant proprietor, and a bad tenant the
reverse.   The plan must be carried out gradually, and
the purchaser find *bonâ fide* a substantial part of the
purchase-money.   Some such plan, by the help of
Land banks, would probably do good in England and
Scotland too, as it is believed to do in Prussia.   The
change of tenure will not make a bad tenant, who is
in debt, into a good solvent peasant proprietor.   The

worst misery in Ireland has been on a few small estates, one of them belonging to the Crown, on which the tenants were in fact proprietors, and allowed to do just as they liked. There are plenty of long leases, long enough to make the tenants substantially owners. As I have already said, adjoining my property there are a number of tenants with leases of 2000 years. None of them show any improvement tending to prove that small proprietors would do better than the present tenants, but rather the other way. My tenants are far better off than these men.

No doubt the number of owners of land in Ireland is too small. It will be no remedy for this to do hurt in another direction. It is by great industry, skill, and thrift alone that peasant proprietors thrive in other countries. The class of small landowners in Belgium and elsewhere work harder and live harder than any other class in Europe ; and not only the men, but all the rest of their families too, including women. They have often, too, a skill in farming inherited from many previous generations. The same lesson comes from America. The owners of small farms there, which they farm themselves, are many of them giving up the business. The work is too hard, and other businesses pay more money. It is not too much to say that the Irish peasant is wanting in every quality needful for success as a small landowner. It is seldom that he has either skill or industry. He is clever enough, but he has no backbone. When he succeeds as a tenant, it is mostly because the rent is so light. He lives too in a climate the worst possible for small farming, where corn never grows well, not even oats, whilst grass and turnips thrive by nature with little trouble.

A word on fixity of tenure, or making the Ulster tenant-right compulsory all over Ireland, so that all tenants shall be at liberty to sell their farms to the highest bidder, with little reference to the landlord.

Tenant-right was made legally binding in Ulster because the Ulster landowners had, almost without exception, freely consented to it and acted upon it. The points in the custom favourable to the land-owners (mainly the security for present rent at a time when rents were very ill paid) were the consideration for this consent. A large proportion of the Ulster tenants have bought their farms from the former occupiers with the consent of the landlords, who got their arrears of rent out of the purchase-money. There was therefore a clear equity in the matter. And by the Land Act, wherever else in Ireland the customs "substantially" exist they are as legally binding as in Ulster. And even when a limited sum has been paid by the incoming to the outgoing tenant with the landlord's knowledge, that sum is a charge on the farm against the owner if the tenant leaves it.

It is plain that to make the Ulster customs compulsory where they have not existed, and where a tenant has paid nothing on getting possession of his farm, would be simply to rob the owner of part of his reversion, and give a bonus gratis to whoever chanced to be tenant. There is just the same objection to the three F's, so much talked of. They are the same as Tenant-right, and more thoroughly unjust to owners. It is quite different from the case of the tenant having himself paid a predecessor for the right of occupation. That a tenant is to get ten to twenty years' purchase for that which cost him nothing, and which the landowner never thought of giving him when he let the farm, will not bear discussion.

No doubt it would give great satisfaction to tenants who never paid a shilling for it, that on leaving their farms (even for non-payment of rent) they should get a large sum from the owner or succeeding tenant. But besides the question of wrong, the custom of an incoming tenant paying a large sum to his predecessor must be hurtful to all, except the man who pockets the money. It clears out of capital every man who takes a farm, except the very richest, and shortens the available capital even of these. The competition is far keener than under the most rack-renting landlord. The payment occurs at the very time when a tenant most wants all his capital in order to stock and manure his new farm. In Ulster not only all the capital the new tenant has is thus paid away, but all he can borrow besides, for the sake of getting more land. The practice is very opposite to that of the landlords and agents of well-managed estates in England and Scotland, who never accept a new tenant till he has shown that he has sufficient capital to farm the land thoroughly well. By the Ulster tenant-right it is secured that a new tenant shall have insufficient capital, or none at all. What happens in Ulster proves that the assertion that tenants mostly save money to buy more land, is quite untrue; very few do so.

Such a custom is really more injurious to the tenant than to the landowner. All landowners in other parts, with any knowledge of their business, guard especially against it. I can say that I clearly saw the evil forty years ago, and have taken the utmost care since that no tenant of mine should ever pay a shilling to a predecessor, though I have very few tenants to whom I either have not let his farm or let him such an addition to it as to make it in substance a new letting. I always took precautions to keep it, to the last moment, so uncertain to whom I should give the land, that all were afraid to pay anything to the outgoing tenant, knowing that a suspicion of their having paid anything, would secure their not getting the farm.

No tenant in Ireland that I ever knew had capital enough to farm his land well, and I think it suicidal for him, and a sure loss to me, that any part of his capital should be paid to his predecessor instead of being available to farm his land well.

Whenever good farming becomes general, the customs will be found to be ruinous in Ulster too. So long as the linen trade, and especially hand-loom weaving, prevailed in country parts, the injury of tenant-right was not felt. The weaving supplied capital to buy small lots of land, and farm them afterwards. That the Ulster tenant-right is no security against starvation or distress is clear from the state of parts of Donegal. The Ulster tenant-right prevails to the utmost height in Donegal, and the distress in Donegal now is quite as bad as in the worst parts of Connaught, if not worse.

I now come to my own doings for the improvement of an estate of nearly 4000 acres. I have said the estate had been thoroughly neglected. My grandfather never saw it in his life. My father never saw it but once, when he drove along the mail-coach road that skirts it in a carriage, stopped for half-an-hour to talk to the tenants who met him, and then drove back again. The agent was bad, and about 1838 turned out dishonest and took a large sum of rent for his own use. It was needful that some one should look after the estate. I had been brought up at Harrow and Balliol, and was a lawyer about London on the Home Circuit. Having been born and lived much in Suffolk, on the very edge of Norfolk, where some knowledge of farming, like Dogberry's reading and writing,

comes by nature, I undertook to look after the
estate. In fact I knew all about the theory of
good farming, but very little of the practical
working details.

I soon made up my mind to do without any
agent and manage the estate wholly myself, going
over two or three times a year to receive the rent
and do what was needful. There was not a house
upon it where I could put up for a night.

At that time Mr. W. Blacker, of Armagh, was
considered the most successful agent in Ireland. He
had done wonders on some ill-managed estates, and
as I was well known to some of his principals, he
kindly received me for a fortnight, showed me
all his doings, and took me to stay with some other
owners in the neighbouring counties, where the same
system was at work.

Of course there were bad and good among our
tenants ; many were in arrears, some largely. The
first step was to get rid of the arrears. A few, who
were well off, were asked to pay them off gradually.
The same form was gone through with all. But, in
fact, much the greater number were forgiven wholly,
and were only asked to pay future rents regularly.

There were a good many old leases, of farms of
100 acres, made before the year 1800. These had
been subdivided into four farms, the old lease still
existing ; and of course the four tenants were legally
answerable for each other. Though it involved some

legal risk, each was allowed to pay his own rent, and the mutual liability abolished, so as to give a better chance for exertion to the good ones.

All tenants were allowed to understand that, lease or no lease, they should hold their farms at the same rent for their lives, and the rent should only be raised to those who came after them. The only exception was in case of gross misconduct of any kind; but it was duly impressed on all that whatever rent any one had contracted to pay, must be paid regularly on fixed days. The principle acted on was that every man should fulfil whatever contract he had made, or give up the land to me as owner.

The most convenient times for paying rents were early in July for spring rents, and early in December for harvest rents. A month before the day fixed, a printed note was sent to each tenant to say I should be in Ireland that day, and requested payment then. No turnips and very little clover were grown by any tenants; potatoes followed by wheat, and then oats, oats, oats, whilst the land would grow any; paring and burning often for potatoes. No grass seeds were sown when the land was left to "rest," as it was called; *i.e.* to grow weeds till another skin had formed, that could be pared and burnt again.

This was the blessed system by which it is now said that the tenant of former days brought the land into cultivation, and is supposed to have conferred

a benefit on the owners, for which the present
successor of the tenant ought to be compensated;
but by which, in truth, the soul was worked out
of the land by exhaustive cropping and little
manuring.

A Scotch grieve was brought over to teach the
tenants to grow turnips and clover. It was necessary
to go myself to every tenant and urge him to grow
half an acre or an acre of turnips. Seed was distributed. The clover seed (of which he knew the
value, and which was got good and cheaply from
London) was sold on credit till after harvest. The
Scotchman's business was to watch the plots for
turnips, help in the sowing and thinning, and
advise in all ways. Prizes of Scotch ploughs were
offered for the best turnips. Before, there had not
been a good plough on the estate; wooden things
only, that would only scratch the surface, and with
which no man could turn a furrow. That grass
seeds should be sown in all corn crops was insisted
on. The land never having grown clover before,
it grew like a dwarf wall. Such crops I never saw
before or since; they were a pleasure to look at.

These steps told very quickly; the additional
food grown for cattle, made all stock rapidly
thrive and increase. It was easy to rear a few
extra calves; better-fed stock gave more and better
manure, and thus crops of all sorts improved too.
The improved payments of rent were a surprise.

Except those who were too far gone for recovery, all rents were paid on the days fixed; and, till the famine came, all trouble seemed to be over. I have often begun at eleven, and by three had a full half-year's rent in bank, without one defaulter, or one angry word.

The first tenant who did not pay—a lazy schemer as ever lived, and a Protestant—was turned out, and his thirty-one acres (divided into twenty-nine fields) started as a model farm under the Scotchman.

At that time many of the tenants had farms which were very much scattered, fields in four or five separate parts, often far off, the waste and inconvenience of which were a great loss to them. The first improvement aimed at was to get each man's land about his house and yard, joining the rest that he had. The regular payment of rent on fixed days, so that there were no overhanging arrears, was very beneficial to the tenants themselves. Every one felt that when his rent was paid the surplus was his own; and many began to prepare for the next payment from the time the previous rent was paid. This lightened the difficulty much. It soon appeared that some were too far gone to recover, and they gradually failed. They were offered forgiveness of whatever they owed, allowed to take away freely all they had, and given a small sum—usually £10, if they left without causing expense for law. Hardly any refused the offer. There were scarcely any

ejectments. At that time there was no doubt we
were greatly over-populated. Emigration was the
great resource, and most went to America.

As I did my own business, and kept my own
counsel, no one could guess, when a broken tenant
gave up, to whom I should let his land. I used it
in consolidating the farms of others. I offered A
(the next neighbour perhaps) ten acres of it, provided he gave up five outlying acres he had in a
distant part. Then I offered the five acres which A
gave up, to B who was near to them, provided he gave
up two acres, another separate bit of his, to C, and so
on. Every good tenant soon found out that a broken
tenant being put out might mean a substantial gain
to himself, one very dear to his heart; he got the
field close to his own house that he had coveted all
his life, his very Naboth's vineyard, which had been
the cause of endless strife from the mutual trespass
of his own and his neighbour's cattle. I gave up all
thought for the time of getting more rent for land
thus added to farms. The old rents were charged.

Thus public opinion on the estate, when any
tenant was put out, became wholly on my side.
They knew better than I did that he was quite
broken, and that not paying his rent was only the
last symptom. And as all hoped to gain by his
misfortune, he met with no sympathy. Anything
so different from the difficulties and heart-rending
scenes supposed to happen when a tenant in Ireland

is dispossessed I suppose was never seen. The men put out knew that they got better terms than they could get by going to law, and so were satisfied; and everybody else was glad. Improvements made by the tenant there were none, and of course he had the rent forgiven to cover any supposed value he had added to the farm.

In this way in a few years every tenant's land was put near his house and yard, where he could farm it with most advantage, and at least cost of labour; and as he paid no more per acre than under the former system, the gain to him was great. Besides, some farms were much enlarged which had been small before, and so were enabled to employ a pair of horses fully.

The next step was to arrange roads for each farm, so that every part of it might be accessible to carts for drawing manure on the fields, and drawing home the crops. Before, though the country is not mountainous, but only somewhat hilly, many farms had large parts that no cart could approach. Whenever manure was carried out, it was in panniers on the backs of horses; and, of course, very little was thus carried.

To utilise the existing roads and lanes, widening them, and adding bits of new road where necessary, was not a very heavy job, and a couple of years' work did all that was wanted in this way, and made every farm practicable for an industrious tenant.

These things were hardly completed when the famine of 1845-6 fell on us. In 1843 I went to live in Ireland. It is not too much to say that the famine knocked the whole previously existing social state into chaos. Our tenants stood the crash much better than their neighbours. There was no starvation, or even want, among them. With good stock, and food for stock, they easily got through 1846. Farmers then had many labourers living on their farms, for all of whom I provided work in draining. I do not remember a single application for work from a tenant whilst he held on as such.

But the spring and summer of 1847, especially when it appeared that the potatoes were again diseased, altogether upset most of the less well-off tenants. America was the only bourne. No one who has lived in Ireland can doubt that farmers with their habits could not get on there without potatoes. Potatoes were twisted into every thought and idea they had, and they were utterly ignorant of all else, except the modicum of knowledge of turnips and better farming which my Scotchman had put into them. The gain of even this trifle was evident in those who remained, and helped them much, as it did also neighbours who were near enough to copy them in part. Especially it lessened the hopeless feeling amongst them that it was impossible to live and farm without potatoes. Still it was the common saying amongst the farmers, " The landlords and the labourers will soon have all the land to themselves." That was the universal feeling. Many hundred acres, the land of those who gave up, were thrown on my hands. I tried to let at the old rents to those who remained, but such was the state of prostration among all that no one was willing to close. The rents were low before, and I was unwilling to make a greater sacrifice, so I had to undertake it myself. At first I meant to hold it only till I could let it fairly. In Norfolk, where most of my knowledge of farming was gained, landlords' farming was thought never to pay. And I knew no instance in Ireland of such farming and land improvement having paid. Sheep, however, did not require buildings, and lambs were luckily very cheap. Useful lambs, fit for any farmer, were bought for five shillings each in July. Four hundred lambs for £100 was not a serious pull on capital; they were equal to such as would now cost twenty-five shillings each. Weaned calves in autumn cost twenty-five shillings to thirty shillings each.

Draining and improvements went on, for though many tenants were gone, many labourers remained and needed work. There was much wet land on the farms given up. Any tenant who failed was offered work on the improvements. Often they were allowed to stay in their former houses as labourers till I could build better ones. Some of the most trustworthy labourers I have had were these broken tenants. I have them still, after thirty-five years, and sons of

such. Their pride has been to go to mass better
dressed than the small farmers around. No one can
doubt that they have lived more comfortable lives.
As to ill-will between us, there never was a bit, but
thorough friendship.

For many years it was very up-hill work. The
land was so utterly worn out that it seemed as if no
manuring would recover it. At length folding sheep
on turnips, for which at first I thought the climate
too wet, began to tell. But from not fully understanding it, we killed the sheep horribly. I have
seen five or six sheep hung up by their heels on
the hurdles in one morning. So the balance for rent
and interest at the year's end was for a long time
small. Then it improved, and made a jump. We
gradually learnt how to meet the difficulties, till the
hope arose that we could make the land pay more in our
own hands than if let to tenants. In time the profits
took to making a jump every third or fourth year,
and passed the old rent, and so went on till there
was a clear net balance of profit for rent and interest
of over forty shillings per acre, the old rent having
averaged a good deal under twenty shillings per acre.
And as the quantity of land in hand had now increased to near 1000 acres, I need not point out that
such a profit as £1000 a year above the former rent
was comfortable. The balance-sheets since 1845 can
all be produced. At least it is certain from them
that I have not cheated myself. The accounts are

made up each year to May 1, because crop and fat
stock are then all sold, and the least is left to valuation. May 1, 1878, the profit was only thirty-four
shillings per acre; May 1, 1879, only twenty-seven
shillings and sixpence. We are sure from prices
that May 1, 1880, will be much higher again, and
have no fears for the future. This guess came true :
the net return was 38s. per acre. Gradually the land
has been farmed much more highly, bought manures
and feeding stuffs being largely used. The outlay
for these on May 1, 1879, exceeded twenty shillings
per acre of the farm, all charged in full to the year ;
and the quantity used increases every year steadily.
Without good feeding with cake and corn we could
do nothing, though our best fields of swedes are
often 35 tons per acre, grown by 12 cwt. per acre of
bought manure, besides what is made on the farm.
The gross produce yielded by the land now is fully
four times what it was in the hands of small occupiers.

The course of farming followed has been mere
commonplace—simply manuring the land well and
feeding the stock well. There has been no fancy
stock kept. A good bull or two, and rams, and a
stallion, have been kept, of which the tenants have
had the benefit too. The worst fields have each year
been ploughed for the sake of manuring them. There
has been no plunging in any way. Gradually, as it
was seen to pay, more bought manures (especially
bones, as we have a bone mill) were used, and more

corn and cake for feeding stock. All improvements, including manures and cake, have been paid for out of income; of course out of the profit returned by the manures and improvement itself. I have thus gradually felt my way into success; because of the uncertainty of what would pay in Ireland it was more prudent thus to act. The outlay on manure and cake now exceeds £1000 in the year. Very few new machines are used. There is nothing done that any common farmer of fair means who is industrious cannot carry out on the scale that fits his own farm.

From the way we have taken up the land, that which I hold has been the poorest by nature and the most exhausted by the worst tenants. In fact, speaking generally, I hold all the worst land, and the tenants all the better land, on the property. Anything more miserable than its state cannot be conceived. I have often laughed at tenant-right advocates who urge that they have a claim to compensation for having reclaimed the land from a state of nature. The truth is the bad tenants took every good thing out of the land that nature at first put in it, and left it as near a _caput mortuum_ as possible. By paring and burning and over-cropping they had brought it so down that it would not even grow couch. A few docks and thistles, and a tuft of hard grass here and there, with the bare red soil between, was not uncommon. I have seen turnip drills, made ten years before, from which the few small bulbs had been pulled, and the tenant had not thought it worth while to plough the field for corn. Three or four good manurings with intervals of grass have not brought such land up to a fair average state. I had to pay for the neglect and faults of those who went before me, bad tenants having been the doers of the mischief. I do not say this to complain, but to show why the land was so many years before it paid, and what had to be faced. All was terribly run down; some worse than the rest. The true trouble in Ireland is, What to do with bad tenants?

No tenant was ever turned out because I wished for his land on account of its goodness, or to round off other land in hand. I just took up what the tenants could not live on, and made the best of it. I heard myself described lately as a man who had a passion for taking up bad land and making good land of it.

Whilst this has gone on the rest of the tenants have gradually come to thrive thoroughly. Of some, on the deaths of their fathers, or when large additions have been made to their farms, the rents have been raised. This has been done on my own practical judgment, as farming like land myself, but making allowance for the tenants being ignorant and bad farmers still. As a body they are far better off than an equal number on any neighbouring estate. Except from his own personal faults, chiefly from drink, that a tenant should fail is unknown. But we have had some cases of the fathers having been worthy, industrious men, who did well, and their sons having turned out worthless. The bad times and prices of the last three years made five tenants last winter unable to pay their rents. Every one of the five was an habitual drinker, who had been going down for the last ten years, but struggled on by the help of friends and chances, till the present bad times brought the crisis. Two are already gone. Two more, one of whom holds near fifty acres, have not a four-footed beast, beyond a cat, on their land, and are sure soon to follow, and the fifth likewise, unless unusual luck should cause a respite. There is the very best of goodwill between the tenants and me and my family.

To act strictly in any way is so unusual in Ireland that it is impossible for the course I have always taken to be popular, and indeed the rules I act on are often not liked. But the tenants thrive and are richer than others, and it is hard to get over that. I am sure there is not one of them who does not know that I wish to see him thrive, and will do whatever is reasonable to help him. They consult me on all sorts of subjects (outside their position as tenants), and act on my opinion. I have had one who deals in guano send me £500 of his own to London to buy guano for him.

A firm, resolute hand—which gives scheming no chance, and will not listen to a whine, but which acts fairly and on proper occasion kindly, because it is right to do so, and not from that favouritism towards the individual, which is one of the curses of the country—is a positive help to tenants, because it encourages self-reliance. Above all else it is needful that whatever one has once said should be strictly kept to; that no one should have the least doubt that, whatever advantage he has been allowed to look for he is quite certain to get, is a most powerful lever for influence, and gives tenfold force to any threats it may be needful to use.

I have stated fully what I have done with my own farm because I think it tends to prove my point that the evils of Ireland are *moral.* There is nothing to hinder any one else from doing what I have done. It has not been done by large wealth. The estate at first was only half its present size. Happily the famine forced me when still young to live well within the income, and in the then doubt whether farming or improvements in Ireland could be made to pay, it was necessary, if one was not to go into it as a speculation, to meet all outlay, even that for farming stock, out of surplus income. It was of course hard work; as one who did the same in another county said to me, "We had to live on bread and cheese for many years," but it has repaid itself since in money and in self-satisfaction twenty times over. The estate begins to be a pleasure to look at. If men will not live within their incomes they can do nothing good, and are only a sort of showy paupers.

As to the tenants, though they farm better than their neighbours, and have quite given up the worst bad practices—such as two corn crops running ; and though many have sufficient capital to farm well the quantity of land they hold ; they are still very far from being good farmers, or making the most profit from their land. It is quite certain, however, that they are far before any small proprietors in Ireland. The profit they are able to make in good years, and are known to make, is very large. If Parliament gave them a large part of the interest in the estate that now belongs to me, there is no doubt they would prefer it. But there could be no advantage to any one from such a change of property. The land was all bought by me and those from whom I have inherited. The tenants agreed freely to hire it, and have all had the benefit of their bargains. The majority have made, and are making, good profit, and those who have failed have done so from their personal faults. If the same system is persevered in, there is no doubt, that as the tenants' knowledge, skill, and capital increase, they will be able fairly to pay higher rents for the land and make a larger profit for themselves besides.

All the draining on the estate has been done by me ; and none, except one bog, on which turf is still cut, remains to be done. Sometimes I have drained for the tenants and charged them an increased rent of 5 per cent on the outlay. When, however, more than a few acres of a farm needed draining, the tenant usually begged me to take it off his hands, and allow him a reduction of the acreable rent for the number of wet acres taken. This was a gain, of course, to him, but I agreed to it, his real reason for asking it being that he had not horses strong enough to plough rough land, nor skill or courage to turn it to profit. After a time it paid me far better than worn-out upland that did not need draining.

At the present time buildings and all kinds of other improvements are going on. In fact for over thirty years there has been a steady outlay for improvements of £700 to £800 per annum. This for more than thirty years amounts to upwards of £25,000 laid out on permanent improvements. Of course the early improvements now yield, directly or indirectly, the money required for the annual outlay on more improvements. And so the work goes on. When I began I can remember having thought, that if I had the estate for ten years, with liberty to spend as much of the income as I liked upon it, it would be in good order. I have now been at work for the best part of my life, and I see it will be necessary that my son should work at it, as I have done, for his life too, before the estate will be in the condition it ought to be in.

It is only by spending capital upon it that land

can be put into good condition and supplied with
the buildings necessary for its full productiveness,
whether it be in Ireland or anywhere else. The land
of Ireland needs all the available capital of all its
landlords and tenants together, for two or three
generations, to put it in a proper state. And yet
wiseacres tell us that if only the landlords (who own
much more capital, and have much larger credit than
the tenants) are thrown overboard, the tenants will
be able to do it all by themselves, both their own
proper part and the landowners' part too. Any one
who likes to believe this, I advise to make himself
acquainted personally with what the average Irish
tenants really are, and with the improvements which
they make, where circumstances of tenure are favourable.

It will be found that much the larger part of such
improvements as have been made has been done by
landlords. I have often asserted that I have drained
more land than all the tenants together for twenty
miles round on every side. If I said I have drained
twice as much, I believe I should be still far within
the truth. I have said that my tenants are much
before most of those on neighbouring properties in
wealth and good farming. In a previous chapter
I have shown how small an outlay the tenants had
made on improvements. It can be judged therefore
how far the claim for improvement by tenants really
goes. Add to this that tenants now employ very

little labour at miserable wages. They cultivate only as much land as their own sons can work. The rest lies in grass. An old and infirm man is alone paid.

A friend who has seen what I have done asked me lately, " Would the plan you have followed answer in Connaught on estates subdivided into from seven to twenty acres?" I answered, I do not know Connaught, but I think there is no other practical plan that it is possible to follow, and in time it would answer.

Let any one soberly consider what it is possible to do with a bad tenant of seven to twenty acres of land (whether he is bad from drink, or idleness, or poverty, or any other fault or misfortune) except to take his land away, and give it to his neighbour, who is doing better, and to whom it will be a means of doing better still?

What is it possible for a half-ruined tenant (which these men in debt really are) to do on a patch of inferior bog, and rock, and mountain, without potatoes? Even in good years he can only just keep his head above water. And in bad years he either gets more in debt, or has to get relief somewhere to keep him alive. Even in our better district nearly all the small tenants were half-ruined by the famine of 1847, and got thoroughly in debt. I have watched them ever since. They have never recovered their position in the days of potatoes. When a few good years came they did fairly, and were better off; but every bad year upset some wholly, and crippled others, however low their rents were. That rents are low does not set a poor tenant on his legs, as can be proved in thousands of cases. His habits are his true enemies—what I have called his morals. And then comes the question, which patriots and agitators always ignore. What is to become of the pauper-tenant's children? But if he loses his land, and turns labourer, or takes up some other occupation, or emigrates, his children grow up in his new occupation as useful as any others. I know myself many children of broken tenants thoroughly useful men and women, whom I have gladly employed. They often claim an acquaintance with me on this ground :—" My father was so-and-so, who you turned out." If they had continued to clem over their bit of ground they could only have been as useless as their fathers and mothers were.

In my judgment this difficulty, What will become of the children? is by far the most weighty objection to small occupiers of any tenure.

For the last thirty years there has been no difficulty whatever in young men and women getting employment in Ireland at fair wages. Thousands and tens of thousands have risen and thriven in this way, and are now far above any small occupiers in every respect.

It is not half realised how backward and barbarous the state of Ireland was half a century ago. My memory goes back beyond fifty years, and I can tell the impression which visits to Ireland then made on a public school boy. One felt the difference from the tone in England all over. It was a totally different state of society, and principle, and thought. The very stories one heard about what was going on were like those of another state of existence. Any suggestion for improving an estate was laughed to scorn by every one, as the dream of an enthusiast, and no one then believed it possible to improve either the Irish land or tenant.

The communication with England then was very different from what it is now. I can remember crossing in a sailing packet from Cork to Bristol, and having what was thought an excellent passage of only three days. The passage often lasted for weeks. I have heard of six weeks. I believe that nothing has done so much good for Ireland, in all ways, as the improved facilities of communication with England. The effect has been incalculable in a hundred unobserved ways.

The best symptom in the present distress is the number both of landlords and tenants who are borrowing money for draining. It makes one hope that knowledge is at length penetrating to the dark places of the land, and that permanent good results may appear hereafter. The previous apathy of landlords in neglecting to drain and improve their land was incomprehensible and sadly wrong.

To these difficulties let it be added that the

country has been made into a political hotbed. We live under that most liberal constitutional principle that one man is as good as another, if not much better; though those who claim such rights have not one quality to fit them for properly using them, and are wholly the tools of others. How can any one wonder that such results as we see are daily produced? Home Rule M.P.'s have done great good in proving to men elsewhere the true nature of Irish doings. They are the *crême de la crême* of the large part of the people they represent. The changed tone of opinion in England is their work; and they should be thanked for it.

I have lived for a great many years in the country, and every year that passes I find more kindliness and good-will, and like those better with whom I am brought in contact. No one can be more alive to the good qualities of the people than I am. To me, too, life in Ireland has been very gainful, as it is to all honest men who take pains and have any sense. Moreover, I see that in many things the country has much advanced since I first knew it, and I thoroughly recognise what is so often overlooked, that improvement in the habits of a people is the work of generations rather than of years. But I am sure that the sentimental view of Irish questions which was acted on of late, and accepted as right and true, is of the very opposite character, and actually hinders improvement. Truth and facts are before all things in

Ireland. Sentiment they ascribe wholly to fear of them and to their merits. And the return they make for it is only to demand more of their own way, as all can now see.

The faults and neglects of landlords justly caused a prejudice against them, and the blame for the state of the country was laid at their door. The mistake was in the further inference that the tenants were all that could be wished. In truth there is not one point in which they were better than the landlords, and they had their own faults besides. If they had been angels of light, they could hardly have been more bolstered up than they were. As these measures applied to good and bad alike, it is easy to judge what has been the effect on the bad. It has been all that could do harm and check improvement. The thing wanted was to discourage the bad and to encourage the good, just as the natural course of the world would do. Men's own faults, the same as I have described in Irish tenants, make some unprosperous; the opposite good qualities make others prosper. And so the good take the place of the bad. In no other way short of a miracle can improvement come about. My estate is better off than others, simply because there are more good tenants on it, and fewer bad ones. If the bad as well as the good had been kept, it would be simply where other unimproved estates are.

To keep this bad and inferior class of tenants, is

the end aimed at, for their own purposes, by one
party in Ireland. Every day may be seen statements
in the papers, as if it was the duty of landlords to
preserve the occupiers of these seven to ten acre
plots of bad land, supply them both with seeds and
potatoes to plant their land, and afterwards forego
the rent, and much else. It is nothing to save their
lives from hunger: the aim is to preserve them as
tenants. The truth is, landlords are greatly to blame
for ever having permitted such miserable holdings to
exist; and the only possible course of amendment is
to treat the land as neglected estates would be treated
in England or Scotland—to remove gradually the
worst tenants and let their land to the best. If any
one reckons the value of their plots, he will find that
if they had them rent free it would not support them.

I do not know Connaught, but I know Munster
well, and the talk that the Irish people dislike emigration is not true. My part is poor, the extreme
south of County Cork, and it is believed there is not
a poor family in that part of the country that has not
near relatives in America; my own tenants, labourers,
and servants all have, as we often hear from their
letters. There is no reluctance to emigrate, hardly
so much as natural feeling would be expected to
cause anywhere. They have gone to all parts of the
world. One thoroughly thriving tenant has two
daughters in Queensland, both married, one to a
shopkeeper so well off that when the son of the

squire of the parish at home went to Queensland with wife and children and good capital, and failed in one of their bad times, even falling into want, she and her husband helped them all to return home again. The other daughter is married to a " Chinee," and seems to like it, which is odd. She writes that " Chinees" are considered to make good husbands out there. There is no doubt she is well off in money. A housemaid, a good servant, who had saved money after four years with us, went lately to New Zealand because she thought her chances of marriage at home were grown rather stale (to use the Irish expression). She writes in great prosperity. It is quite certain in our part we consider ourselves to be Citizens of the world, and are ready to take advantage of any opening in any part of the globe that promises success and gain. It may be different in Connaught. But is it realised what a patch of bog and rock in Connaught really is, to which such patriotic attachment is supposed, and which therefore will be clung to, in preference to the magnificent land of Manitoba and North-West America, where splendid crops of corn grow in succession without manure ?

One thing at least is certain, that the spread of education and intelligence that has made the Munster peasant glad to emigrate anywhere, and even marry a Chinese, will produce the same effect in Connaught, so soon as it reaches the same point there. The contrast of the patch of Connaught bog *versus* the corn-fields of Manitoba, is beyond what human nature could bear. A benevolent person could not do a greater kindness than to print large handbills with descriptions of North American corn-lands, and directions how to reach them, to be posted in all parts of Connaught and distributed to every national school child on its way home from school.

In my district there was no distress last winter beyond others. Not so much as before winter. There is nothing that the poor-law was not more than able to cope with. February 1, there were three more paupers in the union than in 1879; March 1, there were ten more. But nothing is more certain than that where the carcase is, there the eagles will be gathered together. Any amount of relief will be gladly accepted. The feeling is simply universal, "Why should we not get our share of what is going?" I contend, therefore, that the natural way of meeting the Irish difficulty is the true and only sure way—that bad tenants should lose their land by the effect of their own faults, and good ones should get it instead of them, and that the artificial course of trying to bolster up bad tenants should be abandoned. A bad tenant may be useful as a labourer, or in some other occupation. If he is not, his children will probably become so. As an emigrant he surely betters his own condition, and gives his children a far better life than at home.

All the capital of landlord and tenant united, and much more, is wanted to put the land in the condition it ought to be in. If permanent improvements will pay 5 per cent on the cost, the landlord is well paid. Whereas manuring his farm will almost always pay the tenant 20 per cent, and often much more. The natural and right thing is for the landlord to do the permanent improvements, charging an extra rent for the outlay, and tenants the manuring.

It will not have escaped notice that some of the Home Rule M.P.'s objected to loans to landlords for draining, because it would enable them to charge higher rents for such drained land. A better proof could not be given of the narrow ignorance of such men. As if draining does not benefit all round—landlord, tenant, and labourer—and can't be hindered from doing so!

Outlay of capital on the land is the *sine quâ non* of the improvement of Ireland. Whatever else is done or not done, that must be done, if the country is to be improved. It adds to the wealth of all, and is the surest evidence that a country is emerging from backwardness and poverty.

There is one strong recommendation of the course I have urged: every step taken in it is so much secured for good. Whereas it is always the danger of heroic remedies that they may make the last state worse than the first, like that of the man in the Gospels. It will, of course, be said I write as a

landlord. No doubt I do; and if I had not known
the real value of sentimental talk, I should have had
no business to live in Ireland, and could not have
succeeded there.   But I write as one who knew from
the first that his own prosperity was involved in the
prosperity of his tenants, and who, after forty years'
experience, has found his course to succeed.   Above
all, I write in the certainty that the owning and
improving of land is a business, as much as cotton-
spinning, and nothing else; that it can only prosper
when managed on business principles, whether it
be in England, Ireland, or Scotland, and that the
tall talk of politicians in Ireland is only an empty
wind-bag, full only of scheming, and sure to collapse
when met by a resolute will.

CHAPTER XI.

IRELAND—ITS SOCIAL STATE.

JULY 1880. (From *Macmillan's Magazine.*)

I AM told that it will be useful to give some explanations touching my paper on " Ireland from 1840 to 1880 " in April last, and to add what I can on the Social state of Ireland, a question which underlies all particular questions like that of land. I fear it will be impossible to write about the social state of Ireland without saying things that will give offence. I shall be sorry if this proves to be so. It is far from my wish, but in Ireland men fear to speak the truth when unpleasant. It is right and necessary the truth should be told. These then are the motives with which I write.

The *Freeman's Journal* spoke of my paper in a friendly tone on the whole, but objects that, as my grandfather never saw the estate, and my father never saw it but once cursorily, their neglect was the true cause of the state in which I found it.

The fuller facts, I think, show whether this is true.

1. My grandfather, in the busy practice of a profession, bought the estate when past mid-life as an investment. His only son, after eighteen years in the Dragoons, married and settled in England. It was more than twenty years afterwards, when he was on the wrong side of fifty, that the estate became his. Less than ten years after that time I took it in hand. My grandfather's and father's view of management was to let the land at moderate rents, and allow the tenants to do as they liked in most things. As to using any harshness, even when the tenants neglected the primary duty of paying their moderate rents, such a thought never crossed their minds. Their fault was, that they were not before their time, and were too easy. No doubt the tenants would have prospered more if the estate had been managed with business-like strictness. Still there was nothing, except their own faults, to hinder them from prospering; and the burthen of their being in the condition in which I found them lies on themselves and on no one else. It was just a case of land bought for ordinary fair motives, in confidence on the law of the country, and treated in the ordinary fair way of that time. I believe this was the case with nearly all purchases within the last hundred years, in which time a large part of the country has been bought.

There seems to be a notion that owners of land in Ireland acquired it in some other way than it was acquired in England. Except perhaps a few great estates that were forfeited in old times, such was not in any way the case. I have seen much land change hands in forty years, and never knew a case in which it was bought for other than honest reasons, such as prevail elsewhere.

2. The *Freeman* thinks that I speak too favourably of emigration as a remedy for Irish ills. I doubt if any right-minded man who knew the country parts of Ireland from 1835 to 1845 could have any doubt that emigration was then an unmixed blessing to the poor people. They were simply eating one another up alive. I distinctly remember feeling that to give work was the greatest of all charities, and that whilst that state of things existed, it was a pressing duty to spend every shilling one could in that way. Though no effect seemed to be produced on the mass of poverty, still the payment of the small wages then current made all the difference in life to those who were lucky enough to be employed.

Can any one doubt therefore that the departure of half these poor people to where work at good wages abounded, was a blessing to themselves, and a blessing too to the other half who stayed behind—because they got more work at better pay? This is the very cause of the rise of wages from 3s. and 4s. per week in 1840, to 9s. and 12s. in 1880.

And when emigration is looked at by the light of the knowledge we have of how Irish emigrants have prospered in America and elsewhere, any objection to

it must be scouted as cruelty. In my part it is getting common for emigrants to come back, sometimes
with money, meaning to stay permanently; others
only for the winter, or a time, or because they have
been ill. There is but one tale with all—of the good
wages and prosperity they found in America. Then
all our people have near relations there, many whom
we employed, or knew as children, before they left.
They are a frequent topic for talk—what and how
they are doing; whether they are married, and to
whom, etc. They usually marry some one from the
same neighbourhood at home, and we sometimes hear
of visits between the old people here, who before knew
nothing of each other, on account of the marriage in
America. Letters are often given us to read. Sometimes there are inquiries about every member of our
family by name, and messages of good-will. In these
ways the evidence is conclusive that emigration has
been a mere blessing and source of prosperity directly
and indirectly.

Once more, every one, man and woman alike, who
gets into any "trouble" at home, whether it be by
breach of the criminal law or social or moral law, or
by misfortune, is sure quickly to emigrate, partly for
the sake of a new start, partly because their means of
living at home having been shaken, if not destroyed,
they can more easily make a living in a new country.
I believe this to be the whole explanation of the
favourable nature of Irish criminal statistics. The

criminals go away, and so offend no more. Again
and again the police have come to me, as a magistrate,
asking for a warrant to arrest some offender, and
adding, " If he is not taken at once, he will surely be
off to America." Whenever the offence was such as
at all to justify it, my answer has been, " That is the
very reason I will not issue a warrant. You could do
nothing to him if you caught him that would be half
so good for the country as his running away to
America; so let him go." For these reasons I value
emigration.

3. In an agricultural paper there is an explosion
against me by a tenant-righter from Lurgan. This
writer knows nothing whatever of me or my doings,
except what he read in the newspapers; yet everything I said I had done, every motive I showed, is
misrepresented and sneered at. I only notice him
because he affords a convenient peg on which to hang
some things I wish to say. He has, like the rest of
his set, but one idea, and that is what is best described
as a belief in the Divine right of tenants. The Divine
right of kings was absolute wisdom compared with
this. It had at least a noble theory to rest on—that
a king embodied all virtues; and it relied on principles that raised men above selfishness and their own
personal gain. But this supposed right of tenants
has no theory or principle at all to rest on. It is a
mere scheming for private gain, by which the most
indolent and worthless tenants will gain most, often

at the cost of honest men. That because a man hires
a farm, large or small, yearly or for a fixed number of
years, on quite definite terms, the agreement being
often in writing, he thereby becomes entitled to large
rights of property that formerly belonged without
doubt to the owner from whom he hired it, and which
that owner never had a thought of giving him, could
never be conceived anywhere out of Ireland. An
abstract name is put to the thing the tenant wishes
for. We hear of "fixity of tenure," simply meaning,
that instead of holding the land for the term agreed
for and promised, the tenant is to have it for ever and
ever. Then, it being seen that, if the previous owner
could raise the rent as he thought proper, fixity of
tenure might not be of much value, it is claimed that
there shall be a valuation for rents by the Government. The valuation for poor-rates and other local
taxes was made by Sir R. Griffiths for the Government
many years ago. It was meant only as a relative valuation for taxation. The prices of different sorts of
produce were laid down by the Act of 15 and 16 Vic.
c. 63, according to which the valuation was to be made.
These prices were—wheat, 7s. 6d. per cwt.; oats, 4s.
10d.; barley, 5s. 6d.; flax, 49s.; butter, 65s. 4d.; beef,
35s. 6d.; mutton, 41s.; pork, 42s.—all about half the
prices at which such produce usually sells for now.

Yet, because this valuation is so low, it is now
spoken of as the highest standard by which rents
ought to be fixed; and above all things there is to be

no competition as to the rent to be paid to the land-lord, though the keenest competition is wished for as to the money to be paid to the outgoing tenant for his goodwill.

But the right to hold farms for ever and ever, and at rents fixed without any honest competition, is not enough. Idleness or drink might still ruin a good many. So the further claim is put in that if, from any cause, whether non-payment of rent, or having quite exhausted the farm, the tenant has to leave it, he should still be allowed to sell his right of occupancy to the highest bidder, and so, if times are good, put a large sum in his pocket; and whoever buys such occupancy is to have a similar right of selling it whenever he sees fit, without regard to the landowner.

Any one can see that this simply deprives the landowner of part of his reversion and gives it to the tenant. The owner may have spent a large sum on improving the reversion, as I have done (£700 to £800 a year, for between thirty and forty years—equal to £25,000). Again, on the faith of the law of the country, that honest right should prevail, he may have trusted, as I did, that those who were to succeed him should reap the profit of his outlay. It is to be taken from him, and given to the present tenants, good and bad alike, without repayment even of the money that can be proved to have been spent upon it. If the State has sufficient grounds for taking away the re-

version from its owners, let it do so honestly by paying for it, as has been done in other cases. Even
the Ulster tenants paid for their tenant-right. The
landowner may be able to show that he let the farm
to the tenant himself without any such rights; in
many cases by lease. In my own case about three-
fifths of my tenants hold by lease, and the rest only
have not leases, because having been promised their
farms for their lives at the old rent, and my word
always kept to them, they prefer the benefit of the
promise to a new bargain and lease. A great number
of landlords have spent largely—some more, some
less—upon their land, and so have the same rights
that I have. Why are landlords to be deprived of
what is theirs honestly? All this applies to every
plan of free sale no less than to Ulster tenant-right.

Others propose to confiscate the land itself, paying
for it twenty years' purchase of the Government
valuation already mentioned (which is about half the
present true letting-value), and sinking the value of
the reversion. Their plan is, by refusing rents, and
making it hard for owners to get them paid, further
to beat down the value. The Government is to have
the privilege of paying the purchase-money and
getting back from the tenant what it can of it by
instalments.

Let it be added further, to show the small weight
of the tenant party, that the whole population of
Ireland is less than five millions and a half. In 1871

it was five millions three hundred thousand; next year it will probably be less; of whom one million and a half are Protestants—a very different state of things from what I can remember, when in many parts, like my own, the proportion was twelve to one. Men forget that the fact of a majority does not lessen the strength of a resolute minority. Of the remaining four millions, it is believed that the small tenants, who would gain anything by such measures, are less than half a million, besides their wives and children. This is not a great number, nor such as to give any sufficient justification for setting aside sound principles of dealing with the land, even as a question of policy.

4. The simple fact is, that, with very few exceptions, tenants have not improved their farms; they have not been industrious, or skilful, or sober; a large proportion are indolent and scheming; the rents have been less than the value; nor has there been any general oppression or hardship put on them to hinder their prosperity.

Though the evidence given before the Duke of Richmond's Commission on agricultural distress has not yet been made public, yet the nature of that evidence is known. Professor Baldwin of Glasnevin, who is one of the Assistant Commissioners for Ireland, has sent in a report, and has been partly examined besides. He is, at least, a disinterested, and not a landlord's, witness; yet I believe it is not possible that anything could be stronger than the opinion he has given on the faults of Irish tenants and their worthlessness as farmers.

5. I suppose there was never a question the facts and statistics of which were so little taken into account. Everything has been taken for granted on sentiment. The only important question to the great majority of the people is, in what way the general prosperity of the country will be best promoted? in what way the most capital will be laid out? how the best wages will be paid, and who will pay them? so that the comfort of the whole people may be most advanced in better houses, clothes, and all else.

There is no doubt Ireland is a poor country compared with England, and all the capital of all classes, including the landlords, is not enough to lay out in developing its resources. The capital of the occupying tenants is not enough for farming their land moderately well in their own backward style. For anything like good farming, with better stock and enough bought manures and cattle foods, it is wholly insufficient. It is only a chance tenant who has any money to spare that he could lay out on draining or permanent buildings. The Land Act is said to have failed; the true reason is because tenants cannot get compensation for improvements which they have not made. The tenants' friends in Parliament are now asking that the owners' power of ejecting for non-payment of rent may be taken away for one year and a half and treated as a capricious eviction.

What chance is there that men who ask this will be able to lay out hundreds of pounds in permanent improvements and improved farming? The truth is, that to look to the tenants for such an outlay is a mere pretence. They cannot do it, and have not the qualities to enable them to make it succeed, even if they had the money to pay for it. I have had well-to-do tenants ask me to let my men do some special job for them that was properly their own, and offer to repay me the cost. They said I should do it so much cheaper than they could get it done, that it would be a considerable gain to them. Nearly all the improvements now existing have been made by the owners of the land, except a certain number of dwelling-houses, about which a not unhealthy vanity has grown up; and even of these in most cases the landlord has paid a large part of the cost—usually half. The statements made of tenants having made improvements are very rarely true, unless thatched cabins and a multitude of useless fences are improvements. The tenants are unable to carry out any heavy job of reclamation, as much for want of knowledge as of means.

Further, the improvements in farming during the last twenty years have been almost wholly the effect of the example of the landowners' Scotch bailiffs—"stewards" as they are called in Ireland. Some landowners, not satisfied with their own knowledge of farming, have sent their sons to Scotland to learn the very best system and ways of treating land.

In the past winter most of the loans for giving employment to the poor were taken by landowners. In a Barony in the remotest part of County Cork, where there was really some distress, two landowners undertook to employ every poor man in it. Who are able to do the draining and reclamation if the landowners give such works up ? Some landowners have built good labourers' houses for their people, with gardens, etc., attached. The wages they pay, 9s. to 12s. per week, and sometimes more, are without exception far above those paid by farmers. My rule has always been to pay a little over the usual (not the farmers') rate of the district. When a family is industrious, often two or more members of it are employed as labourers. I had a family for the last few years—new-comers to the parish—of whom I employed the father and two sons at 9s. per week each, and the mother and daughter at 6s. each—39s. in all, besides house, etc., free. At the end of three years they were no better off than when they came, and I had the satisfaction of finding that my good wages had gone to get their house blessed, to drive out the fairies, who were suspected of haunting it !

The farmers in my part now employ scarcely any labourers. They only till so much of their land as they can manage with their own help, as they call it. They will not pay the wages. A few employ a servant boy who lives in the house, and sometimes an old or very inferior man who is miserably paid, and whom they also feed because he could not work at all on his home-feeding. It is still a kind of conacre system; house and potato land, grass for a sheep or two, at a price agreed on, to be paid by the man's labour reckoned at 6d. per day. During a part of the year, when potatoes are over, a certain number of sacks of Indian meal are got from a dealer at usurious interest till the next harvest; the farmer giving security. This and the interest are paid for in the same way by the labourer. It is a sorely oppressive system. Bad work, badly paid for, with scheming and trickery, and law at all corners. If the labourers depended on the work given them by farmers, their position would be quite hopeless, except by their leaving the country. From first to last the landlords who give employment are the only persons who have done anything for labourers. The hardness with which the farmers treat their labourers is grievous; very few show them a trace of the consideration they so loudly cry for to their own landlords. If the landlords treated the tenants with half the hardness the tenants show to the labourers, they might very justly complain.

6. Nor does the matter end here. The produce of the land when well farmed is far greater than when farmed by ordinary tenants. I had occasion a few months ago to talk over with my Scotch bailiff

what was the increase of produce from the land in my own hands compared with the produce of the same land when let to tenants. I cannot prove how much the land yielded when let to tenants ; so that no certainty could be attained on that point; but we were both clearly of opinion that the produce was more than four times as great now. Several things lead me to think that it is much more than four times. The net profit—after paying Scotchman and all else —is near four times the Government (Griffith's) valuation of the land.

7. It is easy to judge what is the effect of good wages on labourers, and on the many other persons of all sorts who depend on the expenditure of money wages, or on dealing that is paid for at last out of wages. In my village of a dozen houses, a baker has set up. I built him a large oven that is in work every day, where since the time of Adam a loaf was never baked before, and where until the last few years scarcely any bread was used. He has opened a general shop too, where almost everything may be bought. What has happened on the small scale of my village is going on everywhere else on a much larger scale. The former tenants of my farm spent nothing on bought manures, or on bought foods for stock. Now, we spend over £1 per acre yearly all round on such things, and could not make the farm pay without them.

Such gains as I have described are just what

absenteeism deprives the country of. That some one should spend money on such improvements is the necessary root of any prosperity in Ireland; but, as the toes of the Divine right of tenants are thereby trodden on, the evils of absenteeism are overlooked, and the shouts are directed against the wicked improving owners, who lay out money, and look for a return in better rents. The whole argument is, that outlay of capital on the land and better farming cause the prosperity of the country and of all classes in it. Those who have lived there as long as I have, see the change unmistakably, and in those parts of the country where the largest outlay has gone on, the comfort of the people is much the greatest.

It may reasonably be asked,—If this is so, what is to be done to make things go on in Ireland, as they do in England and Scotland ?

To answer this question we must realise what is the general state of Ireland, what are its shortcomings and their causes ?

1. It may be doubted whether the intermixture of races between England, Scotland, and Ireland is not much greater than has been often supposed, though there are differences of race. The great difference does not probably lie in that.

In very early times the state of Ireland was one of constant conflict between tribes. Like the Ishmaelites, a man's hand was against every man, and every man's hand against him. The country was very

thinly peopled, especially inland. In the reign of
Queen Elizabeth we know that the troops had to cut
their way through the woods in the West Riding of
Cork to reach the rebels in remote parts after the
great Tyrone rising. It was a state of constant war.

2. In such circumstances tribal virtues and vices
would be strongly developed. Fidelity to one's own
tribe, and utter treachery and deceit towards its
enemies (*i.e.* all others), with constant violence,
would be the normal state. This in substance is very
much what we find now. Men are singularly faithful in many relations of life and to comrades even in
ill-doing. They readily combine for all sorts of ends,
especially for their own personal interests. I have
long believed that the force of Trades Unions both
in England and in America owes much to the Irish
element. It is easy to see how such tribal feelings
would adapt themselves to differences in religion and
to class differences, and would be kept alive by the
disturbed and half conquered state of the country
from the time of Henry II. to the present century.

The most striking illustration of the readiness to
form parties and "Factions" (which differ little from
tribes) that I know of, was that of the Two Year
Olds and Three Year Olds in Tipperary, of which so
much was heard a few years ago. The whole original
cause of dispute was that there existed a bull on the
borders of two parishes, which the people of one
parish said was two years old at a certain time,

whilst the people of the other parish said he was three years old. So, as neither faction would admit it was wrong, they fought, and battered, and killed each other at fairs and markets, and Sundays and holidays after mass, according to the approved system of faction - fights of fifty years ago. The Two Year Olds and Three Year Olds spread wider and wider over a considerable district of Tipperary and Limerick. They were again and again cursed by archbishops, and bishops, and priests. After seeming to die out they revived several times, and subsided only after many years.

No Irishman ever breaks the law without having one eye watching over his shoulder, to be sure his way of escape is open. I remember when I first went over, a characteristic story was current. A man was under sentence of death for some bad crime. A gentleman, near whom he had lived, chanced to know that the man had meant to shoot him. He went to the jail the day before the man was to be hanged, and said to him, "You might as well tell me, Pat, since it can now make no difference to you, why you did not shoot me; for I know you meant to do it." The gentleman was a capital shot, always carried arms, and was known to be very resolute. The answer was, "Well, your honour, it's true it will make no odds to me now; so I'll tell ye. I had ye covered twice from behind a ditch, and as I was going to pull the trigger the thought went through

my head, ' By ——, if I miss him, it's all up with
me.'"

Whenever the law is enforced, it is vastly powerful for good, all appearances to the contrary notwithstanding.   The common saying among themselves
when quarrelling and before it comes to blows, " I'll
forgive you the law, if you'll strike me," is conclusive
proof how strong a deterrent the law is, and how
every man keeps it before his eyes.   The influence in
his neighbourhood of an active magistrate, who is just
and determined, is another strong proof.   The unmixed and unvarying hatred shown in Parliament by
all Irish patriots, to the law, and police, and to all
that helps to make these efficient, shows that they
know who are their real enemies.   The curious readiness to go security for neighbours who borrow money,
or in any way want security, comes from this same
clan feeling.   It is nothing short of folly, and ends in
the ruin of numbers.

It is sadly certain, too, that untruth towards all the
rest of the world grievously prevails.   It is the most
painful part of living in Ireland.   It meets one at
every turn, and among all sorts and classes.   One is
forced to become as hard as the nether millstone, and
simply believe nothing at all, if one would not be the
prey of every schemer.   No doubt there are individuals who speak the truth.   God forbid there should
not be.   And there are degrees of truth (or untruth)
that one learns to recognise.   There is a common

expression, which I can never hear without laughing.
When any one wishes to convince you that another
may be believed about something in which his interest is not concerned, he will say, " You know, sir,
Jack is a man who would not tell ye a lie for nothing." There is, no doubt, a distinction in this,
though the moral attainment of Jack may not be of
very high value. One has to judge mainly by proba-
bilities. Happily everybody in his heart is alive to
the untruth. The man himself feels it, and does not
expect to be believed, though he may hope it. Then
there is the enemy with his story on the other side;
so that practically it is easier to make up your mind,
if you thoroughly know the people and their interests,
than could beforehand be thought possible.

The first thing needful for any one who has to
deal with Irish questions, but who does not know the
people, is clearly to recognise this universal untruth.
If he takes that fairly and fully into account, he has
no great difficulty in forming a sound judgment.
Otherwise he is the prey of whoever can get his ear.

It is not only the deliberate falsehoods, but the
unreliableness throughout, that has to be met. There
is an atmosphere of untruth and half-truth surround-
ing everything, so that those who are true themselves,
but have been brought up in this atmosphere, seem
unconscious of it, and treat want of truth with a for-
bearance it does not deserve. Nobody seems to
expect that truth and right shall prevail. When, as

a magistrate, one has decided against a man, there is
no wonder he should think you have decided contrary
to truth and right; but when one has decided in a
man's favour, it is a hard case when he meets you
and says, "God bless your honour; it was only
through you I got the better of that blackguard."
The man does not believe in the truth and right of
his own case, and thinks he won by favour.

Untruth is at the bottom of the universal scheming and jobbing that prevails. Without that such
scheming would be impossible, and the plausible
assurance and confidence with which it is all done—
the assertion of the very highest motives only—often
puts one in doubt whether to laugh or cry.

The most painful proof of the depth to which untruth prevails amongst us is the way in which some
of the Bishops and most of the clergy of the Church
of Ireland have acted under the Disestablishment Act.
The jobbing and money-getting that has gone on, especially under the power given of Compounding, was such
as no one could have believed possible. The Act gave
the power to compound, *i.e.* of selling out his annuity
for a lump sum, free from the claim the Church Act
gave, that the clergyman should continue to do duty
in the Church. It required the consent of the Representative Body, plainly in order that Compounding
might only be done under such arrangements as would
not be a loss to the Church. Compounding in some
cases, and to a moderate and fair extent, was a gain,

but if carried far was a great loss to the Church. The Representative Body was very soon induced to give the full right of compounding at their own pleasure to all clergymen. We were assured they were so conscientious, that the right might be granted safely.

It has come to pass that almost all men promoted to better livings, compound for their former incumbencies before they finally accept the better ones, and so, besides the income of the better livings, put large sums in their pockets for ever, that otherwise would and should have remained to the Church! I could quote cases within my own knowledge, in which a Bishop appointed to a see, with a thoroughly secured income of over £1500 a year, compounded for a living he had held before, and put more than £5000 besides into his pocket for ever, that otherwise would have gone to the Disestablished Church. I could tell of a Dean having a small living, and being promoted to a much better living, and compounding for the smaller living, and pocketing £2000 out of it, besides the larger income of his new parish.

I am thankful to add that we have a few cases of clergymen who refused to take a shilling of such gains, because they said the money belonged to God's service, and not to themselves. All honour be to them!

3. There is no such thing as a healthy public opinion in Ireland among any class. There is nothing and no one to put anybody to shame, what-

ever his conduct may be. Men often do acts, after
which, if done in England, they would never again
venture to look an honest man in the face. In Ireland they walk about as confident as ever, as if
they had done nothing to be ashamed of. Nobody
treats them as worse than others, or seems to think
them so.

4. There is no royal road to better the condition
of Ireland or to improve its land. A country in
such a backward and undeveloped state is simply in
a state of childhood. For this reason the strictest
application of sound rules of right and wrong, and of
those economical principles of free and open competition that have so helped the prosperity of England, are of supreme importance.

5. That the law should be always enforced is one
of the greatest needs of the country. When there is
any difficulty in enforcing it, it is a sure proof that
the law needs to be strengthened, so that it may be
enforced. No one should be left the least hope that
he can evade the law. It is not severity that is
wanted—it is the certainty of punishment for wrongdoing.

I believe that a sure punishment of one month
on the treadmill, if it might be inflicted summarily,
on the same principles as are held to justify arrest
when the Habeas Corpus Act is suspended, would
keep the most disturbed district quiet. I acted on
this view during the Fenian troubles, only of course

I was bound by the rules of evidence. Whenever I could, I sent all who broke the law to the treadmill for a month. The result was capital. The punishment seemed so light that their very friends laughed at them. But their own remark, after the month was over, was, "Whisha, 'twould kill Samson." It did come sharp on men of a sort not much used to hard work. Afterwards I got a message from some of them that I was so impartial that they would not object to be tried for their lives by me. So it is clear I did not sin in over-severity.

If indicted, they would have had the chance of a "friend on the jury," who would not find a verdict. Under Lord O'Hagan's last unfortunate Jury Act, there are very few counties in which a conviction for many sorts of crimes can be got. In Ireland, this "friend on the jury" is one of the institutions of the country, and one of its curses. Magistrates in Ireland have often to serve on juries, and I have often done so. Whenever a prejudice of religion, or any other, could be brought into a case anyhow, though it was a purely civil case, the end was certain. It was utterly disgusting work, and added to one's conviction of the grievous untruthfulness of the country. Any one who had been a lawyer could see the counsel on one side fighting to make a case for influencing a juror to stand out, and so no verdict. There is a public butter market in Cork, where business is done to an immense value, but which is a wholly close market, and has no legal rights whatever. In my memory there have been five actions tried against it with a view to open the market. In every one the Judge summed up strongly against it; but a friend on the jury (the market is very influential) refused to agree to a verdict, and so the market went on again as before, and does so still.

It can be judged of from this, what are the chances of a verdict in criminal cases in which religion or class interests are concerned. The effect of the new Jury Act is, that whilst in form promoting impartiality in the selection of a jury, it really enables the criminal to escape scatheless, whether he is guilty or not, because the jury is not impartial.

As proofs of the effect of enforcing the law, I would recall O'Connell's trial after his agitation for Repeal. A conviction was got, he was put in prison, but not long after escaped by a writ of error in the House of Lords upon a technical fault in the proceedings. Yet such was the effect of its being seen and felt that the Government would put the law in force, and no longer allow itself to be trifled with, that the agitation collapsed, and he never again could recover his influence. So in the Fenian scare, the same night that it was announced in the House of Commons that the Habeas Corpus would be suspended in Ireland, the steamers to England were full of Fenians getting out of reach of the expected Act; they thought the Standing Orders would be suspended, and the Act passed at once. When lately the Westmeath Act passed, which in substance gave power to suspend the Habeas Corpus in proclaimed districts, they knew there was not so much hurry, so waited for the third reading in the House of Lords. There was a complete reign of terror in Westmeath, kept up by only about twelve or twenty ruffians, all known to the police. They murdered the stationmaster at Mullingar, because he was strict to the porters, and others. A labourer could not be discharged without danger. As soon as the third reading of the Act passed, the whole set went together to America from Queenstown, and the country was quiet.

I never took a serious view of the Fenian affair. I thought it one of those Irish follies only needing to have a firm foot placed on it to be put down.

In the small town near me a set of silly boys and others " began the war " as they called it. Beginning the war consisted in trying to rescue any drunken men the police arrested and were taking to Bridewell. They did not succeed in rescuing anybody, but in a few days two or three attempts were made, and the police were hustled and struck. Summonses for the next Petty Sessions were issued, and threats were used by the Fenians, that, if any one was punished, it would be the worse for the magistrates, etc. etc. I did not hear of the matter till the day before the Petty Sessions, and having then asked what precautions had been taken to prevent a rescue and protect

the magistrates, was told that a good many extra
police had been ordered in. I at once said that was
quite enough to make a successful fight, but not
enough to prevent a row from taking place (the only
right principle to act on in Ireland), and as there
were dragoons thirteen miles off, I signed a requisi-
tion for a small party of them to come over next
morning. At ten o'clock there they were, drawn up
outside the town, and waiting for a magistrate to
billet them.

The result was the most amiable quiet. The
officers sat with us for their amusement all day. I
went to Court resolved, if possible, that some one
should go to the treadmill for a month for his
country's good. Too much fuss had been made about
the first cases, and it was necessary to send them to
Quarter Sessions for trial, which had the effect of
letting the offenders out on bail. At length three
unhappy fellows had cases proved against them, and
I persuaded the other J.P.'s to sentence them to one
month on the treadmill. In ordinary course they
would have been forwarded to Cork gaol next day.
And I knew that there would be an ovation of
Fenians, and perhaps a row, when they started.

It was a frosty evening, and I asked the officer of
the dragoons how fast he should go home if we let
him go. "About six miles an hour," was the answer.
I replied, "The door of the gaol at B. is just opposite
your barrack gate. Will you take charge of these

men in a car and lodge them in it?" My friend was
only too happy to go home on such conditions. In a
quarter of an hour the soldiers were at the back door
of our Bridewell, mounted. The prisoners were in a
car with two policemen, and all trotted off, whilst
their friends knew nothing of what was happening,
and there was not a soul to cheer them. A note to the
county jailor requested him to give them as much of
the treadmill as the law permitted. And a grim answer
came back, that he would take care they should return with a salutary dread of that establishment.

So there was no more war or trouble with Fenianism in that place. Some time after the men had
done their month, happening to meet the head con-
stable, I asked how his friends were going on. The
answer was, " Oh, sir, you might send them for a
message down the pump, if you wished. When they
meet me in the street, if they are the same side, they
cross over to the other, for fear I should say they
jostled me."

6. Home Rule is even a more pitiful sham than
Fenianism. In O'Connell's agitation the leaders were
at least men of intellect and power of mind. Everybody knows what the Leaders and the Led are now.
The one good they have done is to make this known
to all. A firm grasp by the Government would put an
end to them.

It is this artificial character of Irish agitations, and
that they are not caused by real present grievances,

that makes much of the difficulty. Agitations are in substance got up by the agitators, upon the remains of the ill-will of former days, and are purposely contrived to give all the trouble possible in every way. Every one in them means to go as far as he can, without getting himself personally into trouble. The more bad motives and ill-will he can infuse, and the more alarm and excitement he can cause, the more his end is attained.

Yet all this time the real danger to the peace of the country is very small, as all sensible men, and even the agitators too, know well. Of course, the classes which would gain by the agitation, if it could succeed, back it up as well as they can. Why should they not do so? If agitators in England proposed to give a great dole to some poor class out of the pockets of another class, would they too not shout for it? What does the fear of Socialism on the Continent, especially in Germany, mean? Its root is the same as that of Irish agitation.

But in Ireland the class that hopes to gain by it has no idea of committing itself. If the agitation succeeds, it will gain something. If it fails, it loses nothing that it had before. It is just making-believe, like all the rest. I firmly believe the mass of the people are quiet and willing to obey the law, only they cannot resist trying what can be had at the cost of others by scheming, when the hope is held out to them.

7. Another great need of the country is more

industry. They are not an industrious people. Hard work, however gainful, is disliked. They will work hard by fits and starts; but the steady backbone is not there. There is nothing to hinder any man from reaping the fruit of his industry. Many do so. Things are not now as they were before the famine, when, if a tenant lost his bit of land, there was little for him to fall back on. Labour is now well paid, whilst there is every facility for earning still higher wages in England and America. The man who clings to a wretched bit of land in Ireland, that is unable to support him and his, is just a pauper, and must be so for ever if he stays.

What Mr. Robert Chambers, with Scotch canniness, calls the "peasant proprietor craze" needs qualities that are very rare in Ireland—great industry, skill, and self-exertion.

Instead of being a sort which the State should strive to root in the soil, the State (if it is to do anything) should put paupers like these somewhere where they can earn a better living, and the children can grow up in comfort and decency, different from the state of their parents. Such paupers are useful to agitators, and to no one else. They form, in fact, the agitator's stock-in-trade, and the agitators accordingly do their best to preserve them. The more that is done for them by the State, or any one else, the worse they will be. They are in the position of a protected interest under the very worst circumstances, because they never had any industry or exertion in them. To treat them as some seem to wish is pure protectionism. And as with other protected interests, Free Competition, in the same way as it has been brought to bear on all the other protected interests of the kingdom, is the only way to cure the evils that arise from it.

Those who propose heroic cures are, without exception, men who have no personal knowledge of land or of farming. All the powers on earth cannot improve land, except by the expenditure of capital of some sort, or of labour which is capital. These men have no sort of capital, they hinder those who have it from expending it, and will not work hard themselves.

The principle of the Land Act was economically unsound. It was really a measure of protectionism for one kind of business—small farming in the hands of the least industrious class in the three kingdoms. The business of small farming needs the stimulus of free competition more than almost any other business; and protection to small farmers was sure to produce, and has produced, the same effects on them that it has produced everywhere else.

8. One thing that makes the progress of Ireland slow is that it is only within the last ten years that the personal recollections of the Rebellion of 1798 have passed away. Ten years ago there were many alive who could tell of the crimes and horrors they had actually seen or heard. And there is a reality in

the accounts of such things by old people who have been eye-witnesses, that makes them very different from hearsay second-hand stories.

It is not many years since, taking shelter in a cabin from a shower, an old woman told me all that happened during the rebellion of 1798 in my own neighbourhood. Chancing to repeat what she had told me to a friend, a General Officer of Artillery from another district, he answered, "Remember it? why, I was out, and helping to put the rebellion down." It appeared that his father, having fought manfully as a Royalist in South Carolina during the American Revolution, and lost in it wife and child and all that he had there, when the rebellion of '98 broke out, was put in command of a camp of volunteers, etc., twelve miles from his home in Ireland. My friend was twelve years old, and when his father started for his command, his mother hid the boy's shoes, to prevent his following. When his father got up next morning, there was the boy without shoes in the corner of the tent. So he was allowed to stay and go through it.

Soon after, talking over the subject with an old poor-law guardian, he said, "Oh, I remember all about it. I was a boy and lay behind the ditch, to see it all, when there was the fighting at the cross above."

This fighting is known in history as the Battle of Ballinascarthy, which I well recollect to have heard of often in childhood, because our best tenant had been killed at it with a year's rent in his pocket, which was never seen after.

Part of a regiment of militia from the north of Ireland had been quartered at the small town near, to keep the district quiet. It was known that some of the men had been tampered with by the rebels. So the militia were ordered to march one morning for Cork, whilst some regulars were sent from Cork to take their place.

My friend the guardian described it :—" They went along the old road as far as the Big Cross (marked on the Ordnance map still as Croppy's Cross). There the rebels were waiting for them in the fields. The captain was on horseback, and he stood upon the bit of grass in the middle, where the roads meet, and the sergeant by his side. Jack —— he put up his gun to shoot the officer, and before he could do it, the sergeant shot him. Then Jim —— he shot the sergeant; and they were just going at it hammer and tongs (no doubt in hopes to master and kill the officers and loyal men) when, sure enough, the army from Cork was seen coming over the hill along the road, not a quarter of a mile off. Then they ran away down the fields as hard as they could go, and the soldiers after them. And then Peter ——, and Mick ——, and Pat ——, and Denis ——, with a dozen others—whose names he mentioned as fathers, or uncles, or related to people one knew about—were all killed."

Can it be wondered at that, when living accounts of fights like this, and of many others worse and far more barbarous, could be heard from eye-witnesses, breaking the law should be thought little of ?   I can remember how the horror of the stories I heard fastened itself on my imagination in early youth : such as the burning of the Shea family in the county Tipperary, the murder of another family at Wild Goose Lodge, and many others.

Whilst such things as these are present in men's minds, not as matters of history, but as realities, a country cannot be peaceable ; everything in the way of outrage seems possible and easy.

Then wherever men have the idea of outrage in their minds, intimidation is sure to present itself as advantageous. In fact, in Ireland, in any difficulty, the first resource of many is intimidation.   The frequent threatening letters we read of in the papers are a proof of this, though ninety-nine out of a hundred are rubbish—only attempts to frighten.   The threats are by no means always threats of outrage, but of all kinds of indefinite wrath, loss of favour and of help, which the unhappy offender will or shall encounter. Many will threaten, and try to intimidate, who never really intend to commit an outrage.   Then the people are curiously afraid of each other.   Again and again, when I have suggested to a man that he should do something that was likely to be unpopular with some of his neighbours, I have had the answer, " How

could I tell, but may be when I was not expecting it
I'd get a blow of a stone on my head, from behind
a ditch, that might kill me ? "

9. The idea that a man is independently to act
on his own judgment about public questions does not
seem to exist. 1 remember many years ago, during
the reign of Lord Palmerston, his Attorney-General
was member of Parliament for County Cork. He
had to seek re-election on his appointment, and
though a thoroughly respectable Roman Catholic, the
Roman Catholic priests opposed him, to punish Lord
Palmerston for something he had done. The Attorney-General was a native of the small town near me,
where he had many relatives, and was very popular.
So the people and Roman Catholic clergy of it were
all with him, but not so in other parishes. I went to
vote for him, and when I got near the polling-place,
I saw a mob, which, as soon as they saw me, started
off towards me. I soon found they were townspeople,
who had caught a very respectable and thriving
tenant of mine from a neighbouring parish, going to
vote against their popular Attorney-General. They
had had him some time, arguing that I was going
to vote for their man, so he had no right to vote
the other way, and when I came, I should make him
vote as they wished. He declared he was sure I
should not ask him. So all eagerly rushed at me,
entreating me to make him vote right. The coolness
of the man, who was only gratifying his priest, and

the excitement of the crowd, were most amusing to
see. I told him, of course, to do as he liked, to the
sore disappointment of my neighbours. It was most
characteristic. Nowhere are the mischiefs of government by party so evident as in a country in the condition of Ireland. The questions that divide parties
in England and Scotland are only on the surface,
compared with those that are at stake in Ireland.
It is not alone differences of religion, but all the
rights of property, as hitherto understood, that are in
the balance.

10. The system of competitive examination for
all the minor Government appointments, as Excise,
Customs, etc., has done great good if only by lessening the party patronage to be given away. The
number of successful candidates has been much beyond the proportion of the numbers of the people.
A good schoolmaster, able to grind up youths for
the examination, does great good and gets well paid.
The successive masters of a national school in the
small town near, of which I am the manager, have
more than once passed three or four candidates,
out of a total of eighty to one hundred vacancies for
the three kingdoms. The school is only attended by
Protestant children, of whom we have many. But
for grinding youths for Government examinations,
Roman Catholics come to our masters as freely as
Protestants. Religious differences don't count when
there is something to be got, and Roman Catholics

succeed as well as Protestants when they have an
equally good teacher.

11. Whatever appointments, high or low, are
made for party reasons are often grievously jobbed ;
and there is no difference in that respect in my experience between the two parties ; one is as bad as
the other. Thus, the appointments to the magistracy
are often very bad. Men are not seldom appointed
who are wholly unfit, without education, knowledge,
character, or even property. Religion or politics are
the only motive. The queer thing is that some of
the worst appointments are those of men of a different religion from that supposed to be allied with the
party by whom the appointment is made. We have
men nominated of whom it is doubtful if they can
read and write, and others who, unless direly maligned,
have themselves been guilty of all sorts of offences.
No one can believe the harm such appointments
do. The Stipendiary magistrates, too, are appointed
for party reasons, and many of them are very inferior, and of no value ; in no way men of the high
character that well-paid Government officials ought
to be. Of course, some are fit men, but others are
such as a magistrate who knows his business would
prefer not to have with him, if there was any difficulty.

The same evil is visible, though in a less degree,
in the Chairmen of Quarter Sessions. Having attended Quarter Sessions for nearly forty years in

Ireland, I have of course seen a great variety, and many whom I knew are dead or have left. Whilst some were men to be respected, I have seen things permitted by others, and done by them, and a want of uprightness, that, as a lawyer, made one's blood boil. Going to Ireland fresh from years of Circuit and Sessions, and having also acted for years as a magistrate for Suffolk, with a colleague on the Bench who had been himself a lawyer, and was quite the best magistrate I ever knew, I grieved from the first over these great defects in the administration of justice in Ireland, and have never ceased to lament them.

Appointing the best man to be found, and making the administration of justice the first object, is not cared for as it ought to be ; and though the outward forms may be carefully kept up, yet on many questions there is an evident bias, which is very hurtful. Let what I have said of the absence of a healthy public opinion be always remembered, as well as the backward state of things fifty or a hundred years ago. The improvement since that time will then be seen to be great, and in spite of all drawbacks, it is still going on.

The object to aim at is to raise into a higher state poor and backward people, who by help of potato cultivation had grown up in numbers that potatoes alone could barely support, and who have neither industry, self-reliance, nor knowledge of anything fit-ting them for such higher state, now when potatoes can no longer be relied on. And the question is, whether this can best be done by acting on plans which are partly speculative theories about peasant proprietorship, partly the scheming of those who have their own ends to serve, and partly the sentimental views of politicians, all seeking to employ means hitherto unknown among us, and which would be unjust and dishonest to the class of owners; or by following the plain common-sense ways of practical men, who understand land, and which have succeeded in their hands, and whether they wholly succeed or not, must do good so far as they go.

CHAPTER XII.

ULSTER TENANT-RIGHT.

DECEMBER 1, 1880. (Partly from *Macmillan's Magazine*.)

IN discussing the proposed remedies for Irish difficulties it is needful to bear clearly in mind the facts
that have been established in former papers, before all
things, the thorough Scheming and falsehood that run
through everything said and done in Ireland. It has
been suggested to me that out of Ireland it will not
be understood what is meant by scheming. It is the
working to make personal gain out of everything,
small or great, without respect to truth or honesty,—
e.g. saying that tenants have brought the land out of
a valueless state by nature into productiveness; that
they have made valuable permanent improvements,
that they are charged unduly high rents, and their
improvements taken advantage of by the landlords;
that they are treated with hardness and capriciously
evicted—these are statements almost wholly untrue,
and if in a few cases true, are only so in part. They
are put forward as the ground for every sort of unjus-
tifiable claim, in hope of getting some personal gain.

The real state of the country is one of great backwardness in civilisation. Education, habits, and ideas,
are those of a semi-barbarous people. They have both
the virtues and vices of that state. Read the daily
account in the papers of outrages committed. To
say nothing of shocking murders, consider what such
facts as these mean.—Not long ago the house of a
poor man in County Limerick, who had given offence,
was beset. They tied him down in bed and cut off
his ears. Of course this is better than burning him
and his wife and children alive in their house, as
was done in the same district within the memory of
many. Only to cut off the man's ears shows progress.
But what a progress! It is still grievous barbarism,
if less horrible than formerly. Since then other poor
men's ears have been cut off. Cutting off ears or
slitting them is fast becoming an institution in Ireland. It has become a positive cause of fear to harmless people. Yet there are a large number of Irish
M.P.'s who feel no shame in stirring up an agitation,
of which these acts are the sure fruit, and when such
cruelties have been done, palliate and excuse them,
and deny that they are answerable for such wickedness, and think it is enough to assert it is the fault
of the Government or landlords, and face it out with
vehement assertion.

The country being in this state of semi-barbarism,
with parts on the eastern side more advanced, and
parts on the western side more backward, the first

fact to be observed is, that the average Irish peasant has no desire for progress and civilisation. His view is that he ought to be left all the rough advantages of his uncivilised condition, and that besides concessions ought to be made to him (at whose cost he cares not), to make up to him, and more, for all the disadvantages of that condition. The strongest ground on which he asks for such concessions is his poverty, and he and his M.P.'s urge the extreme poverty of the poorest part of Connaught as a sufficient reason why concessions should be extended over the three-fourths of Ireland that are much farther advanced. He has no thought that concession, not founded on strict right, must be ruinous to the country, and in the end even to himself. The present moment and his personal gain are all he can think of, and by this importunity of poverty, like the clamour of the sturdy beggar, he does influence those who act on sentiment rather than on facts. It is these very men who use threats and commit outrages to keep up, as far as possible, a Reign of Terror. Nearly all the fine sentiments of patriotism and the rest, that are put forward, are the merest shams, invented for the occasion, having no foundation in fact. The strongest feeling of patriotism is jealousy of England. The legislation of 1870 proceeded on the view that most Irish tenants are good and worthy men, and most Irish landlords the reverse; the truth being, that the proportion of bad tenants in Ireland, indolent, drinking, and use-

less, is grievously large, and though some landlords
neglect their duties by not laying out money on their
land, the proportion of those who treat their tenants
with any harshness is very small.

The Devon Commission in 1844 visited every
corner of Ireland and investigated every case of hardship that could be heard of. The result was so trifling
that for a generation complaints of hardship ceased.
Lately such complaints have again begun, it is believed
with less foundation even than in 1844. Whenever
definite complaints have been made, they have been
shown to be untrue. One good of the new Commission is, that it will test all such complaints. This
is the reason why it is objected to by the Land
League.

We who live in the country know the men and
the details of the cases in our own districts that are
brought forward. I know the facts about two such
cases that have been the pretence for neighbouring
land meetings, and assert that, from first to last, they
rest on mere untruth. It is upon men in this social
and moral state that the franchise has been conferred.
They are placed in what is to them a constitutional
hotbed, with the same rights as sober, intelligent,
and educated men in England and Scotland enjoy.
A better illustration cannot be found than in the
Borough Franchise. In England in boroughs every
householder has a vote. In Ireland a £4 valuation
is required for a vote. If a household franchise was

given, the occupier of every thatched hovel would
have a vote, and the whole political power in such
boroughs (not including large towns) would be put
into the hands of the occupiers of these hovels. A
hovel is a house, and a house may be a hovel. Therefore the immense difference between the occupiers of
hovels in Irish boroughs and houses in England is
put aside.

What wonder can there be that dwellers in such
wretched hovels as can be seen in the purlieus of
every Irish town think that the only use of a vote is
to try and get some personal gain for themselves, and
are ready to follow the foolishness of agitators, who
are really only the worst of their own sort, much
worse than most of the poor people, having all their
faults and none of their good qualities? The one
argument in favour of the extension of the franchise
in Ireland is, that the members returned now are
such a thoroughly bad set, that it is impossible worse
can be found, whatever the franchise may be. It is
hard to answer this.

The extension of the Ulster tenant-right custom
to the rest of Ireland is often spoken of as a remedy
for all the evils of the country. Such an extension would be contrary to all principles of honest
dealing towards the owners of land. By the Ulster
tenant-right, whenever the tenant leaves his farm
from any cause, he is usually entitled to sell (what is
called) his interest in it to the highest bidder, pro-

vided he is not a bad character. The transaction is wholly between the outgoing and incoming tenants, the landlord having nothing to do with it, except that any arrears of rent due are paid out of the purchase-money. The landlord may object to the purchaser if he is of bad character. But the faults that would justify such an objection are not of the kind that are common among those who have money enough to buy a farm. So that this right in the landlord is of little consequence. In theory, too, the landlord is at liberty to raise the rent. But the practical difficulties in his way, unless the rise be very trifling or the rent unduly low, are so great, that it is very seldom he can accomplish it. The rate of purchase is sometimes as high as twenty years of the rent and over. Ten years' purchase is thought an ordinary and moderate rate. The price depends upon the acreable rent, and all the other incidents that affect the letting value of land, especially the demand for farms at the moment. Whether the times are good or bad makes a great difference in the price of tenant-right. It has been asserted that tenant-right existed in Ulster more than 200 years ago. The proof of this, however, is very indifferent. Whether it existed or not, it is certain its great extension occurred at the latter part of the last century, when the great improvement of the linen trade took place. Hand-spinning of linen thread and handloom-weaving were then universal in many parts of Ireland. They went on in every farmer's and labourer's house. The land in Ulster had already been very much subdivided. When the linen trade flourished, it enabled industrious families to make money and pay great sums for the tenant-right of the small lots of their neighbours, willing to sell from any cause.

The spinning-wheel and the loom afterwards earned the means of stocking and manuring the land bought. Tenant-right can only live when the rent is under the true value of the land. If the land is let at the full value, the tenant has nothing to sell. Very little thought will show it is impossible men should go on, from generation to generation, paying the full value of the land in rent, and a great sum of money besides on entry. In those days, and long after, rents were very ill paid in Ireland ; the landlords lost in this way very largely. As under tenant-right all arrears of rent due were paid out of the purchase-money, most Ulster landlords acquiesced in the system, and sanctioned it. The purchaser paid his money into the landlord's office ; the arrears were taken out of it, and the balance handed to the outgoing tenant. It was well known that often incoming tenants thus paid away not only all their own money, but also all they were able to borrow from their friends besides, in order to buy Tenant-right.

When thus stripped of capital it was impossible a tenant should farm the land well. If a few bad years chanced to come he was ruined, and had to sell his interest again for whatever it would fetch, submitting to the loss. Any arrears of rent that he might have accumulated in his turn were stopped out of the money that was payable to him, and thus he often became a pauper, or near it. The immense effect of bad or good years upon Tenant-right has never been duly observed. It is much greater than upon tenants holding in the common way. Further, Tenant-right is a chattel. It may be sold by a creditor for debt, and it may be left by will or settled independently of the farm itself. Sales by creditors are common, they are just the same as ejectments in effect. Tenant-right, too, is left often to wife and younger children as a provision, and so has to be paid over again by the son who gets the farm, thus pumping the farm dry of capital every generation, at the very time when a young, energetic man enters on it, who could do much good if he had the capital. Tenant-right rested wholly upon custom; the custom is said to vary in nearly every county in Ulster. It had no legal authority, but the customs were so undoubted that hardly any one thought of disregarding them, or indeed would have ventured to do so. The Land Act gave the customs legal right. Having been acted on by landlord and tenant alike, there was a clear equity in favour of the customs, and it was right that any legal doubt about them should be removed.

There have been disputes under the Land Act, but they have been about small accessories of the

customs. These have been decided on appeal by
the judges of the superior courts named for that purpose. It has been established that a limitation of
the customs on estates to four years' purchase is good.
This was settled as to Lord Erne's estate in Ulster,
where the tenants are very flourishing. Four years
was insisted on, because by paying more the new tenant stripped himself so bare of capital as to have none
for farming the land. There have been other like minor
points. The decisions, it should be observed, wholly
turn on the question, What was the custom of the
estate ? The tenants had bought their several rights
in their farms expressly under the custom of the estate,
well known to them and the landlord. What they had
bought and paid for, the same, and no other, they
had a just claim to sell. The tenants' efforts of
course have been to claim and get the utmost custom
that prevails anywhere. Whenever a decision was
made contrary to their interest, of course a howl and
clamour rose up about it. Several small attempts
have been made in Parliament to get an Act passed
reversing the judges' decisions. All have failed.
The custom is the universal rule of right everywhere.

About 1840 I went to Ulster to inform myself on
the management of land there. Previous to that
time the difficulties in the management of land in
Ulster were as great as in other provinces. Tenants
were usually as badly off and unsatisfactory as elsewhere. The linen trade had led to great subdivision

of farms. The arrears of rent on many estates were grievous. The intermixing of fields of different occupiers caused a great loss to the tenants. How is it possible to farm to advantage when the farmer has several fields, an acre or two each in different parts of the estate, that he must go a quarter or half a mile round to get into!

As I have said before, I happened to know Mr. W. Blacker, of Armagh. He had started the plan of getting over a Scotch grieve and fixing him on an estate, whose whole business it should be to go amongst the tenants to teach them better farming, and especially how to grow clover and turnips, before quite unknown. This answered well. The increased food for stock soon produced more and better manure; this gave better crops, and a wonderful change was effected. I stayed some time with Mr. Blacker, and remember going over an estate with him which he had bought for a friend. It was bought with a large arrear of rent upon it, every shilling of which by this plan was paid up in a few years, and the purchase-money thus largely reduced, whilst the tenants prospered much.

Nothing could be more interesting or instructive than the results Mr. Blacker showed. His example had been followed by many other landlords, sometimes by getting Scotch grieves, sometimes by transplanting one of Mr. Blacker's good tenants into one of their farms as an example. Having gone with him for a tour in the counties of Tyrone and Fermanagh, to see what was going on there among his pupils, I remember at one place we went to visit one of Mr. Blacker's transplanted tenants, and found he had given up all the good ways in which he had been instructed, and had relapsed into barbarous native habits.

Whilst Blacker was reproving his erring sheep, an old neighbouring tenant, who had joined himself to us in our walk, as the way is in Ireland, came up to his landlord and me, and said, "Whisha, your honour, ye brought that fellow to be a parable to us, and sure he is as bad as any of us." It was too true.

It will thus be seen that though the looms were then in almost every house in a large part of Ulster, Tenant-right did not save the country from the common troubles of Irish bad farming and subdividing land, nor raise the condition of the people. It never could do so. Still less can it do so in the other provinces, where very few are able to pay large sums to get possession of farms but shopkeepers who have made money in business. What is the gain from such men as farmers? A great trade in Ulster for many generations has enriched many of the people, and Scotch blood and habits have helped to make Ulster more prosperous. That is all. After the Land Act passed in 1870 we had several very prosperous years for farmers. The prices paid for Tenant-right rose higher and higher; and the years

being good, and, as usual, Hope telling a flattering
tale, all were sure that prosperity would be eter-
nal, only greater prosperity still. Sellers and buyers
both could not praise Tenant-right enough. Though
those of us who remembered that after the famine
in 1846 the price of Tenant-right fell to almost
nothing, and knew its unsoundness in principle,
always predicted what would happen in the changes
and chances of time. The last three years the tall
talk in Ulster itself in favour of Tenant-right has
greatly come down. Of course there are many who
still praise it, and the interests of all who now occupy
land are involved in it to the extent of hoping to be
able to sell out of their farms well. The present
discontent in Ulster is wholly caused by a heavy fall
in the price of Tenant-right. Let the account of
Donegal in Mr. Tuke's pamphlet on *Irish Distress
and its Remedies*, p. 8 *et seq.*, be read. These letters
give the most instructive view of Tenant-right that I
have ever seen. They prove that it in no way meets
the farmer's troubles and difficulties.

It will be seen then that Tenant-right is no security
even against starvation. Tenant-right is as strong
in Donegal as in any other part of Ulster; yet, as
Mr. Tuke tells us, whole parishes were starving last
winter, though every man had this valuable Tenant-
right, as it is supposed to be, which he could have
sold not long before for ten to twenty years' purchase.
A few with better or larger lots, that could still find

purchasers, sold out at a low price to go to America.
(Page 11.) The rest were fed by charity. Large
parts all over Ulster, in spite of Tenant-right, are no
better than the rest of Ireland. And this is put forth
as a system to cure all the evils of the country! The
sure result of a bad system is, it breaks down when
the pinch comes. For forty years past it has been
my clear opinion, as a practical farmer, that the time
would come when Ulster would be the poorest part
of Ireland, because Tenant-right sucked away from
the land the capital that ought to enrich it. Nor are
the difficulties at all confined to Donegal. Wherever
the effect of the linen trade is not felt, the tenants are
in the same state as in Donegal.

In the *English Agricultural Gazette* of August
30, there are two letters from an Ulster farmer who
is plainly a man of some education, and, we are told
by Mr. Morton, the editor, has often sent him valuable practical notes on farming subjects. The letters
are nothing else but a prolonged scream against rents
and landlords, with really piteous and pitiable appeals
to landlords and to Parliament to lower rents out of
charity, and every other motive he can think of. Of
course he does not say that he or his predecessor
bought the Tenant-right of his farm from the previous
tenant for a large sum, knowing perfectly the rent it
was subject to, and without any thought of the landlord, thus proving the farm to be worth more than
the rent he pays. He calls himself one of an

oppressed and down-trodden class ; talks of landlords
rolling in wealth, and tries to excite every prejudice
and ill-feeling that the Land League habitually relies
on, because, having made a bad bargain in buying
Tenant-right, his landlord does not save him from
the consequent loss.

Well may Mr. A. M. Sullivan, the Home Rule
M.P., suggest, as he does, that the price of Tenant-
right shall be fixed by arbitration as well as the rent.
I wonder how the tenants who have Tenant-right to
sell will like that proposal.   It is a blessed foretaste
of the wise principles on which Ireland will be
governed under Home Rule.   Why should not everything be decided by arbitration ? prices of corn and
meat, *e.g.*   As one wrote lately, why should tenants
get a great boon in price, and buyers of bread and
meat pay as long a price as ever ?

To any one who can read between the lines,
both Mr. Sullivan's letter and Mr. Tuke's pamphlet are more than instructive.   The Land Act
makes Tenant-right legally binding in all parts of
Ireland as much as in Ulster, *wherever like customs
exist*.   There are many estates in other parts, of
which Lord Portsmouth in Wexford is a leading
example, on which the custom of Tenant-right has
been allowed to grow up.   Whenever this has
happened with the consent of landlord and tenant,
no one has a right to say anything against it.   If it
is unsound in principle, it must be left to cure itself

in time, and meanwhile it does not hinder others
from acting on sounder principles, or stop, except to
a small extent, the general progress of the country,
which depends on sound principle and on nothing
else. Tenant-right is liked by agents, because it
greatly lessens their trouble in collecting rents and
getting rid of bad tenants, who must be turned out.
The rent is always safe, and a broken tenant goes
out with much less trouble when he is to receive a
lot of money on doing so; though to oblige the
landlord to pay a fat, idle, drinking tenant because
he ruins himself would be absurd. Naturally when a
tenant paid nothing at all for his farm at hiring, he
finds it pleasant and profitable if he leaves it to
receive a great sum also for nothing.

Forty years ago, I remember, it was much discussed in the South, among landowners and agents,
whether the introduction of the Ulster Tenant-right
on their estates would be advantageous.

Having thoroughly seen its working in Ulster, I
have never had any doubt that the common way of
fair contract between landlord and tenant was much
better for both ; that the tenants would gain far
more by using their money in better stocking and
manuring their farms, and that they need every
shilling for those purposes ; that paying away their
capital to outgoing tenants who had to leave land
they had utterly exhausted, and which could only
be restored by more capital, could only be ruinous.

N

Besides, in those days very few of my men had any money. What could they have done under Tenant-right, and with their farms often intermixed in four or five separate parts of the estate? Unless by going in debt, not one of them under the Ulster custom could have got an acre more than he had, or a better situated field.

The payment of the arrears of rent out of the purchase money of Tenant-right differs nothing from the payment of a fine to the landlord, which in England everybody understands is ruinous to any estate, and so has been almost wholly abandoned there. Nothing but the great ignorance in Ireland of sound principles relating to land prevents such a system being scouted as the utter folly it really is. Whether the incoming tenant pays his money to the outgoing tenant for Tenant-right, or to a landlord as a fine, equally drains him of capital. It is in substance a fine far beyond the amount ever heard of anywhere else, or that the hardest landlord ever exacted. Such fines as seven, or ten, or twenty years' value were never dreamed of in business; the usual copyhold fines never approached such a sum. It is certain that if Tenant-right was made compulsory throughout Ireland, all understanding landlords would be forced only to let on heavy fines to secure themselves.

This ignorance extends to men of ability and character. A man so much respected as Judge Longfield, whom I wish to speak of only with the regard I feel for him, is as ignorant in this way as others. Judge Longfield's article in the *Fortnightly* for August shows throughout that he knows nothing of practical farming and management of land. Yet it is on such knowledge of land that the question turns, and no legal knowledge will make up for the want of it. Judge Longfield does not say a word on the undoubted evil of stripping a tenant bare of the capital wanted for better farming his land, but proposes that somehow the tenant should pay seven years' rent to the landlord for Tenant-right. Seven years of £50 a year rent of a farm is £350. Where are many tenants to be found with capital enough to pay this, make all permanent improvements, and farm the land besides? My tenants are richer than most, yet only one or two would be able to do this, except by going in debt. Judge Longfield's whole scheme is a milder Ulster Tenant-right, honestly recognising in part the rights of owners to their land. Why have they not the same right to the whole as to part? It is open to the same difficulties and objections still, as a breach of the rights of owners, unless he means it to be left as voluntary. He suggests the rent may vary every ten years, upon principles as complicated as a Chinese puzzle, just as if nobody had ever heard of the working of leases for nineteen or twenty-one years in Scotland, and their benefit, and that the best farming authorities in the kingdom believe such twenty-one

year leases are the greatest gain to landlords and
tenants alike; and that under the modern system of
high feeding and manuring, which alone pays, it is
impossible in less than nineteen years to recompense
the tenant for honest outlay in good farming.

CHAPTER XIII.

TENANT-RIGHT AND THE THREE F'S.

THE sentiment of some politicians in England has caused the Tenant-right system to be spoken of with tolerance. It will not, however, bear discussion on principle. That on which legal Tenant-right wholly rests is custom. In Parliament it was put on the same ground as copyhold custom in England.

In forty years no tenant of mine has ever paid or received a shilling for Tenant-right. If the custom is to be acted on in my case (and thousands of others), Tenant-right is simply impossible. I have given ⸺ nearly all my tenants larger, many much larger, farms than they had. Every field is near the homestead, and none of them are scattered about. Most are paying smart rents, but there are no arrears. Many tenants have become wealthy. The two rent-days are fixed at times most convenient to them for paying. No excuse except positive misfortune is taken.

I shall be happy to show them against the tenants of any equal number of acres on Lord Portsmouth's estate, or any other, where Tenant-right is allowed, in wealth, condition of their farms, and good farming.   If any one thinks Lord Portsmouth's example is of weight in the question, I ask him to come and see my land.

The simple fact is that money laid out by the farmer in manuring exhausted land will pay him many times better than any other way he can spend it.   Ten, twenty, fifty per cent is a common return. Often all the money comes back in the first crop, and pays well for years after.   What money my men had they thus laid out, instead of stripping themselves bare to buy Tenant-right.   In consequence, the condition of their farms is much better, and when times were good they were fast making money.   Many are now wealthy men.   There are few who are not comfortable, or whom I should wish to change.

Thus the fatal objection to the Ulster Tenant-right is that it absorbs, in buying it, all or a great part of whatever capital an incoming tenant has, and leaves him often without the means of farming well, and always crippled in means.   There can be no doubt that in Ireland the farming class is far less wealthy than the same class in England and Scotland. Yet whilst there every care is taken to let only men with sufficient capital into farms ; it is said here it will be for the advantage of all future Irish farmers to pay away a great part of the small capital they have to the outgoing tenants, who nine times out of ten failed because they were indolent or drank, and that a heavy fine in the shape of arrears of rent should be paid to the landlords. The money he gets will be probably spent by the broken tenant in idling and drinking, instead of his being forced to work and earn an honest living as a labourer, which any one in most parts of Ireland, out of Connaught, who likes, can do now as easily as he could in England or Scotland.

An actual case will enable the best judgment to be formed. Last January I ejected a tenant for non-payment of rent who was a drunken rake. His farm was fifty-two acres, at £52 a year. It was good land, but for many years he had done nothing to it in manuring or anything else. Twice I have seen his corn left in the field till winter, being not worth paying labourers to cut it, and he too lazy to do it himself, though idling about all day at the public-houses, that were unluckily near him. But he kept his eight cows, which he let to a dairyman, his own wife, a strong young woman, being too idle to manage them. The cows paid his rent, and more, till last year, when I was glad to get rid of him as an eyesore and discredit to the estate. I relet the farm at once for £64 per annum to a Scotchman. I engaged to put up good buildings that will cost £200. There were a good house and barn before, a large part of the cost of which I paid more than thirty-five years ago for the tenant's father, an honest thriving fellow, who lived comfortably and prospered. All other buildings were wholly ruinous, the land dirty and exhausted. If there had been Ulster Tenant-right

at ten years' purchase, at least £520, should have been
paid to this worthless man for nothing. The land
was all dry by nature : there were no other improvements on it. The Scotchman would have had to
pay the £520 Tenant-right, though without any consideration for doing so. And he would of course have
had to put up buildings for himself costing £200—
£720 capital spent for a farm of fifty-two acres.
Where was the capital then to come from for stocking, manuring, and farming it ? £10 an acre, £500
was wanted for this purpose. Nowhere are men to
be found with £1200 capital to lay out in occupying
a farm of fifty-two acres. The interest on the money
alone at 10 per cent would be £120 a year, 47s. 6d.
per acre, leaving the rent of 24s. per acre, a trifle by
comparison. In England or Scotland a farmer with
£1200 would hire 150 acres of land. With that
quantity he could do something, and earn his 10
per cent well. No one with that capital would hire
fifty-two acres, nor would any one who knew his
business do so in Ireland. Having added largely to
nearly all my tenants' farms, without the increase of
land having cost them one shilling of capital in any
way, I am able to give any number of similar cases.

Here is another illustration. Soon after I came
home from London last July I met in the street a
prosperous old fellow who has a large farm from a
neighbour, and with whom I had very long been
friendly. After mutual inquiry after each other's

health, which in Ireland often takes a sort of *Oriental*
character, I said, " Well, Andy, how are you getting
on these times?" " I've got a new farm of forty-
seven acres," was the answer. "At what rent?"
"Oh, the rent's cheap enough, 10s. per acre. Sure
you know the land, it's bounding you and me. 'Tis
that ——'s farm, and under my own landlord too."
" I hope you didn't pay much money for it, Andy?"
" 'Deed I did—a dale too much. I had to pay £300."
" What could make you such a fool as that, Andy?
I thought you were a knowing man." " Sure that
——, who bounds it the other side, offered £300 for it.
I knew well it was too much, but my family made me
give it, though I knew it was not worth it." " What's
the interest of your £300, Andy?" " Sure it's £15 a
year." " And what term of the farm have you? You
know you ought to get back the £300 by the time
the term is out." " I've no term at all. There is no
lease of it, but I have great confidence in my landlord." " You are an old man. Suppose you die, and
your landlord dies, and the estate has to be managed
by trustees for his children, how long can they leave
your son land at 10s. an acre that is worth 20s.?"
And so I went on to show my friend his folly, and
that it would have been much better for him to have
kept his £300 in his pocket, and hired a farm at 20s.
per acre, with thirty-one years' lease. His £300
spent in manuring would have come back quickly,
and made a rich man of him. In his case I have no

doubt the stocking of his new farm was got by skimping his old farm, and so cost double its true value. No doubt in law he got Tenant-right for his £300, but he paid thirteen years' purchase of the rent for it, much beyond its worth.

So much do I feel the importance to myself of a new tenant having his whole capital available, that I do not make him pay any of the expense of his lease, or even the stamps upon it. What would be thought of a landlord who took £300 yearly for a farm of forty-seven acres? Yet Parliament is asked to make such a system compulsory as a boon to tenants.

Another objection to Tenant-right is the great competition when land subject to it is so hired, far more severe than the pressure the most screwing landlord ever puts on his tenants. The usual rent of the country is much below the value of the land. Even those who look for higher rent, take care that it is not more than the tenant is able to pay, else the rent is only promised, and cannot be paid. But with Tenant-right, the competition is wholly unchecked; it is extreme, and often ruinous. The outgoing tenant of course wants the last penny. He cares nothing at all for the future of the farm. With the jealous habits of our people towards each other, they often bid quite without sense from boastfulness. It is here the influence of a landlord with judgment can usefully come in. If he had any real power, he would not accept a tenant who got the farm by such competition, nor allow a son who succeeds to the farm to be stripped bare of the capital needful to farm the land for the gain of the rest of the family.

Once Tenant-right is made compulsory by law, there is an end of the landlord's power for good, though men in Parliament often talk as if after landlords have been fleeced at pleasure they are still to co-operate, as it is called, in carrying out the measures for their own injury. Some complain that landlords do not thus co-operate in working the Land Act. It would be just as reasonable to expect that a sheep should co-operate with the shearer who clips it, or with the butcher who cuts its throat. What is the use of expecting that landlords will exert themselves, and take trouble, and incur odium in regulating well an estate, when they will gain nothing by its good management, nor lose if it is badly managed ? Let it be observed, too, that if the Tenant-right system was made compulsory in the rest of Ireland, it is only the present tenants who would gain anything. Their successors would have to pay the utmost farthing of the value of the land. It would put a great gift into the pockets of existing tenants out of the landlord's reversion, with great injury to the incoming tenant.

It is overlooked, too, that even now there are estates in the south on which though nominally the tenants are allowed to sell their interest, a large fine to the landlord, in spite of the Settlement, is besides required to be paid. The Tenant-right dodges the part of the Settlement that forbids fines. The money nominally is paid to the outgoing tenant, who hands it to the landlord. I know a large estate on which this is the custom. One hundred pounds is the least sum to be paid to the landlord on any sale. This cannot be stopped. It can be done secretly, if forbidden openly. And it is not worse in any way than Tenant-right, though ruinous to both parties.

Another bad effect of Tenant-right is, that it deprives the owner of the power of selecting the best tenants for vacant farms, nor can he re-arrange farms, the fields of which are scattered and intermixed. Whoever will give most money to the broken tenant must get the farm just as it stands. On neglected estates these intermixed farms are very common. It is impossible the tenants can improve till they are re-arranged. It would have paid me best to hold myself this farm of fifty-two acres I mentioned just now. I let it to the Scotchman, because I thought his good farming, as a man who had to make it pay, would be a capital example, and do good. In parts of England and Scotland, it is not uncommon for a clever, industrious labourer, who has saved some money, to hire a small farm, perhaps with the help of friends, and if times favour him, to work himself up gradually into the position of a considerable farmer. These are often the best farmers in the country, and their rise is thoroughly wholesome and useful to all. But under Tenant-right such choice of good tenants would have no place. The first step, where Tenant-right exists, is that to hire even fifty acres of land a man must have large capital to pay for the Tenant-right, besides enough to make all permanent improvements himself, *and of course farm the land afterwards.*

This brings me to another objection. It is never worth while for a landlord to lay out money in improvements where there is Tenant-right. Practically he could not raise the rent enough to pay the interest on any large outlay for improvements, and if he made such, he would be adding to the value of what the tenant would have to sell at leaving. There can thus be no sufficient profit to the landlord to lead him to lay out money in improvements.

Thus all money laid out in improvements in every case would have to be found by the tenant alone. Those of us who now do all improvements ourselves would cease to do so. The greater number who now pay part of the cost of improvements or draining, since the Land Act law don't, would also stop doing so. Loans for draining, of which so many have been taken by landlords, would cease to be taken; though all the available capital of landlords and tenants together for generations is wanted to make the necessary permanent improvements on land in Ireland. Those who wish the landlords to leave the country, could not do better than promote the extension of Tenant-right. Whoever knows how much the good working of every part of Local government is the work by the much-abused landlords, had better well consider the question. It may be relied on, there is no need to add to the inducement for any man of education not to live in Ireland, and but for the pleasure and profit of seeing an estate improve, very few would undergo it. To few can it prove more profitable than it has done to me. Besides the gain from an improved estate, the rent of which hitherto has been paid with very little trouble and no ill-will from the tenants, and from very successful farming, I bought much land after the famine, which has paid me well.

Yet, in spite of such gain, and the pleasure of seeing one's people thriving, and being on such terms with them, it is a sorely heavy drag to live here. And though I have seen as lovely a place grow up under my hands as can be found in the South of Ireland, if the Government likes to pay the honest value of it all, I shall gladly leave it, and think my son a gainer by the change. This by the way.

These are some of the practical objections to making the Ulster Tenant-right compulsory, and to that modification which some have described as "The Three F's—Fixity of tenure, Fair rents, valued by County Court judges, and Free liberty to the tenant to sell his interest. All these plans have the same evils as Ulster Tenant right.

There are other objections on principle in every way. A number of witnesses in favour of Tenant-

right were called before the Duke of Richmond's
Commission on agricultural distress. This question
was put to each of them: "A man hires land for the
purpose of farming it. He lays out a considerable
sum in improvements, which repay him, both principal and interest. Where, or on what principle of
right, does he get a just claim to be paid a large sum
besides if he leave the farm?" Of course no one
could answer the question, and the chief witness, who
was sent over to expound Judge Longfield's plan,
lost his temper wholly over it.

The claim of tenants who have not, with the
assent of the landlord, paid their predecessors for
Tenant-right, to receive a large sum on leaving the
farm, is, as lawyers would say, wholly without consideration. The tenant has paid or done nothing to
give him a just right to be thus paid. At best, it is
a case of *nudum pactum*, and therefore, void for want
of consideration, even though there had been an express
contract. ˙And, besides, the payment is really taken
out of the reversion, which belongs to the landlord,
and the value of which it reduces. If an incoming
tenant is to pay £500 for a farm of fifty acres, the
interest on that sum at 5 per cent is £25 a-year,
supposing he gets his money back on leaving. This
is 10s. per acre on the farm, and if he had not to pay
his £500, but had to pay 5s. an acre extra rent
instead, he would be a gainer of £12:10s. a-year. If
he had to pay 10s. per acre extra rent, he would still

be better off, because he would have his £500 capital to lay out in manure which would help to make the rent. The 10s. per acre, therefore, is a clear reduction out of the landlord's reversion.

However it may be concealed, the future rent of the farm is lessened, and in the long run must be lessened accordingly, by these payments for Tenant-right. The landowner loses whatever the tenant gains.

According to all principles of right, the State cannot justly thus take away this reversion or any part of it. If there is good cause for the State taking away a man's property, it is bound to pay the honest value for it. There is no escaping this result, if right and justice are still to prevail among us. I know of no way in which this duty can be escaped. There is talk sometimes in Ireland that by tenant-right the tenant gains, but the landlord does not lose. This is mere ignorance, the ignorance of men who do not understand the business of dealing with land. If the landowner knows how to make his land pay by farming it himself (as at least some of us do), the payment of tenant-right to a broken tenant at once appears in its true light. I have already shown that it is only the lowness of the rent that enables ten or twenty years' purchase to be given for tenant-right.

We have further positive evidence now, such as we never had before, of the value of land in Ireland.

M. de Molinari is a Belgian, and a political economist, familiar with the subject, and a man of influence and weight in France, a thoroughly sound authority on such a question, and plainly disinterested. After carefully seeing the land here, he states without hesitation that it is let at half the rent similar land would let for in Belgium. This quite agrees with my own experience. As I said in a former paper, for many years I have made double the rent that used to be paid by tenants on 1000 acres in my own hands.

If the drawbacks and greater expenses there must always be in a gentleman's farming are fairly taken into account, it is certain this 1000 acres is honestly worth double the rent the tenants used to pay for it, thus corroborating M. de Molinari's opinion. Again and again, when an exhausted farm has been given up, I have put as many cows on it as the broken tenant had. It has paid me a net profit of double the former rent. This was before I had time to manure and improve the land. In all the years I have lived here I never once had a farm in fair condition given up to me.

At a Land meeting near me lately, though the object was to attack others, I received the larger share of the abuse. As they had not a word to say of any tenant being ill-used, they said, as they came they saw on both sides of my property many gables of ruined houses, but on my land they could not see one. They were sure I had turned out many tenants

to get possession of the 1000 acres I farm myself.
I must have pulled down the gables on purpose. No
doubt 16 or 17 tenants held the land I now farm.
Though their rents were very low, and less than half
the net amount I now make out of the same land,
and they had never been raised, all lived in great
poverty, and many gave up their land freely. There
are now 22 good labourers' cottages on the same
land, besides three or four of the old tenants' houses,
which, repaired, do duty at present for labourers.

Some one told me the other day my labourers
are "claner, nater dressed, and fatter looking," than
any body of men in the country; they, their wives
and children, came to the house last summer (as
they do every year) for some small festivity. A
more hearty, healthy lot could not be found in the
three kingdoms. This is not wonderful, as I pay
fully £25 per week in wages. I can prove they
have now as many blankets to their beds as they
want. Forty years ago I am assured there was
not one blanket in the whole land. At our Cloth-
ing Club, which has now existed for so many years
that there is no doubt in the minds of most but that
the Queen sends the money for it in some way, our
own people have for some years begun to take sheets
instead of blankets—a pitch of luxury which is considered to be rather a scandal.

One tenant who had an old lease of thirty acres,
was a widow without children; she brought in a

stout nephew, with wife and children, to work for
her, who hoped to succeed her in the farm. They
held on at the rent fixed in 1796, till they had
not one four-footed beast left—neither horse, cow,
sheep, nor pig. They used to let the grass to
neighbours who had stock, and cultivate without
manuring any fields that gave the chance of a crop.
My Scotchman passing their house one day in spring
during an ordinary year found the whole family
actually starving. The wife just confined, and
without a morsel for herself or baby, and all the
picture of hunger; so that he gave them money out
of his own pocket for present relief.

They then gave up the land. The man was
taken as a labourer; he is an honest worker, and
they were allowed to live in a tenant's house near
their former farm, till it tumbled down, when a good
cottage was built for them. Through the rest of the
summer we could see the man, his wife and children,
all visibly swelling out in face—they were naturally
ruddy hearty folk—till their fatness became a joke
among us. They are with us still, twelve years after,
except that the old widow is dead. We take no
excuse for labourers not working. A more prosperous
set, leading more comfortable lives, does not exist.

My next offence, stated at the land-meeting, was
that my garden wall bristled with broken glass, which
I suppose was taken as showing an unworthy dis-
trust of the Irish people. The main public road

goes by the wall, and the carmen who carry loads along it at night, found out that, by drawing them close to the wall, they could step from the top of the load to the top of the wall, and the fruit-trees inside were a regular ladder by which to climb down and up again. They did not take much, as last year having been so wet, the peaches ripened badly. It amused us to see the stones and half-eaten sour fruit of those they had tried.

My third offence was that, in an account I printed of the International Dairies at the Kilburn Agricultural Show, near London, 1879, for the information of the farmers of our county, I contrasted the bright, clean German dairymaid, wearing blue ribbons and a smart cap, with the dirty drudges so many dairymaids are in Ireland. A man who could so speak of Irishwomen was declared unfit to live in the country. What is to be thought of those who could put forward such a mixture of rubbish as serious blame to anybody?

There is still a further difficulty in the way of compulsory Tenant-right, that much land is let on lease. Leases are definite contracts between landlord and tenant. What is to be done about them? I have still an old middle-man's lease of four lives with one left, aged nearly seventy. There are 340 acres for £105 a year, worth £340 a year to let, and double if I farm them myself. The occupiers are a gentleman and two ordinary farmers. What should be done with such a case?

On one of the lands I bought, a tenant, having another large farm adjoining, has a thirty-one years' lease of 124 acres of splendid land, at a low rent. The farm, when let to him, had been in the occupation of the owner, and there was a clause that by paying at any time £100 (probably a fine the tenant had given) possession might be resumed. They bound me not to take advantage of this clause. The lease will be out five years hence. I can easily make five times the rent out of this farm. I have elsewhere 150 acres, let for 5s. 9d. per acre, on thirty-one-year leases, worth three times the rent, or 15s. per acre. This, too, was bought with the leases running and the value taken into account in the purchase-money.

It will probably be answered at once, Definite contracts cannot be touched. Even the Land Act excepted leases from most of its provisions—from all important ones, and made future leases for thirty-one years the alternative for such provisions. Accordingly since the Land Act great numbers of leases have been given. Three-fifths of my estate is let on lease.

Since the establishment of the Landed Estates Court, it has sold all the land that has passed through it, with most careful statements in a schedule to each conveyance of the precise rights of every tenant by lease or otherwise. This schedule is absolutely binding between landlord and tenant as if a contract. How can Parliament vary it, except by consent? Besides, on many estates there have been contracts or promises as definite as any leases, and that have been acted on in favour of the tenants, without one exception, for near half a century. These have been more favourable to tenants than if they had leases under the Land Act.

Forty years ago I let my tenants know that, with the single exception of gross misconduct, each should hold his land for his life without increase of rent. The rent should only be raised to his successor. This was, of course, equivalent to a lease for thirty years. Practically it has been more. Out of kindness one had to make a concession to the widow and children, if a man died young. There were a few old leases, and an old verbal promise of thirty-one years to the tenants of one ploughland. The holders of these had to be given the same advantage of my promise as the yearly tenants.

Nearly two-fifths of my people still hold under this arrangement. These are now all old, and a few years will place their successors under leases. I have given these details, because they show plainly the arrangement under which great numbers of tenants, in all parts, hold under respectable landlords. The State would have to recognise such contracts and promises, whether legal or honourable, because tenants have profited by them for long courses of years. A compulsory Tenant-right in such cases would be an outrage on right. If ever the question is gone into as one of right, many such cases will be proved in which thorough consideration and indulgence have been shown to the tenants.   Knowing England better than I know Ireland, I assert that Irish tenants, as a body, are treated with a consideration and indulgence, especially in the rent charged for the land, such as English tenants never asked for nor expected.   The statement of the Land Leaguers to the contrary are bare lies.   If they had any facts of this kind to prove, why should they hesitate to prove them before the new Commission ?

In Mr. Courtney's speech lately at Liverpool, advocating fixity of tenure and fair rents, he said there must be a revaluation of rents throughout Ireland, undoubtedly, else easy-dealing landlords would suffer where hard ones gained.   It is certain that such a revaluation would be necessary, if any approach to honest dealing was desired.

What the process of such a revaluation will be I cannot imagine.   To me it seems that Mr. Courtney must be in a condition of primæval innocence in his knowledge of land, and what belongs to it.   The valuation of land by the best valuers, though quite honest men, is very uncertain.   To settle the value of land by evidence, and such evidence as can be had in Ireland, before such men as County Court Judges, would be simply robbery of the owners ; and, unless such robbery was perpetrated, the howling of those who howl now would be louder still.

Then what is a fair rent? Is it what an honest, industrious tenant of reasonable means can make of the land? or what an indolent, ignorant man, perhaps a drunkard and a pauper, can make? The most easy and liberal rule on this point, strictly and honestly applied, would cause ten evictions for one that is now made by landlords. The strictest landlords among us do not evict one quarter of those who ought to be evicted, if the good of the country was duly considered. It is industry that makes the whole difference. In no business can any one get rich in any way, except by self-exertion. Half the time spent in work that is now spent in trying to get something out of landlords by scheming, would make rich men of numbers of tenants. No part of M. de Molinari's letter to the *Journal des Débats* was more striking than that in which he described the sadly low social and moral state of many Irish tenants, and divided them into two classes—one with fair-sized farms at moderate rents, who were industrious, paying their rents and living comfortably; the other with small farms at equally easy rents, but idle, in debt, and steeped in whisky, who could not support themselves if they held the land rent-free. Professor Baldwin's evidence before the Duke of Richmond's Commission on Agricultural Distress is also very remarkable as to the entire badness and worthlessness in all respects of the large class of bad Irish tenants. Even if the County Court Judge had to decide what is a

fair rent, what good would be done by his decision to
bad tenants ?   They are sure to fail sooner or later.
But, to decide what is a fair rent, it must first be
decided what is the fair price of corn, and mutton,
and beef, and pork, and butter, and all other agricultural products which vary every year; and after
a fair price for these has been fixed, no progress has
been made till it has been decided what will be the
demand and supply of these things for the next
thirty-one years.   And there are half a dozen other
questions, equally hard to answer, that must be
settled before an honest decision can be given.

The truth is, there is no fair value of land; the
value varies in England, in Scotland, everywhere,
with the skill, the industry of the farmer, with the
climate, with the prices of particular sorts of produce, and the cost of production, just like the price
of other kinds of goods.   The true point is, what
profit can the farmer make by the land ?   That is
all that matters.   Acts of Parliament cannot regulate prices nor values ; neither can arbitrations,
which are at best only lawsuits.   Shades of departed
free-traders and anti-corn-law leaguers ! what are
your former colleagues and successors coming to ?
They think they can direct by Act of Parliament how
the businesses of landowning and farming shall be
carried on, and by the same means regulate the
price of the chief raw material of those businesses,
viz. land.   To a man who began life nearly seventy

years ago as a Tory, and was made a free-trader by
facts which common sense would not let him ignore,
one view alone is possible, of the reason why so
many Liberals, in dealing with Ireland, set at naught
every sound principle of free-trade and the universal
gain of free-dealing, with which they thrashed us
formerly into good sense. The curse of party politics
is upon them. Partly for party ends, and partly from
sentimentalism, they have for years flattered the imagination of the farming classes in Ireland with hopes
of what is really Communism, and what cannot be
realised till England has ceased to be England. Talk
about the upas-tree, and rooting natives in the soil—
that an eviction is the same as the death-warrant of
a tenant; it is these words of Mr. Gladstone that
have done most of the evil. We are reaping what
he then sowed. No declarations, like Mr. Forster's
excellent one, that the law shall be enforced, weigh
in the least. The flattery is believed, the threats are
disbelieved, as is natural. We, who see and know
what becomes of broken tenants, are sure such words
have no shade of truth in them; but the hopes they
raise are unbounded. Playing with fire in a straw-
yard is nothing compared to such talk, and this too
from the Prime Minister. It is not for me to draw
the moral.

Hitherto the immense magnitude and difficulty of
such a task as the Government settling rents has been
felt by all independent men of any intelligence and
forethought.

It is a task such as no Government in the world ever attempted.

If Government is to protect tenants in their own bargains as to rents, there is an end of free-trade in anything, and Protectionists have been right all the time.

Such things rest on no principle if free-trade means anything. The object is to do away with competition among tenants. Nowhere is competition so much wanted to enforce better farming on tenants.

Fixity of tenure leaves the tenant to go on as badly as before; and, besides, it does this by confiscating part of the landowners' reversion.

CHAPTER XIV.

WHAT WILL DO GOOD IN IRELAND.

EVERYBODY who is interested in such subjects is inclined favourably towards any plan for promoting Peasant Proprietorship in Ireland. At first sight it seems that with tenants used to small farms, for which they have to pay rent, a plan that shall make them owners of their farms, and after some years free them from having to pay rent, must much promote their prosperity.

It is certain too, that both in England, Scotland, and Ireland, the land is in too few hands, and any honest plan by which more men would become owners of land would be a gain to the country.

But when the whole case is looked at in its details, it is by no means certain that any such plan can be made to work, except to a very limited extent, in Ireland. There is very much to be said for the view that, whilst realising to the full the good of Peasant Proprietorship, yet it is one of the goods of an earlier and simpler stage of civilisation than that which we have reached in the end of the nineteenth century,

that small landholders belong to a time when men
were content with a harder and humbler way of
living than even labourers are now satisfied with;
and that we cannot now produce artificially by
any efforts of our own a large system of peasant
proprietors, because the necessary conditions are
absent. Now and then, and here and there, individuals may chance to have the qualities that will
enable them to succeed as peasant proprietors; but
on any large scale it is impossible. There is no
people in all Northern Europe in whom the necessary
conditions are so wanting as the Irish.

The conditions needed for success as peasant
proprietors are great industry and skill in farming.
In every country of Europe where small farms and
peasant proprietors have flourished, these conditions of
industry and skill have existed in an unusual degree.
The skill is often hereditary, coming down from
several generations. It is enough to mention Belgium,
parts of France, and the Channel Islands, the latter
having a further advantage in the immense quantity
of sea-weed thrown on shore, affording an unlimited
supply of manure gratis, and no part of any
island being more than three miles from the shore.
Let any one read the report on the farming of
Belgium by Dr. Vöelcker and Mr. H. M. Jenkins in
volume vi., Second Series, of the Journal of the Royal
Agricultural Society of England, and he will find the
facts reported at length by two of the most competent

authorities we have. He will find Belgium contrasted with Ireland in this respect, and the result established that small owners of land work harder and live harder than any other class in Europe. Again, in M. de Molinari's first letter to the *Débats*, September 22, is this statement:—"Examples in support of this system are not wanting. Men please themselves by citing especially that of the peasant proprietor of France and Belgium, only they forget to add that the small proprietorship of France and Belgium was created by the work of ages, and that the peasants began by acquiring the qualities of order and economy that are indispensable for the good carrying on of proprietorship before they became proprietors. They worked and saved penny by penny the capital which they have employed in the acquisition, and later in the increase, of their small domains. Nothing of the sort is required of the Irish tenants; it is proposed to suppress the apprenticeship of landowning in their favour, and the worst result will be to consolidate in Ireland agrarian pauperism."

He goes on in a very striking passage, too long for quotation, to show the similarity between the small Irish farmer and hand-spinners and hand-loom-weavers in England and elsewhere, and adds that such farmers will be at last only more miserably overwhelmed in the ruin of the false system to which their unwise friends are trying to attach them. All these letters, as giving the opinion of a wholly disinterested witness, and one used to the consideration of such questions, and an authority upon them, deserve the most earnest attention.

My own feeling is very favourable to peasant proprietors, whenever men can be found who have the qualities that will enable them to succeed in such a position. As a practical farmer, I know that unless a man has the habits that M. de Molinari speaks of—industry and skill—he can never do well in a farm, either as a tenant or proprietor. In the County Cork there are a great number of tenants with long leases, that put them substantially in the position of proprietors. On one side, joining me, there is a property let to all the tenants for 2000 years. It is very improvable, wet and stony, only wanting labour to make it good useful land. On the other side a tenant has a lease for 100 years, and a splendid tract of wet land, with a capital slope down to the river. He has never made one drain in it, though to drain it would pay him twentyfold, and he could have borrowed money at 1 per cent last winter from the Government to do it. He and the tenants for 2000 years, who also did nothing but work under 1 per cent loans, are not half as well off as my tenants, nor their farms as productive.

These are some of the difficulties in the way of Peasant Proprietorship.

I think it is certain that it is only by carefully selecting fit buyers, that selling land to tenants will answer any good purpose,—a bad tenant is sure to make a bad proprietor. That is the key of the question and of all the plans of fixity of tenure. All cut off or limit the common chances of improvement. All end in small gains to present occupiers, confiscated from the owners, and leave the occupiers just where they were, not raising them a single peg, but more firmly convinced than before that scheming is much better than industry. Instead of having the good habits needful for thriving as proprietors, inferior and bad Irish tenants have bad habits, which ensure their failure, whatever position they may hold in whatever walk of life. Trying the experiment on the scale that the Church Act and Bright's clauses in the Land Act sanction can do no harm. Bright's clauses might be made more effective, if the Government was empowered to bid for land that is offered for sale. Having bought it, Government might sell the farms to any tenants likely to do well as proprietors, and who would honestly pay one-third of the purchase-money. Much has been urged by Mr. Shaw Lefevre and others, who believe in Peasant Proprietorship, in favour of tenants being required to pay only one-fourth of the purchase-money, instead of one-third. I believe such a difference is insignificant. It is the difference between 13s. 4d. and 15s.; whoever could pay the one would have no serious difficulty with the other. I prefer one-third because it is rather a more substantial part.

I would only sell to those who were fit to buy. It would be a positive benefit in Ireland to have the distinction between good and bad farmers drawn thus definitely. To those who could not buy, or were not fit to do so, let thirty-one years' leases at the true value be given, which nine times, out of ten would be more than their former rent. And if within three or five years they still did not come in and buy, I would sell the land, subject to these leases, to the best bidder. In this way there would be no loss to the Government, because the higher rents would make the fee even of residues of this kind sell better. There would be no injustice nor even hardship to any one, landlord or tenant, whilst those who were fit would become proprietors.

Let any one read in Mr. Tuke's pamphlet his account of the peasant proprietors he saw, who had bought under the Church Act. It is clear that of those he saw, whoever were thriving tenants throve as proprietors, whilst bad tenants went to the wall as proprietors, thus proving my statement. Professor Baldwin gave an account to the Duke of Richmond's Commission of what he saw on another estate, bought under the Church Act by the tenants. Before the Act passed they had been a very fairly thriving body of tenants. Ten years after, he found them nearly all pauper proprietors. Common sense suggests, as I have said, that the habits of Irish peasants are not changed by their ceasing to be tenants and becoming proprietors. And I believe there is conclusive direct evidence to the same effect to any extent. If it is not clearly recognised that the great number of bad tenants who lose their farms from any cause, nineteen times out of twenty are just useless poor creatures who in no circumstances can do good with land, it is impossible to remedy the troubles of the country.

This, then, is the working of the other panacea— peasant proprietorship. It is no panacea at all. Carefully worked, it may be made to do some good; as it might too, I think in England and Scotland. I have long believed that by a system of Land Banks, more or less on the model of the Prussian Land Banks, advances might be made without risk to help any one in the three kingdoms who wishes to buy a limited portion of land, and thus the number of landed proprietors be fairly increased, and those appeased who suffer in any degree under land-hunger. Such advances, if made gradually, and with a firm resolution to enforce repayment, would be quite safe.

In Ireland the curious readiness to place money on deposit in banks, and the great sums so deposited, enable a Land Bank to be set up with great advantage. Depositors now only receive usually 1 per cent for their money; the offer of 2 per cent would procure a great sum. By arrangement with the Bank of Ireland, which now has many branches in country places, the Government, by offering 2 per cent, could probably get any sum wanted for advances to enable occupiers to buy their farm. I would suggest that only a definite sum yearly should be advanced, say £100,000, so that by the time a really large sum total was reached, a substantial part of the first advances would have been repaid. With firmness there need be no loss, as there has not been a shilling of loss on the millions advanced to land-owners for drainage, who *ex hypothesi* are so bad, whilst tenants are so good. The only risk of loss is if we have a Government that for its own political pur-poses does not care to resist the beggar's whine. Any doubt in Ireland whether money need be paid or not, is sure to settle itself the wrong way, against paying.

Of course advances by the Government for such a purpose cannot be justified on the highest economical principles. But the object of increasing the number of owners of land is a good and important one. And if it can be brought about without cost to the tax-payers and with no serious risk, it is worth trying. But the same advantage should be given to persons in England and Scotland who wish to buy land to a moderate extent. With like limitation as to the amount to be advanced, and with proper selection of borrowers, so as to avoid speculators, there would be less risk than in Ireland, and no less advantage.

To do away with the invidious feeling that land is a monopoly in few hands is no small object. A

few men have a genius for the cultivation of land.
It is to these men that land-hunger is a real hardship.
The excessive wealth of the country does raise the
price of land to an artificial and perhaps undue value,
which loans on easy terms to small buyers would in
some degree remedy.

It will be said a bank like this, to enable tenants
and others to buy land for themselves, is the proper
work of private persons, especially of the patriotic
and benevolent class, who in Ireland profess such
anxiety to help the tenants. No doubt this is true.
O'Connell founded a large bank, which has thriven for
over forty years, and holds many millions on deposit
at 1 per cent. Another patriotic Home Rule M.P.
has also founded a successful bank, which also holds
a great sum on deposit at 1 per cent, and which pays
a dividend usually of 10 per cent. It is clear these
banks could lend to farmers the money they hold at
1 per cent, at a moderate rate for making purchases
of their farms, and at no risk. No more useful or
good national object could be imagined.

But, alas, these patriotic banks can also lend the
money, for which they pay 1 per cent, on small bills
to the same farming class at the satisfactory interest
of 8 per cent, and the temptation to do this is irre-
sistible. So these virtuous M.P.'s pocket their 10
per cent dividends, and join in the cry to rob the
landowners, to enable their farming customers to go
deeper in debt, and give better security.

It is the undue facilities for borrowing, given by those very banks to farmers, that cause the grievous indebtedness of the class I have heretofore spoken of.

It is gravely suggested that such troubles as these can be set right by robbing the landlords, and above all by driving away or crippling every landlord who improves his property. I again suggest that it will be wise to look to the end.

M. de Molinari here too leaves no doubt of the right direction.

He asserts that no people in Europe at present are so wanting in all the qualities needful for successful peasant proprietors. No one can doubt that he is right, and the practical question at once arises— Can those needful qualities be acquired ? And how ? No remedy is worth anything that does not lead to this end. If the proposed remedy will not do this, no choice is left but to look deeper and in another direction.

That which lies at the bottom of the trouble is the thorough untruth that prevails in Ireland, especially among politicians. The whole agitation is got up, in hope of gaining something by it. It is only money-grasping, without one high idea. The extreme party urges confiscation, and the more moderate party Ulster tenant-right. Present private gain is the only end of both. For any man to succeed in dealing with such people it is necessary he should see and understand their faults. The

exact temper wanted for dealing with them successfully is downright intelligent honesty that will not
be humbugged. The present agitation deliberately
aims at causing such a state of disturbance as may
be unbearable, and so force unjust concessions on
the ground that something must be done.

In one word, all in Ireland is more or less mixed
up with scheming; nothing is simply true. It is
quite as easy to advocate Mr. Parnell's views as
Tenant-right views. Untruth is as necessary to one
as to the other, only slightly different untruth. The
real mischief of the sentimental flattery addressed to
these poor people is that it encourages this scheming. If any of us who live here, and has to manage
his own concerns, and take his part in the local
business of the country (justice business, etc.), acted
or talked in this sentimental way, he would be simply
drowned in the flood of lies that would pour in on him.
Our mode of proceeding is the very opposite. We
believe nothing at all until it has been proved to be
true, and even then we know it is sure to be hugely
exaggerated; or facts, more or less true, perhaps,
applied to circumstances in a relation that makes
them untrue. We are careful to raise no expectations, but simply to do what is just and right.

The fault of Mr. Forster's Disturbance Bill
was this. There was distress last winter in the
western and mountainous parts of Ireland, but very
little in other parts, even of scheduled Unions. When

it was known that money could be had for relief,
wonderful exaggerations sprang up in all directions,
according to the universal principle here, "Why
should we not have our share of what is going, as
well as another?" The poor can hardly be blamed
for this; the ordinary poverty of every winter is
enough to make them glad of whatever they can get.

In Ireland there are very few men of any class who
can resist such a movement. Love of popularity, or,
more accurately, fear of unpopularity, makes nearly
all, Governments as well as others, as easy as possible about giving relief; and Mr. Forster's feelings
being moved by the distress in some parts, he ceased
to realise the difference between scheming and truth,
and took untruth to be true. So he proposed a
measure in the teeth of every sound principle of
estate-management, and which must have ruined
more tenants than it helped, and besides been a
grievous wrong to many landlords who know their
duty and have done it. To keep the tenants clear of
arrears, is the first principle of good estate-management. The condition of any estate can be unfail-
ingly judged of, when it is known, what is the amount
of arrears upon it? so, too, from the same facts, can
be known, what is the comfort the tenants live in?

I should myself have suffered great loss had the
Bill passed, though I have no arrears. I am in a
scheduled Union, in which, on February 1, there were
three more paupers than in 1879. I had my summer

rent-day on July 10, when the Bill was still in doubt. About two-thirds of the half-year's rent was paid, where commonly nearly the whole would have been paid. A number of the largest and best-off tenants did not appear; even some thoroughly wealthy shopkeepers, who held town fields. It was easy to guess who were readers of newspapers. The next day two of the best tenants came, in the main worthy industrious fellows; the half-year's rent of whom was £49 and £67 : 10s. They said they had no money. I answered I could not afford that they should not pay some rent. They might pay half in the next ten days, and the rest at Michaelmas. I got a short reply. They had no money and could not pay, but might pay something after harvest. I then said, as they took that tone, I would accept nothing less than a half-year's rent in full; and if this was not paid before Michaelmas, I would eject as soon as I could. I never again asked for the rent. About September 1st, the £49 tenant came suddenly with the rent in full in £5 notes ; the large notes being a sure sign it had been lying ready for some time. Two days after the £67 : 10s. tenant came in such haste that he would not wait to change some Cork butter-buyer's cheques for his butter of this season, dated before July 12, the day when he told me he had no money. The cheques were for more than I had asked him to pay in July. If the Bill had passed, both would have gone into arrears, and probably have ruined themselves in the end. I know one (and believe that both) had joined the Land League.

Not to press for the payment of rent and to let arrears accumulate is just the common old way of dealing in this country, by which to go in debt is considered to be of no consequence, so long as you are not forced to pay it. It is hoped Providence may provide some good years, that may make it easy to pay the arrears or reduce them; and, if not, it is hoped they may not be pressed for. In either case they are a dead log round the tenant's neck, which depresses all his energies, because in a good year the surplus is not his own, and does him no good, and in the bad years he is more likely to be ruined, and lose everything.

Here is another fact. Just before September 29, a neighbour brought a young Liberal English M.P. to see our doings. He had come over to inform himself on the Irish question. *Inter alia,* I asked if he would like to see a distressed tenant under ejectment for non-payment of rent. Nothing he would like so much. So I sent him to a widow, a poor woman, with beautiful land, and faults enough to ruin five tenants. She owed a year's rent, and was to be ejected in ten days. I did not go with him, that he might ask and see all he liked. His many questions had the effect of convincing the widow he must be the sheriff's officer, or some one who wished to take her land, or had to do with her ejectment. So when he went away, having made his investigation, she ran after him, and told him she had the year's rent all ready in her house, and meant to pay it; and an hour after he had left us she ran over in hot haste to me with the rent in full. I sent a card after him to beg if he was in Ireland another year he would let me know, because, should I happen to have any more defaulting tenants I should be so glad to take advantage of his assistance.

The true remedy is to act on simple sound principle — on that which is the true principle of free trade—that the natural liberty Providence gives of buying and selling, and dealing with what belongs to any man, is best for all, and promotes the greatest happiness of the greatest number. The ingenious hair-splittings now so common to try and justify confiscating that which honestly now belongs to landowners, are instances of the opposite manner of dealing. Nothing else can do real permanent good, and raise the condition of the people. It is astonishing how any one who has ever grasped the principle of free dealing can lay it aside in regard to such a country as Ireland, and fancy that continual concession to indolent, ignorant men can promote their prosperity and raise their moral condition. The lazy, bad tenant is sure to be lazy and bad though he got Tenant-right or was made a peasant-proprietor, or put in any other employment. To talk of rooting such men in the soil, as Mr. Gladstone did in the debates on the Land Act of 1870, is proposing to do that which is worst for the country. The vanity of the ill-affected class in Ireland is pleased by flattery, as it is by every word of respect and every empty compliment they can pick up; and so that self-important, fractious, untrue character is formed, without a grain of sense, even for attaining its own ends, which is now so common in the House of Commons and elsewhere, and which it is impossible to deal with reasonably. Sound principle and strong downright common sense can alone answer. Let the flattering way of dealing with indolent men be tried in any other industry, and the results will be the same as have been produced in Ireland.

The business of landowning or of farming can no more be regulated by Act of Parliament than any other business. Each is a true business, and can only thrive when conducted on business principles. No bolstering up, or favouring, or helping by Parliament, or any other way, will make the business thrive. Industry and skill and capital can alone do this. All else is only an attempt at protection. Like other systems of protection, it is popular with those who think they shall gain by it. It may seem to succeed for a time. But the state of Donegal, and other parts of Ulster where the linen trade does not exist proves clearly that one such mode of protection, viz. Tenant-right, is unsound. Moreover, more than half Ulster at this moment is dissatisfied with the Tenant-right it has. Like all other protected trades, more protection is wanted—that more should be taken from landowners and given to tenants without payment for it.

I believe these facts cannot be met. Parliament has never yet taken away from one body of men that which it has recognised for centuries to belong to them, and given it to others, however strong the reasons of public policy may have been, except by paying the owners honestly for what is taken away. Nor could the principles of the Land Act, passed so lately as 1870, be thrown overboard without the forfeiture of all self-respect.

I have been forced to use hard words about lying and untruth much more often than I like. But there was no choice. The extent to which these faults prevail upon the subject cannot be realised out of Ireland.

The opinion expressed by M. de Molinari, that there is no royal road to prosperity in Ireland, is the very same that I have constantly expressed and acted on for forty years past. He says, increased production can alone make men to be better off. The production may be from land or manufactures, it matters not which, but more production there must be for more prosperity. Misery may be relieved by poor-laws or charity, and, rightly, from another motive. It is only from increased production in some way a

country can be better off. The poor fellows who
raised from the land I farm one-fourth of the produce it now yields, not only lived like paupers themselves, but sorely hindered the prosperity of the
country too, because they added nothing to its trade.
My labourers now, who work on the same fields, not
only spend much of their 10s. or 12s. a week in ways
that do good to trade, but the increased produce they
raise, beyond what the poor tenant used to raise, adds
greatly to the trade of the country. This truth lies at
the bottom of the whole question. Men may shut their
eyes to it, but they cannot escape it. Unless there is
increased produce, things can never be better. All
this is ignored by the Land League people. Their
end is that every man in Ireland should live at ease
under his own vine and fig tree, without rent or aught
else to disturb him, and work and drink as much or as
little as he likes. This might perhaps answer in a
way, if it could only be shown where the money is to
come from that will support him and his whilst he
thus lives like a gentleman. The idea of living at ease
like a gentleman has more to do with Irish troubles
than most men see.

But to take the subject in order.

M. de Molinari asks, If any one told the *ouvriers*
of Montmartre and Belville, Paris, that hence-
forth, on account of their poverty, they should only
pay half the present rent of their *appartements*,
or none at all, what effect would it produce upon

them?   He adds, This is just what has been done in Ireland.

The agitation now going on is meant to produce its true work in England.   The agitators believe that people in England are really afraid of them—that the Government will yield more in proportion as they can increase this fear.   The Land Act raised the expectations and excited the imagination of ignorant men here, that Parliament could be induced to take from the landlords to give to the tenants; and Mr. Gladstone's unwise talk which I have quoted above, and which is cited at every land meeting, inflamed all such ideas.   In parts of Ireland, no doubt, the agitation has produced a dreadful state of things, but still we have seen disturbances of the same kind, even greater, at intervals of a few years, again and again, since the beginning of the century.   We know what such agitation is worth, or rather, what it is not worth, and how it ought to be met and put down; and that it is sure to collapse at once, directly it is known that the authorities are in earnest, and mean to put it down. During nearly a generation that Lord Chancellor Blackburne practically ruled Ireland, when the difficulty from over-population and far greater poverty was much worse, if outrages became numerous from agitation or any other cause, the law was simply put in force.   A special commission was issued, a few convictions obtained, and, without bloodthirstiness or undue severity, all were convinced the law could not be set aside, and quiet quickly followed. When O'Connell had to be thus met, Blackburne met him and put him down : whether the Government was Conservative or Liberal, it was the same. Lately a milder course has been taken. By the Westmeath Act, ten years ago, the Lord Lieutenant, when a county was proclaimed, could order the arrest and detention in prison, at the pleasure of the Crown, of any dangerous person. As all those who had been doing wrong, and knew they were therefore in danger of arrest, forthwith ran away to America, where they were harmless, this plan answered every good purpose. Scarcely any persons were punished or even caught and shut up under the Act. It was the highest sort of moral rule. Men's own consciences judged them, and they bolted or not accordingly. Quiet and no more outrages were the result. I have already told how much Lord O'Hagan's Jury Act has added to the troubles.

No one can doubt that law and order must be enforced. To leave this uncertain for a day does an injury to the poor people themselves, worse than the worst injuries their agitators complain of many times over, even if such were true, which they are not. There is no trouble or difficulty in thus producing quiet. Only Mr. Forster's plan cannot answer, of using strong words one week in behalf of law and order, and the next week watering them down by speaking against the landlords or the House of Lords, and so convincing the agitators that something may be got out of him, even if he does put the law in force.

Mr. Froude's article in the *Nineteenth Century* for September is as powerful a proof as could be that law and order must be enforced, unless grievous injury is to be done. It is no question of landlords or the House of Lords. The moral mischief that is being done by delay is immense. Let any man of decision be sent to Connaught with the commission of the peace for Galway, Mayo, and Sligo. Give him the command of the police and as many extra men as he needs. Let his directions be to enforce law and order. He will not have been there a month before Connaught will be at peace. All that is necessary is that a man of will and brains should be in command, who will not let himself be trifled with.

But it is impossible that any sudden change for the better can be made in districts that are now bad. The popular cry may be yielded to, no doubt, but this will be only laying up worse evils for the future. Concession is sure to whet the appetite for more; it will not remove the evil. The object sought is personal money gain alone. In 1873 I pointed out in the *Times* that the Land Act had thus only whetted the appetite of agitators. It had satisfied no one. More concession will only add to the same. The ill-habits of the people still in substance exist. It is only as better habits establish themselves that a

better state of things can grow up. Whenever an
estate has been well managed, the tenants made to
know that whatever any one promises will be held
binding on him—the rents undertaken will be required, and no humbug listened to, but honest, straightforward dealing be the rule—bad tenants be removed
and their land given to good tenants, the condition
and wealth of the people steadily improves. Good
tenants invariably make money. When they can do
this, what is there to fight about? When the proper
time comes for a rise in the rent, and such rise is
made, they would be more than human, and much
less than Irishmen, if they did not kick a little.
But when the dealing is reasonable and resolute,
this does small harm. A wise notion has been
started that Irish tenants are so poor they cannot
contract freely. Heaven forgive the man who acts
on that view in Ireland! That a man is not bound
by his contract, is the dodge of every rogue we have.
This is the constant struggle over workhouse and
all other public contracts, that when the contractor
loses by his contract, he should be let off or paid
more. Once it is known that contracts cannot be
got rid of, the attempts to get rid of them cease
miraculously.

The outlay on improvements, both by landlords and
tenants, lately has much increased. An honest census
of what landlords have done for the last thirty years
will show a total that is not anticipated; such outlay

by landlords cannot be disregarded. If order prevails it will go on steadily. A moderate part of men's incomes applied to this purpose will be enough. Money so spent is not lost; it will pay well in the end.

In the past year tenants have awakened to the value of draining, and the loans at one per cent last winter from the Government did great good. Though in strictness of economic principles they might not be justifiable, yet practically I believe the One per cent loans were the most successful step that any Government ever took. The country had advanced sufficiently to profit by them. The gain to those of us who had been draining for many years had been observed, and fruit was now borne by our example. In my Union forty-four loans for draining were taken. I believe half of these were taken by tenants for small sums, £100 and such like. This is a larger total than was ever before spent by tenants on drains within the memory of any one living. The profit certain to be yielded, the drains having been well sunk, under the inspection of Government officers, and having outfalls (whilst many drains they heretofore made for themselves were very shallow and without any outfall), must do great good.

The sense of success will be such, that it might be wise for the Government to offer once more loans for draining to tenants at a cheap rate. Loans at 2 per cent, or even $2\frac{1}{2}$, could be very small loss. More loans would be taken at $2\frac{1}{2}$ per cent (making

the total charge for principal and interest 5 per cent
for thirty years), after last year's experience, than
were taken at 1 per cent; and an effect would thus
be produced in many parts that would secure draining in future going on of itself, to the immense advantage of the country. In a district like this, which is
not mountainous, and where the wet land does not
lie usually in great tracts, but every farm has more
or less of its land wet, such as an industrious tenant
can drain for himself, the general conviction that
to leave land undrained is a dead loss, must work
wonders in a few years.

In much the larger part of Ireland, the only true
remedy is the better management of estates; that
bad tenants should be steadily weeded out, and their
land given to good tenants, without payments that
would reduce their capital. Three-fourths of Ireland
is in this condition.

There are in the country a sufficient number of
good tenants, fairly industrious and steady men, with
some knowledge of their business, who have too small
farms. And there are a large number of thoroughly
bad tenants, indolent, ignorant, and drinkers, who, as
I have shown, in whatever way they hold land, can
never do any good with it. Their faults are their ruin.
This class hardly exists in England or Scotland, and
accordingly its extent or even its existence in Ireland
is not realised. All are looked upon as poor and
honest men; of course the agitators keep up that

idea by vehement but untrue assertion : the ejectment of one of these bad tenants is spoken of as
cruelty and wrong.   Let it be considered what it is
to have in a farm a lazy, drinking, even if not
drunken, man, ignorant, without capital or knowledge of farming, and his land much exhausted.
How is it possible a country can improve when
much of the land is thus held ?   There is no difficulty with any one else but these.   No landlord who
is not an idiot ever quarrels with a good tenant.
These bad tenants are the men for whom Mr. Forster's
Disturbance Bill was made, and who would have
prayed for his soul if he had carried it.

I have three bad tenants, all drunken; two of them
have no four-footed animals on their farms, one holding
forty-seven acres, at 5s. 9d. per acre : what is it possible
to do with such men when they cease to pay rent ?

When such men are turned out there is plenty
of work for them, if they will do it, in spite of Mr.
Gladstone's wholly untrue statement, that evictions
are the same as death-warrants, and, under the obliga-
tion to work, their children grow up into useful labour-
ing people.   In what part of the earth can men be at
once idle and prosperous ?   On what principle should
the land, these men have failed in, not be given to
good tenants, who will farm it better, and benefit the
country and themselves by so farming it ?   This is
the common-sense course which has succeeded with
me and with all others having improving estates.

The principle professed in behalf of the Land Act was that capricious evictions might be stopped, but it was expressly added that no one wished to keep bad tenants on the land. The Act, however, has been put in force in a way that has tended directly to keep bad tenants in their farms.

It has been held that the Act gave an absolute right to every tenant of four to seven years' rent as compensation for eviction. Non-payment of a year's rent alone deprived him of this right. The landlord no doubt might have a set-off against him. But the most justifiable cause for eviction has been still held a disturbance, and still left the burden of four to seven years' rent to be paid by the landlord.

The only right course would have been that, if there was justifiable cause for eviction, the landlords should not incur the penalty.

I have had but one land case myself. A poor old tenant had forty acres of capital land. Before I bought it, he had divided the farm with his eldest son, who was the most hopelessly lazy fellow I ever knew. He soon could not pay his part of the rent. So I had to turn him out, and take the loss of his rent on myself, giving his land back to the father, as he had another son; this other son, when little more than a boy, was convicted of a bad attempt at rape, in one of my own fields, and got twelve months in Cork gaol for it. He used habitually to rob his father's potato pit, to supply money for his iniquities.

So there was an end of his chance as a tenant. The old man had cows on his land, which he let to a dairyman, and so paid his rent; after his wife died, he became so feeble he could not walk across the room to his own door. A daughter had married a rich farmer twenty miles off. She had to take her father home to her house in a cart to save his life, and there he lived for some years. The farm is part of the best land I have : by manuring, it has paid me capitally since. I could not allow it to be thus left half waste, and therefore served a notice to quit, and ejected. The County Court judge agreed it was impossible I could help ejecting in such a case, but yet ordered me to pay four years' rent, over £150, for so doing. I think it was a wrong decision, and so did most others who heard it. Luckily I had a set-off for dilapidations, that saved me in part, and by appealing to the Judge of Assize I forced on a compromise that still more relieved me. This is the effect of the Land Act as it is worked.

No reasonable landlord objected to capricious evictions being stopped. The attempt to make out a bastard Tenant-right, as has been done, has caused great disgust, and turned many against the Act. It is strange, the effect of unfair dealing, by men in the position of judges towards those whom it is impossible to deprive of much power, except by confiscation, is not observed.

Nor is the requirement of thirty-one years' leases

to be complained of. I think this last requirement
might be extended in such a way that all future
lettings of land should be by lease for thirty-one
years. A twenty-one years' lease is long enough
in England and Scotland, and I am convinced is a
great gain to both tenant and landlord, because it
gives security for the tenant's expenditure. Though
thirty-one years may be too long a term, in some respects, yet, with the ideas that prevail in Ireland (I do
not mean the wild view of the present moment), I
think the term need not be objected to.

More drainage by tenants, if landlords do not
themselves drain as they ought, and thirty-one-year
leases in all cases, will give much increased produce
from the land, and so satisfy M. de Molinari's principle.
It might be a condition of the lease that the tenant
should drain all wet land in the first fifteen years, if
the landlord did not do it, and the tenant get a charge
for the outlay in full. I have often thought a justifiable pressure on both landlord and tenant could be
had if the land was valued for rating, not as now at
its present value (but when more than 5 per
cent of the farm is wet and reclaimable), by valuing
it at what it would be worth if drained and reclaimed. Those who now drain their land suffer an
injustice if their neighbours do not also drain. The
sums required for the Poor or the Roads are applotted
on a fixed area, and those who raise the value of their
farms by draining pay a larger share of the sum so

applotted, whilst the neighbour who neglects his
duty is actually relieved of part of what he would
have had to pay. By valuing all as if the land had
been drained, this hardship may be set right, and a
mild screw put on the neglectful occupiers and owners
to do their duty. The gain to all from the general
drainage of the country exceeds all other possible
gains manifold.

M. de Molinari's last letter in the *Débats* of
September 22, deserves the most careful attention.
It is directly on the point I am now discussing,—
What can be done ? He says plainly, Ireland is truly
sick. It is sick of one of the worst forms of pauperism,—agrarian pauperism. There are 200,000 to
300,000 tenants, representing more than a million of
souls, who cultivate an inferior refuse soil, so that in
good years they are only just above starvation, and
in bad years they are starving. It is these small
refuse farms that are the cause of the trouble ;
nothing else. They must be united to other farms,
so as to increase the size, and make each farm large
enough to support the farmer and his family, and
such as he can prosper in. The process has gone
on rapidly ever since the great famine. The Land
Act retarded it. But still it went on, nevertheless, and nothing but the union of farms, till they
can support a family, can produce a better state of
things.

I believe there is no answer to this statement.

In substance it agrees with what I have told as the experience of a life in Ireland, lived not without success. Take the case of one of these small tenants M. de Molinari speaks of, who pays £9 a year. £9 a year is 180 shillings, less than 6d. per day ; so 6d. per day would be his total gain if he had his land rent-free. But much the larger number pay less than £5 a year rent. Well, £4:10s. a year is less than 3d. per day—his gain if rent-free. Can such sums alter the tenant's position from poverty to comfort ? Will 3d. or 6d. per day added to the means of living of a Connaught small tenant raise him to the wished-for condition ? Any one can tell the answer. Compare the state of these men with my labourers earning 12s. per week, with free houses, garden, and potato-land, and remember that, according to Mr. Gladstone, I signed the death-warrant of many of them when I evicted them long years ago.

In County Cork the number of the ejectments in the last three years, that have been by creditors, mort-gagees to whom the tenants pledged their farms for money advanced, turns out to be near half the total. These are the direct effect of the tenant's debts and his faults, with which the landlord had nothing to do. The justification of Mr. Forster's Disturbance Bill was the cruelty of landlords in ejecting tenants in these bad times. Here is the answer.

Again, in this same letter, M. de Molinari de-scribes what will necessarily happen if these bad

tenants are made peasant proprietors, or given a
greater hold on the land by Tenant-right or the Three
F"s : they will get deeper in debt in consequence, and
be more surely sold up by the creditors the first time
bad years come. I believe one cause that my tenants
are less in debt than others is, that all money-lenders
know that I feel no pity for them; as my tenants
and I are on very friendly terms on the whole, the
money-lenders fear we may collogue (as it is called
here), and leave them in the lurch. My principle in
all such cases is, that though some of my tenants, I
am sorry to say, are not so honest as they should be,
yet money-lenders are so much worse rogues, that it
is no part of my duty to think about them, and if
a tenant likes to surrender his land, I decline to ask
what money he has borrowed.

I may be told that the course of gradual amendment I suggest is too slow. My answer is, its slow-
ness is one of its chief recommendations. Amendment of a people's habits cannot be fast, as I have
said before. Improvement will need generations to
effect; but every step is a gain. The proximate cause
of the present agitation is the distress from failure of
crops in Connaught and some other parts. Smith
O'Brien's folly in 1848, just after the famine, proceeded from the very same causes. It must be clearly
understood that the state of Connaught and other
western mountainous and sea-coast districts differs
wholly from the rest of Ireland. Here and there an

out-of-the-way spot in other parts approaches their bad state, but the quality of the land and condition of the people are far different. Before the famine of 1846 the subdivision of farms caused us to approach to this bad state. Since then we have advanced to a quite different condition. In Sir Charles Trevelyan's articles in the *Edinburgh Review* for 1848, and which he has lately reprinted, and from his letter to the *Times*, in July last, it will be seen what was then our condition and what we then went through. He says plainly, that was done then, which M. de Molinari advises to be the only possible thing that can be done now. The distress was fully relieved whilst it lasted. Afterwards the modest part was taken of helping the healing work of Nature, and acting on the sound principle of *Laisser faire*.

This, M. de Molinari adds, does not satisfy modern doctors; but Ireland in time will learn that the doctors are worse than the disease.

The Government of that time was Liberal, like the present. Sir C. Trevelyan is surely a Liberal. He had met the evil in Ireland, and grappled with it for near two years, being then Secretary to the Treasury. The words and acts of men like Sir C. Trevelyan and M. de Molinari cannot be passed over in favour of a brand-new revolution to turn everything upside down.

I believe there is clear proof that poverty is the only evil, and self-exertion the only cure. The district in which I write is only twenty miles from Skibbereen, and part of the Union was cut out of the Skibbereen Union, and runs within ten miles of that town. Every one knows what Skibbereen was in the famine of 1846. This district was not so bad, because there was less congestion of poor people from the poorer districts beyond, yet the suffering and starvation in it were terrible. The whole winter 1846-7 was like a frightful nightmare to those who had to go through it. In the following years more than half our people emigrated. Where an estate had been only neglected and subdivided, with low rent and no pressure, tenants being suffered to do as they liked, they emigrated more than from other lands. They had made a harder pressure for themselves. These spots had become much the same as rabbit-warrens. I knew two such cases from which nearly all went to America, though the rent was a mere trifle, and no pressure or restraint put on them. A large part of our population were labourers. There had been much emigration before the famine, so that many had friends in America: this helped to cause emigration to be looked on with liking. Our land is mostly of a quality that will not yield still without good manuring. So it was not easy to do much here without money. We are now one of the most thriving parts of the South of Ireland, and improve yearly. The land has got into larger farms; and though the farmers only half manure and give very little employment, only tilling as much as their own families can work, still, as prices of all grass products are very good, and wages are higher than they were then, all are much better off, and there have been no rent troubles.

There is a place of 400 acres near, called the Common Mountain, that belongs to no one. It was settled by squatters, who, in potato times, built cabins and reclaimed fields and bits. The fee was in the Crown, and the ownership by squatters was recognised. They are mostly no better than paupers. Last spring a large proportion had to get seed of champion potatoes on credit from the Union. It is quite the most turbulent part of the petty sessions district, and for a long time, as a magistrate, I thought it right to give double punishment to offenders from this part, for the sake of preserving order there.

I believe, if the matter was fairly looked into, this district and the greater part of the County Cork would be found to give conclusive proof of the soundness of the principles acted on by Sir C. Trevelyan and the Government of 1847. If the evil is pauperism—agrarian pauperism—surely to fix the present paupers on the land, bad ones and all, by Ulster Tenant-right, or fixity of tenure, or making them peasant proprietors, can never cure the trouble.

It is the strongest confirmation of this view that the whole effort of the present agitation is, to keep the worst and the most useless tenants still in their farms. They may be doing no good for themselves, and never have done any good even in the best times, and their bad habits and poverty may prove they never are likely to do any good; but there they are to stay and vegetate, neither paying rent nor benefiting themselves or the country.

It is strange men do not see that this means that all the bad habits of the lowest class in the country will be stereotyped among us, and all progress to a better state of things stopped.

The main help in Connaught and that part of Ireland which is the worst, must be emigration. Wherever there is a congestion of more on the soil than it can support in comfort without trusting to potatoes, emigration alone can relieve it. Of course no Government can undertake emigration, still less enforce it; they would hinder it if they tried. But the Government can give every facility for the purpose, and so open the door for it as wide as possible. They can provide, as ought to have been done long ago, proper agents at the ports of embarkation, to advise and help all emigrants asking for such help, and show where to procure food and lodgings whilst waiting for the ship, and forwarding them in every fair way. It is strange this has not been done before. It is done for these same poor people on their arrival at New York by the American Government. There is reason to believe emigrants are often grievously wronged and cheated at our own ports before they embark. A reasonable

care for them in this respect would be a great
encouragement to emigration, and an act of charity
too. Boards of Guardians have power now to help
emigration from the rates. But larger powers might
be given to help, and in poor Unions loans for the
purpose granted, where the burden became too heavy.

When the Prime Minister of Canada, Sir J.
Macdonnell, was in London just before Parliament
was prorogued, he offered grants of the splendid land
in Manitoba, the wheat from which causes so much
fright to English farmers, 160 acres each to able-
bodied emigrants settling there; and he offered to
get an Act passed by the Colonial Parliament to
charge the cost of the emigration and support for
some months of the emigrant upon the land, in case
the cost had been advanced by any third party, as
Boards of Guardians, etc., so that, whether the emigrants stayed on the land or sold it, the money should
be repaid. A proper officer of the Government was to
see to the whole business, and procure repayment. The
proposal was communicated to Lord Dunraven (who
has travelled so much to the Far West, and has personal knowledge of the country) and to Lord Monck;
they brought it before the House of Lords. Though
the climate is no doubt severe, still it must be a
very advantageous offer to poor emigrants. An
advance of £50, with what means he may have,
would be enough to pay for the emigration of most
farmers with their families. This, or even more,

charged on 160 acres of good land, must be quite safe.
Arrangements could be made for large parties going
out together.   If the offer is made known, and
facilities for embarking at this side are given, it is
likely a large emigration will follow, provided all are
convinced law and order will be enforced here, and
that those who stay at home must earn their living
by honest work.   It has long appeared to me that,
if advances for emigration were made personal debts
from the emigrants in any Colony, duly recoverable
in a safe and cheap way by Act of Colonial Parliament, with proper officers there to enforce payment
if not otherwise repaid, it would be a great advantage
to many honest poor people who wish to emigrate.
We are sure that most emigrants do well, and could
repay an advance easily by instalments.   Why should
they not do so?   Some would be lost, perhaps, by
the emigrants passing into the States: such loss
might be borne; the majority would repay.   All the
class of able healthy boys and girls in our workhouses,
growing up and able to work, might thus be sent out,
to their great gain and our relief.   In our great town
workhouses with thousands of paupers, some such
resource is much wanted.   The great workhouses in
the large towns, as Cork, Dublin, etc., are a grievous
evil, that never ought to have been allowed to grow up.
They are a disgrace to the Local Government Board,
and show how little sense prevails there.   In Cork
there are over 2500 paupers in the workhouse.   In

the two Dublin workhouses it is worse. They are born there, marry there, live and die there. The quantity of stimulants consumed in the houses is outrageous. Poor Law Inspectors almost live in them to keep things right, but still the evil goes on unchecked, a huge wen of pauperism. Nothing so bad has existed in the three kingdoms since the old Poor Laws of fifty years ago. I am sure the sentimental thought, that it is a hardship on a poor person to be forced by circumstances to emigrate, is a delusion. Irish people, when removed from the influence of their own class, become better workers, and more quiet and more prosperous. They have many qualities that better fit them for success in a new country than the English have. The faults of home are their bane. The proportion of those who succeed in America is very great.

To sum up: Agrarian pauperism is the true trouble of Ireland, and increased production of some sort the only possible cure, except in those parts where emigration is wanted. In one hundred years bad tenants will not produce more from the land than they produce now, but probably much less, as their land becomes more exhausted. Let, therefore, every opportunity for emigration be given to all unsuccessful and bad tenants and to all superfluous labourers, and let the land they occupied go into the hands of those who already hold land and are doing well with it. There is immense room for profitable employment for some generations in draining, with profit to all. The ordinary loans, at a rate of interest which causes no loss to Government, should be continued to landowners, as they have been for many years past; and for two or three years cheaper loans at 2 or $2\frac{1}{2}$ per cent might be continued to farmers. They will gain from draining thus done much more than they would gain by any reduction of rent.

Until the check of distress that has been felt all over the kingdom from the bad crops of the two seasons came on, Ireland was fast improving, and had greatly advanced compared with the state it was in at the Union, or any time since. It will do so again from natural causes, if only law and order are enforced. The doubt that foolish speeches and foolish acts of men in authority have raised, whether the law and rights of property will be upheld, has caused a hundred times more hardship to individuals, and to the tenants themselves, than all the hard acts of landlords in the same time, and has tended sorely to retard improvement in the country.

Mr. Froude truly says, " These words have raised incendiaries and assassins to the rank of patriots, and encouraged them to go on with their work by telling them that, if they were only violent and mischievous enough, they would have their desires. The one indispensable requirement in Ireland is authority armed with power to make the law obeyed." I cannot add a word to these weighty truths.

Unjust measures, disregarding the rights of property, may gratify the covetousness of some and the ill-will of others, by injuring the class of landowners, but they will never improve the social state of the people by a hair's breadth. Ireland, like all other countries, contains good and bad of all classes. Those of us who understand farming have no wish to let our land at all, because, from the bad farming of nearly all tenants, we can make much more of it by holding it ourselves. I should be glad to farm every acre of the 3900 that belong to me, and could add much to my income by doing so. The labourers I should employ would as a body be better off in all ways than most of the tenants, and their number would be greater. But I have not the least wish to part with my old friends, and have no thought of doing so ; only I can see no sense in rooting bad tenants in the soil to be paupers, and the cause of evil for generations to come.

No one who understands the question can doubt that the price of all farming products, except corn, has risen greatly in the last thirty years, and has a tendency still to rise. The mode of farming, too, has greatly improved. The use of bought manures, and of cake and corn in feeding stock, has much increased the profits of farming in ordinary times. These are the causes of the rise of rents that has taken place. Lately there has been a check, but prices may, and probably will, increase again when times improve.

Landlords have a just claim to a share of such increased prosperity according to what future prices may prove to be. Every man of business is of course ready to adjust the rent accordingly with fairness and consideration.

The same common sense and judgment that produce a prosperous estate and contented tenantry in England and Scotland will do so in Ireland. Whether we are few or many who try to reach this good state, we are doing our duty, and the best hope of the permanent progress of the country rests on our success. Why, instead of being helped, are our hands to be tied and our efforts hindered by what is really an effort to give protection to all the bad habits and backward ideas that have made Ireland a byword? Surely England has not so far lost the qualities that made her what she is, as to be unable to say law and order shall prevail, and upright honesty to all classes alike be maintained. Without these nothing else is worth having, nor can any people prosper.

The difference between indolence and industry is much greater than any difference of rent that any landlord can propose. The difference between order and the rule of the Land League is greater than that between prosperity and ruin.

At bottom the question is whether the dealings between landlord and tenant are to be governed by open free contract, as, since the principles of Free

Trade were recognised, has been done in all other business dealings amongst us. Or whether, because some Irish tenants are poor and backward, and seek to get a money advantage for themselves whether rightly or wrongly, a fixed artificial system is to be set up for this end, depriving owners of their honest reversionary rights. It has never been thought that to give largess to a pauper will cure him of his beggary, still less of indolence and love of drink. Everywhere else in the world industry and self-exertion are counted the only road to prosperity.

CHAPTER XV.

ON CLIMATE AND THE SUPPLY OF LABOUR AS AFFECTING AGRICULTURE IN IRELAND.

1872.

CLIMATE has been well described as the ruling principle of agriculture.

The Irish climate is proverbially wet. Mr. Scott, of the Meteorological Office, the highest authority in the kingdom on this subject, informs me that the rainfall of most part of Munster, all Connaught and Donegal, Cornwall, Wales, and the West of Scotland, resemble each other, all are forty to fifty inches, whilst the rainfall in Essex and the East of England is about twenty inches, over forty inches is the average of County Cork. The rainfall of the West of England, except Cornwall, and of the Eastern part of Ireland does not differ much—thirty to thirty-five inches. The rain increases down to Penzance, where it is the same as in Munster. Meteorological observations are kept at very few places in Ireland, and there is reason to believe that the local rainfall in many places is much greater than any that has been registered. It is certain that there is a damp-

ness in the atmosphere, as shown in the effect on
household goods, clothes, etc., and an absence of hot,
dry weather in summer, especially in the South,
much beyond anything usual in most parts of the
West of England, even where the rainfall is the
same. Arthur Young said, long ago, "The worst of
the climate of Ireland is the constant moisture
without rain." I am inclined to think it might be
said more truly, The best of the climate is the
constant moisture. But, either way, whether for
good or bad, such is the climate. My experience has
been chiefly in the West Riding, County Cork, and
there, beyond a few warm days in summer, sometimes not more than half-a-dozen, we know very
little of what hot weather means. In spite of this
dampness of atmosphere, the soil being generally
rather thin, and so drying very quickly, it is a
charming climate, mild in winter and cool in summer,
of a refreshing softness after the heat of English
summer weather, that causes a sense of actual
enjoyment from mere passing through the air, like
the enjoyment of a drive in the cool evening of a
roasting day.

The one drawback is the force of the south-west
winds, which are, however, the cause of our other
advantages.

Facts from the garden confirm this opinion.
Pears against a wall seldom ripen to their right
flavour. Peaches, except in especially warm and

sheltered places, will not do well. Peach-trees
continue growing throughout the autumn. I have
often seen them as full of leaves at Christmas as at
Midsummer. Of course the wood does not ripen,
and any frost kills this green wood, and often reduces
the tree in the following summer to bare branches,
with a tuft of green leaves at the end of each.
Apricots hardly ever bear fruit.

Such a climate as this plainly must have a very
great influence on farming; a greater influence probably than any other natural cause.

Mr. Buchan, President of the Botanical Society
of Edinburgh, in his address to the society, November
9, 1871, thus speaks on the subject of the effects of
climate on the distribution of plants :—

" Bousingault examined the distribution of wheat
on the continent of Europe, and arrived at the conclusion that it required 8248° Fahr., from the time
it begins to grow in spring, for the proper ripening
of the seed ; and, moreover, that this heat must be
partitioned so as to secure a mean summer temperature of 58° during the development and maturation
of the seed. This minimum amount of heat
required for the maturing of the seeds is a vital
consideration. We have proved in Scotland that a
mean temperature of 56° during the critical period,
with the average sunshine and rainfall of the
Scottish summer, is sufficient to ripen wheat properly. Not only so, but it was found that the

wheat crop of 1864 ripened well with only the average temperature of 54·4°. In that year, however, the sunshine was much above the average, and the mean of the daily maximum temperature was high, being as high as in August 1861, when the mean temperature was 57·4°.

" It is probable that the longer time the sun is above the horizon in Scotland, as compared with Germany and France, renders the ripening of this cereal possible with a lower mean temperature, and when this is combined with a clear dry atmosphere, and consequently a blazing, scorching sunshine, grain of excellent quality is ripened, though the mean temperature rise no higher than 54·4°. From this it is clear that in regarding the influence of temperature on bringing plants to maturity, it is not mean temperature merely, but the way in which the vital element is distributed through the day and night, particularly at the critical periods of the plants' growth, which must be considered. A high mean temperature, with little variation, implies a comparatively low day temperature; and, on the other hand, a moderately low mean temperature, with a large daily range, implies a high day temperature; so that a climate with a comparatively low mean temperature may yet afford the warmth required in carrying on the higher functions of the plant which another climate of a higher mean temperature could not supply.

" Now, that which in the highest degree deter-

mines the mode in which temperature is partitioned
throughout the twenty-four hours of the day is the
amount of cloud and the degree of moisture in the
atmosphere; for a knowledge of which we must look
to the rainfall through the months of the year as
furnishing the best available key.

" The rainfall affects plants directly through the
nourishment it conveys to them, and indirectly
through the state of the sky which its amount or
absence implies.   Indeed, so great is the influence
of rainfall on vegetation, that we cannot be far wrong
in regarding it as co-ordinate with that of temperature.   Whatever the law may be which expresses
the atmospheric conditions that determine the limits
of the growth of species, it must include in its
functions both the heat and moisture of the air.

" Decandolle deduced the law for the distribution
of species over a region whose climates are marked
off from each other rather by variations of temperature than of moisture.   He then endeavoured to
extend it so as to account for the distribution of
the floræ of other regions, the climates of which
may be characterised either as moist at all seasons
or subject to marked variations of moisture at stated
seasons.   Perhaps not the least valuable of the results arrived at by him is the negative one stated in
these words :—' On the borders of the Mediterranean
Sea, the limits appeared so often determined by the
humidity, or by causes still unknown, that the

operations of temperature always escaped my cal-
culations.'

" It may be predicted that when the limits of
species have been drawn with some exactness for
Central and Northern Europe, the regions from which
Decandolle took his examples, they will be found to
coincide with no mere temperature lines, however
calculated and determined, inasmuch as there are
much greater differences in the climates of this
region than are generally supposed, as regards the
rainfall, particularly in the manner of its distribution
over the year." [1]

The practical result of these views seems to be
that the same summer temperature (I mean the
average temperature of each twenty-four hours) may
be arrived at in two ways :—

(1.) By cool days and warm nights; or (2) by
hot days and cold nights. Hot days are necessary
for the growth of good corn crops, and if the days
are hot and sunshiny, cold nights are of less importance. There is no doubt that the moisture and
clouds in the atmosphere of Ireland cause cool days,
with little sunshine; and though the nights are
mild, that does not, for the purpose of corn-growing,
make up for the want of heat and sunshine by day.

Dr. Lloyd, the Provost of Trinity College, Dublin,
who is probably the best authority we have on the

---

[1] "Transactions and Proceedings of the Botanical Society of
Edinburgh," vol. xi. Part II., 1873, pp. 262-264.

subject of Irish climate, has been good enough also
to suggest to me that another subsidiary action,
connected with those of temperature and moisture,
that plays a sensible part in the phenomena, is the
frequent *lowering of temperature* which occurs in
July in connection with the arrival of the mass of
condensed vapour from the Atlantic, and which,
unhappily for the cereals, occurs at the St. Swithin
period, just at the time when it is most injurious to
them, although advantageous to green crops. This
shows itself very decidedly in the annual curves of
temperature as well as of rainfall.

Mr. Whitley, in an article in the Journal of the
Royal Agricultural Society, gives the average summer
temperature of Cork at 65°, being, as he adds, the
highest in the British Islands. There can be no
doubt that this is founded on erroneous observations.
There is no such average summer temperature as 65°
in Ireland. It is probable that the average summer
temperature of the South of Ireland is about 60°.
But 60° is a sufficient average temperature for growing wheat well. It is much more than a sufficient
temperature for growing oats, which are believed
only to require from 54° to 57°. Yet good crops
of wheat can seldom be grown in Ireland, especially
in the South, and even oats, though so much hardier,
do not grow so well as in England and Scotland,
especially on land that is highly farmed. My experience is that it is increasingly hard to get a

proportionately good crop on high-farmed land than on land in worse condition. This is the difficulty. The temperature is high enough, according to received views, to grow wheat or oats well. But they do not grow well. Mr. Buchan's explanation is probably the true one.

There is no series of accurate observations for any long number of years extant. I have been favoured by Mr. R. H. Scott, Director of the Meteorological Department, London, with the following Table :—

TABLE I.—MEAN MONTHLY BAROMETRICAL PRESSURE and TEMPERATURE at VALENCIA and CORK.

MONTHS.	VALENCIA.		CORK.	
	Pressure. Mean of 5 Years.	Temperature. Mean of 5 Years.	Pressure. Mean of 11 Years.	Temperature. Mean of 13 Years.
	8 A.M. Obser. only. 1866-1870.	8 A.M. Obser. only.	1857-1867.	1857-1869.
January	29·754	43·0	29·813	41·8
February . . .	·895	44·1	·934	43·1
March	·874	45·4	·823	44·8
April	·922	49·2	·894	49·6
May	29·861	52·9	·932	53·5
June	30·105	56·7	·998	59·2
July	30·016	60·0	·959	62·1
August	29·964	58·9	·929	60·5
September . . .	·835	56·4	·909	57·0
October	29·920	52·9	·833	51·0
November . . .	30·015	46·8	·881	44·5
December . . .	29·814	46·3	29·933	43·2
Mean for the year	29·915	51·1	29·903	50·9

NOTE.—The barometric values for Valencia are obtained from values kept in the Meteorological Office. All the other averages are computed by Mr. Buchan and published by him.

An interesting illustration has been mentioned to me by Mr. Scott from the climate of the Scilly Islands, which may be taken as an exaggeration of the climate of Ireland. He says :—

" In Scilly the mean monthly temperature ranges only from 45° to 63°, being a less variation than at any other place in these islands. The north of Donegal and Shetland most nearly approach it. The result of this very equable *spring* temperature is that vegetation is always going on, and no crop or fruit will ripen thoroughly. A few bad apples are the only fruit besides gooseberries. The plants that flourish there are sub-tropical, such as aloes, yuccas, mesembryanthemums, and, of course, large geraniums and fuchsias. The produce of the islands is to a great extent vegetables for the London market, especially new potatoes.

" The climate is an exaggeration of your southern climate, such as Cape Clear, the mean temperature for the year being 1° higher. The reason of the very exceptional climate of Scilly is due in some measure to the set of the currents at the mouth of the English Channel."

I think the suitableness of the Irish climate for growing potatoes was one cause that led to the great extent of potato cultivation there before the famine, which has hitherto been ascribed mainly to social and political causes. Till the blight, potatoes flourished in Ireland better than elsewhere, and therefore were more grown.

In the South of Ireland corn ripens, but with difficulty, so that a good or bad crop of corn is more dependent on the character of the season than elsewhere, and the crop is more often inferior. Over thirty years ago, before the famine, when I began to farm in Ireland, the universal rotation in the county of Cork, except near the mountains, was potatoes on lea manured (and such lea as it was!— land left to rest, without grass seeds even, and one mass of weeds; and then the manuring!—earth drawn from the field, with a little calcareous sand and the refuse of the dwelling-house mixed), followed by wheat. Oats only came in as a scourging crop when the land would no longer grow wheat. The wheat was a poor crop, five or six barrels of twenty stones, about equal to twenty-four bushels, being considered good. Half that produce was much more common. But as Corn-law prices then ruled, farmers were content, except in bad years, which in that climate were frequent.

After I had been farming pretty well for some years, with only a moderate increase of crop, I remember thinking the cause must be in the previously exhausted condition of the soil, and that I might get over it and grow good wheat by a rotation of (1) swedes, (2) rape, (3) wheat. The swedes and rape were well manured with bones, besides other manure, and half the swedes and all the rape were eaten with sheep. The wheat looked all that could be desired during the spring and summer till harvest, but it was no sooner in shock than it was enough to lift a sheaf to have a painful proof of the crop's lightness. In fact, it was worse than the crop of the small farmer in the next field, that had not been a quarter so welldone by. There was sunlight enough to ripen his thin, short-strawed crop tolerably. But the ears of my handsome crop were not half-filled, and much of the corn in them was only fit for chickens' food. The same result several years in succession at last taught its lesson.

I gave up trying to grow any corn except oats. The common farmers, too, have gradually ceased to grow wheat, except a small piece for their own consumption (as it is one of the curiosities of our stage of development that every farmer thinks it needful to grow the food of himself and his family on his own farm; so, as potatoes will no longer grow well, he grows some wheat wherever he can for home consumption). They, too, have taken to oats as the chief crop. Wheat being usually lower in price than it was in Corn-law times, and oats much higher, no doubt tends to the same end. There is a general opinion, too, that the local climate has altered. The oats even are not the better sorts of oats. Black Tartary oats, the coarsest sort known, succeed best by far. But even with oats, and thoroughly good farming, the produce in corn is not on the average of years what it should be; nothing

like what such farming would produce in England
or Scotland. The upland soil in my district is a
useful turnip loam, rather thin from the rock being
near the surface, but growing great crops of swedes.
(Manure as highly as we please, we cannot grow
half a Norfolk crop of mangolds, for the same reason,
I think, that we cannot grow good corn crops.) It
steadily improves with good farming in the yield of
grass, and in the quantity of stock it will feed, and
not at all slowly. The bottom land is generally
more or less peaty, with clay below, and when
drained is very good for grass. For years I have
used bought manures and cake largely; last year to
the value of 20s. per acre over the whole farm of
seven hundred acres. Yet the corn hardly increases;
fifty bushels of oats per acre is still as much as we
can grow in a good year, even after sheep folded on
swedes, with hay and cake. I am not able to give
measured quantities of any value, for the farm is
managed in subordination to the needs of the estate,
with sometimes a slice of good land let away in
order to improve a tenant's farm, sometimes a slice
of reclaimed land added to it, sometimes of land
given up by a bad tenant, and worn out to a degree
of exhaustion that will not grow either weeds or
couch (it is something to have come to look on a
good crop of couch as a hopeful sign of land), and
which swallows up all the manure of a year or two
as a starved beast swallows good feeding without

showing it. Rotation and exact quantities at successive intervals thus are made almost impossible; but my conviction is strong, from close observation, that the difficulty of growing larger crops of oats is due to the climate, which, though in ordinary years it will ripen a moderate crop, has too much moisture and too little sunshine to ripen a really heavy crop, except in chance seasons.

On the other hand, the very same climate that is so unfavourable for corn is extraordinarily favourable for grass, which continues to grow often through most part of the winter.

And this is the true explanation of the inclination to grass-farming that is almost universal in Ireland, not only among large farmers and landowners farming on their own account, but equally among middling and small farmers. The small farmer formerly tilled more of his farm in proportion, because it took much of his land to provide the food for his family, but even before the famine the constant argument used by small farmers seeking more land was, "If I get more land I can leave more out in grass." When a farmer failed, it was always said, "He tilled too much of his land." There was never any doubt but that the land paid best in grass, when the farmer could afford to buy stock. The climate was and is the ruling principle, as Mr. Whitley said. Even when the grass farming is bad, as it often is, it still pays better than the

equally bad tillage farming that the same farmer
would practise on the same farm. The views in
favour of breaking up inferior grass so often urged
in drier climates have very little place in our wet
climate. There is very little land so bad that if it
is once in good condition will not grow grass well in
this climate. When the land needs breaking up it
is almost always only as the best means of adding
condition in order again to put it in grass.

Of course what I have said in no way affects the
correctness of Mr. Pringle's complaints of bad grass-
farming. No doubt, too, there is some land that
cannot profitably be kept in grass beyond a few
years. I believe, also, there is a tract of country in
the East and North-East of Ireland, from Wexford
to Down inclusive, where the climate is more
favourable to tillage than elsewhere. When land is
foul with weeds, and much worn out, cultivation
with heavy manuring of green crops, is the most
economical, if not the only way of getting it into
condition; and without some roots and straw for
winter it is not easy on middling land to manage a
heavy stock to the best advantage; but I think the
problem of profitable farming in these times in Ireland is (or at least is fast becoming) with how little
cultivation a farm in grass can be successfully managed. There is a great change since the time when
Mr. Algernon Clarke, whom Mr. Pringle quotes as
his authority, wrote of Irish farming. The price of

stock, and of most grass products, has immensely increased. The cost of labour has greatly increased too ; not only are wages much higher, which is not to be complained of, but labourers in Ireland usually give less and worse labour for their hire. It was bad enough before with low wages, it is worse now with much higher wages, whatever it may ultimately come to. Emigration, too, is steadily lessening the supply of labour year by year. Several years ago, being pretty forward with draining and such improvements, I bethought me that it would be well to devote money to the improvement of labourers' houses over the estate. I had already built good houses for most of the men in my own regular employment. When I came practically to consider the subject I found that everything was in such a transition state that it was wiser to wait a while, and see what houses would be really wanted and where. It was well I did so, for now there are a number of labourers' houses on all parts of the estate standing empty, some of them fairly good slated houses, much superior to the common cabins of the country ; more are yearly being left empty.

Extra jobs of draining, etc., can no longer be done in most years at a reasonable cost, or a fair increase on former prices. Men are not to be had, except a few at slack times of year, and they will not do wet, unpleasant work except for very high pay, and in their own lazy way. It is often said that

one advantage of more and better cultivation would
be additional employment for labourers. I have
always thought this a fallacy. There is more profitable work in draining, etc., wanting to be done in
Ireland, exclusive of the reclamation of real waste
land, than all the labourers could do in two generations, even if they worked well. There is no
good reason, therefore, for the sake of the labourers,
to depart from the sound principle of political
economy, that such mode of farming should be
followed as will leave the largest net profit (true),
whether it be grass or tillage farming. In truth,
even such lightish land as I have described, when it
is laid down in grass in good condition, produces
excellently and for many years. The number of
years that it will produce well in grass without
showing signs of going back, wholly depends on the
condition it is in when laid down, and on the treatment of the grass. In the neighbourhood of towns,
where manure can be bought, top-dressing grass is a
very favourite course, and is thought to answer
especially well. Except in such places manuring
grass is little understood or practised. How far
artificial manures, as recommended by Mr. Thompson, of Kirby Hall,[1] will effect a permanent improvement in grass on such a soil as ours, which is not
strong land, may perhaps be doubtful; but it is

[1] *Vide* Journal Royal Agricultural Society, 2d series, vol. viii.
Part I. No. xv. p. 174.

certain that any phosphates of which the soil is
deprived by milk or grazing can be thus restored at
small cost; and it is also certain that there are
many intelligent men in Ireland, ready to try Mr.
Thompson's prescription, and all other suggestions
for keeping up the condition of grass land.

The conclusion I wish to draw from the facts
and considerations I have stated is, that Ireland,
notably the South and West, is from its climate
a land of grass, and that for farming profitably in
Ireland grass should be the first object, and tillage
only so far as it helps the grass. I believe this is
what all our best farmers are, consciously or uncon-
sciously, working to.   Mr. Pringle's strictures on the
fault of much of our Irish grass-farming are generally quite true, and the remedy he proposes is in a
measure good, but only in a measure—not as an
end, but as a means to better grass. In truth our
grass privileges (as an American might call them)
are very great. Farmers, who know their business,
are doing excellently. It is sometimes said that
landowners farming their own land in Ireland lose
by it. Never was there a greater delusion. The
profit on grass-farming makes it all easy, whatever
scale a landlord farms on; much easier than in a
country fit for tillage alone. Numbers of us are
making more than double the rent we used to get
for the land, when let to tenants, and three times
the present valuation of the land.

When land is well laid down, the first year's grass is very good. The second year is worse, because the artificial grasses are dying out and the natural grasses have not had time to take their place. The third year the natural grasses are established, and a close and excellent sward is the result, equal to good old grass in the West of England, and such as in Norfolk could not be got in thirty years, hardly in twice thirty. I have often said that such land as I have to deal with, in the Norfolk climate would not be worth half what it is in the Irish climate. Again, consider the immense rise in the price of grass products in Ireland. Twenty years ago, butter sold for 5d. to 6d. per lb. Good beef was often at 3d. and pork at 2d. per lb. £2 to £3 was not thought a bad price for a yearling heifer. I have bought good fair stock lambs in July for 5s. each. Now prices are some twice, some four times, some six times these rates, all, be it observed, for grass products. This rise of price has not yet produced its effects on our farming, and on the value of land. Some of it is still recent, at least in part—as the value of young stock—and the argument is still used and felt, " Perhaps these high prices will not hold." But as soon as the prices of stock are felt to be permanent—as the increasing demand for meat from increasing wages in England shows it is likely they will be permanent—that cause alone will be sufficient to turn the balance in favour of grass farming, wherever grass will grow fairly. I can say that in the arrangements for my own farm these considerations weigh more day by day. Corn is not higher in price, the wages to be spent in growing it are higher ; but grass products, that cost little or no more wages, are many times higher in price. Can there be a doubt, from this cause alone, what the intelligent farmer will do in a climate specially suited to grass ?

Grass farming in every form, and with every sort of help from bought manures or bought food for stock, cake, etc., is the true future before us.[1]

Water meadows, the especial advantage of which, in the mild climate of Ireland, was pointed out by Mr. Philip Pusey (in the Journal, vol. xi. p. 62) more than twenty years ago, are a most valuable resource to Irish grass farmers. Mowing upland grass on second-rate land for hay is very exhausting to the soil, and we do it as little as possible. We cut hay mostly from bottom lands. But water meadows in this climate are very productive, and we grow unusual crops of hay on them, yet systematic watering is not nearly as common as it might be. Small farmers are constantly squabbling amongst themselves for the use of any rill of water near their

[1] The new plan of feeding stock with decorticated cattle cake or grass, promises to pay capitally. I have tried it in 1880 on a large scale.

farms. When they have got it, they often let it run the whole winter over one spot, which is thus made into a morass, especially as the cattle are seldom kept out of the field. The opportunities of making regular water meadows are very frequent, and will be made use of more and more. I have found a dressing of five or ten cwt. of bones per acre on water meadows greatly to thicken the grass and improve the quality of the hay. They are applied as soon as the hay is off, so as to be well trodden in by the stock eating the after-grass, and avoid risk of the water washing them away when the meadow is flooded in autumn. I believe they pay well every few years, as often as the hay shows any signs of becoming inferior. My theory, I know not how correct, is that the water must contain the other food of grass in larger proportion than phosphates. The bones thus make up all that is wanted.

The course on my own farm, which has been arrived at simply from experience and the pressure of facts, will, I think, show what we are coming to. For nearly twenty years the course, instead of a regular rotation, has been to choose fifty or sixty acres of the worst grass on the farm each year for ploughing. Most of this is sown with lea oats; but if the land is very poor, no oats are taken, and then it is ploughed with two ploughs following each other, one skimming the grass as lightly as possible, the other turning a good furrow of earth over it.

It is then broken for turnips the next spring. But there is more trouble in getting such land prepared for turnips than after lea oats, and the plan can only be followed to a limited extent.

The ewes are folded on the grass meant for lea oats, before it is ploughed. But still the oats are usually very bad. The older the grass, the worse are the oats. It is plain the sod does not rot in time to help the oats. In some districts they grow two crops of oats in succession, on breaking up the land ; the first is bad, the second good enough, because the sod by that time is rotten. But this plan is exhausting, and leaves the land very foul. With fifty or sixty acres of turnips we have been in the habit of fattening 200 sheep and over 30 beasts, besides keeping 200 ewes and 200 hoggets of the previous spring, 60 cows, and young stock, rising yearlings and two-year-olds, about 35 to 40 head of each age—enough to stock the farm in the following summer with little buying.

We have the last two years reduced the number of acres broken each year to forty instead of fifty, and still fatten and keep the same stock as before, with the help of more cake. This of course lessens the work of men and horses ; and if, as is said, a ton of cake may be reckoned as roughly equal to an acre of turnips (which I do not think it is, of such crops of turnips as we grow), there is no reason that such a course should not answer and keep up the condition of the grass. In two or three years I expect the extent ploughed may be reduced to thirty acres each year, and with still more cake the same winter stock be kept and fattened. Just now I have a tract of cut-out bog that has been drained, etc., coming in. This for its own sake needs cultivation and turnip cropping, and so delays the decrease of tillage. Oats with grass seeds follow the turnips, unless the land is poor, when it is laid down with rape and grass seeds, no corn crop being taken. Experience can alone show how far we can decrease cultivation, and keep up the condition of the grass land. It can clearly be done to the extent of one-half, *i.e.* twenty-five acres instead of fifty, being ploughed each year. The net profit on the farm is more than double the rent the tenants paid for it when they failed, after charging to each year all the cake and manure bought, bailiff's salary, and every expense. The changed appearance of the land is a pleasure to one's eyes. The stock are more than double the number, and individually double the weight of those the tenants kept.

It may seem strange to say it, but religion and politics have been brought in Ireland even into the question of farming, and whether grass or tillage are best for the country is sought to be decided by what is most to the advantage of the Roman Catholic or Protestant interests. The power of the Roman Catholic clergy and their party depends on the number of Roman Catholics; and tillage, as giving more employment than grass, has been favoured accordingly. Even the growth of flax has been urged on the same grounds. I have already shown the weakness of such reasoning, because there is plenty of work for every one for long years in draining and other improvements, far more profitable to all concerned than it can be to try to force one kind of farming instead of another that for any reason is more profitable. But there is no doubt it has been thought the increased employment from tillage would check the emigration.

My own opinion is clear that the decrease of labourers is going on so fast that by the end of the next seven or ten years there will be no choice in the matter, and it is very fortunate for us that the increased price of grass products gives us so profitable a means of escape from what would be otherwise a most serious difficulty. Those who have treated their land best will have least trouble.

On one point alone Mr. Pringle, I think, is quite wrong—when he argues against grass farming because small farmers, holding 7 millions of acres, keep on them stock to the value of $17\frac{1}{2}$ millions of money; whilst large farmers, holding $8\frac{3}{4}$ millions of acres, keep on them stock valued only at 18 millions of money. But the cattle on both sizes of farm are valued at the same rate, £6 : 10s. per head. It is evident that the cattle of the small farmer much more nearly approach this value than the cattle of the large farmer. Large farmers, as a rule, have much larger and more improved cattle of all ages than small farmers; and nearly all the fatting and fat cattle. Mr. Thompson's estimate of the weight of cattle killed in England is 600 lbs. per head on an average, which at present prices would make their value a good deal over £20 each. The cattle of large farmers in Ireland probably do not weigh much less than the average of all English cattle killed, and after all due allowance for the value above £6 : 10s. of the cattle of small farmers, there must be a large excess in the value per head of the cattle of large farmers. If this excess is only fifty per cent, and it is probably much more, it will quite alter the inference Mr. Pringle draws. Considering how few turnips, etc., Irish small farmers grow, and how much they overstock their grass, and that they use no cake or bought food, it would be strange indeed if they thus grew more pounds of meat than are grown on better managed large grass farms.

The last three years have been excellent seasons for grass in Ireland. With the same stock every farmer has had plenty of grass; even those usually over-stocked have had enough, and their stock has profited accordingly. Many have thus been taught the lesson of the profit from the better feeding of stock; the price a well-fed animal of any age has brought in the market has been so out of proportion to the price of an

ill-fed one that the most backward has had the point
driven into his head, and efforts at better feeding for
the sake of the better profit have been numerous.
I think the young cattle sold in the next few years
will show the effect of this better feeding.

Such a number of calves as have been reared this
year in Ireland was never seen since the world
began. It is caused by the great price of young
stock in the past year. The country positively
swarms with calves. Hitherto small farmers have
usually reared only heifer calves and the bulls have
gone to the butcher at once. This year bulls and
heifers have been alike reared. This, too, if the
demand continues, will in a few years help greatly
to improve the quality of Irish stock. When the
bull calves were sold for a trifle to the butcher at
once, and many of the heifers kept as cows for himself, the backward farmer felt little the gain of
putting a good bull to his cows. Where now he has
so many to sell, the difference in the price of a well-
bred calf or yearling on such a number will soon
work more care in the choice of a bull. But most
of the calves must be sold before the winter, since it
is certain farmers have not food for half of them.

The same causes that have given us plenty of
grass have made the potato crop a great failure.
There has not been so much blight since the famine
as last year and this, and the crop has been very bad.
I think fewer potatoes will be grown in future, which

again will lead to less cultivation and more and better grass.

In spite of all the miseries of the famine, farmers and labourers alike have since, as far as they could, gone back to the old conacre potato system. This is the explanation why for years the statistical returns have shown a regular increase in the average of potatoes; only as potatoes did not grow well enough to last the whole year, the system could not fully re-establish itself as of old. Some modification to supply food in spring and summer, when there were no potatoes, was unavoidable. A few sacks of Indian meal, bought on credit, was the means used.

The terms for farmers' labourers in this district have been 3s. per week and the man's food at the farm-house; the cabin, charged 6d. per week, and the conacre another sixpence per week, being stopped by the farmer out of the 3s. On the balance, with such potatoes as grew, wife and children existed. Of course there were some minor privileges—pig, cocks and hens, etc.

The strangest thing is that many labourers preferred such terms from small farmers to 8s. or 9s. a week, with free house, potato-land, etc., from others. I believe the secret is, that there was real work in the one case, and no real work, but half-idle dawdling in the other. This year the potatoes have failed again in earnest, but the people are now so few the effect will not be the same as at the famine. The

3s. per week, however, has broken down, as the labourers have no potatoes. Labourers can now be had in plenty for any job paying fair wages, and next spring will show a larger emigration to America than for years before.

It may seem presumptuous in one mainly connected with Irish farming even to offer a hint to English farmers, but I cannot help saying that I think in many parts of England the difficulties as to labour, etc., are the same as our difficulties, and the remedies that suit us will also suit them. It seems a safe general conclusion that wherever grass will grow well, more grass will lessen labour. Where permanent grass is attainable with difficulty, the Scotch five-course rotation instead of the Norfolk four-course, i.e. two years' grass instead of one, must save near one-fifth of the labour on a farm.

More grass, with higher manuring and more cake, seems to me the remedy, wherever possible, for dear labour, at a time of great demand for all grass products.

It is a very old opinion that the successful farmer is he who, with skill and knowledge of general principles, most clearly recognises the particular facts and circumstances under which his farm is placed, and applies his skill and knowledge to them accordingly. That is all I contend for under the very exceptional climate of Ireland, at a time when labour is dear, and when the value of grass products is such as has never been known or heard of, and seems likely so to continue, certainly in a measure, and possibly to a still larger degree.

No doubt many cases can be given where cultivation to a considerable extent has been profitably carried on in Ireland, but if the circumstances and rotation of these farms are looked into, it will be found that not more than a tenth or a twelfth of their acreage is annually in green crop. This means that a good deal more than half the farm is in grass over one year old, and that the system is something quite different from that of an arable farm in Norfolk or the Lothians. It will also, I think, be found that many such farms have been in bad condition, and their occupiers have been getting them into heart.

I am far from saying that during this process and under this system their farms have not paid well; my own farm has for many years been a proof to the contrary. But the fact is, that once land is in condition, grass in the Irish climate will pay best with as little cultivation as may be, and that there is plenty of more profitable work for the displaced labour in draining, etc. Sound political economy teaches that the most profitable application of labour, whoever may gain by it, whether landlord, farmer, or workman, is the greatest gain to the community; and that all artificial attempts to force labour in a particular direction for the sake of secondary (even) good objects are a mistake, and sure to end in dis-

T

appointment.   I think this mistake is made by some authorities on farming in Ireland; and as political economy is little else than the correct statement of facts that are sure to produce the same results, whether correctly or incorrectly stated, only with serious loss in the meantime to those who are misled, good may be done by putting forward the above views.[1]

[1] Journal of Royal Agricultural Society, vol. ix., Second Series.

CHAPTER XVI.

THE EFFECTS OF THE LAW OF SETTLEMENT OF LAND.

JUNE 1872.

IT is of the very first importance that the bearings and effects of the law of settlement should be clearly understood. The law on this subject now is undoubted. No settlement is valid beyond the life of a person or persons living when it is made and twenty-one years afterwards, *i.e.* till an unborn child attains its majority. But in much the larger number of cases men live till their children reach twenty-one years of age, and if settlements on unborn children were wholly forbidden— leaving owners of land to do as they like about settlements for their own lives, or others living when the settlement is made—a small minority of cases would alone be affected, viz. those of men who are so unfortunate as to die whilst their children are still minors. Practically, very few even of such cases would suffer, because, as the right of an owner whose children are minors to dispose of his property to his children by will could not well be interfered with, it is certain most of these men, when dying or failing in health, would settle their estates on their living children. Nothing would give a chance of attaining the end sought by the opponents of settlements but peremptory prohibition of all limited estates in land, *i.e.* forbidding all settlements whatever, whether on persons living or yet unborn, that the owner of land, on his marriage or otherwise, should be forbidden by law to settle his estate for his own life or that of himself and his wife. If settlements on unborn children were forbidden, but not the power of settling for the lives of persons living, it is clear that every motive which now makes men settle their estates to the extent the law permits, would operate just the same to make them settle their estates as far as the altered law permitted, and they would do so. A father, being absolute owner, whose son was about to marry, would settle the estate for the life of his son and his intended wife, just as those who acquire landed property after they have married now do. If the son was owner, he would do as he does now, and for the same reasons. It is the habits and ideas, I might almost say instincts, of the class who own land, which have been the growth of generations and even centuries, that are the true cause of men striving to keep in their families the land they own. Landowners, with very rare exceptions, wish their families and estates should continue after them. And then as settlements are mostly made on marriage, it is really the influence of the girl a man wants to marry and of her family, that more than anything else causes settlements to be made. Their wishes go even beyond the law, and they would tie their estates up longer if they could. If settlements were forbidden by law, it is very doubtful if to a great extent the same habits and ideas, which cannot be rooted out, would not keep the land in families much as at present. A few spendthrifts might be sold up—the mass of landowners of steadiness and character would act much as they do now.

It has never yet been proved that owners in fee lay out more money in improving their land than limited owners so spend. It is a pity the new Doomsday Book does not enter on that question. It is so probable, if settlements were forbidden, that owners of land would still in substance act as now, that in France, where they are more logical than we are in carrying out consequences, the law goes a step farther, and hinders men from making their own wills. The law makes a will for them to insure the partition of land. But even in France the landowners' instinct prevails, and this instinct is the same in the small French proprietor as in the great English landlord. I think the subject of settlements has not at all been thought out by many of those who have taken it up. It involves settlements of personal property really as much as of land. Different rules could not stand. Distinctions would be impossible between settlements of land and settlements of the money for which land would sell. Lawyers doubtless see the bearings of the subject and its difficulties. Mr. J. S. Mill's late acknowledgment in the *Examiner* newspaper of January 4, that a change in the law of settlement would make little difference in the number of owners of land, reduces the question mainly to one of sentiment, and in substance is throwing up the sponge. The distribution of the land in small quantities among large numbers of the people has something to say for itself, if it can be shown to produce greater happiness to the majority. Hatred of an aristocracy and *doctrinaire* radicalism are not yet English principles of action. The true issue is, are English landowners to be deprived of the right of settling their estates, when they marry, on their intended wives and expected children ?

The weak place in the argument of those who wish to upset the present law of settlement of land is in their facts, or more accurately their want of facts. The utmost they can carry their case to is, that in the opinion of Mr. So-and-So, of more or less authority as a poor-law inspector or otherwise, the settlement of land prevents a due outlay of capital upon it for landlords' improvements, notably the building of cottages. This is not proof, but opinion. Cases such as those cited of settled estates that are unimproved, plainly prove nothing at all; they have no more weight than cases (which could be cited by the score) of estates in strict settlement excellently managed, on which every proper landlord's outlay has been made. To make such evidence worth anything, the cases need to be carried much farther. There are too many other causes in operation besides the fact of the land being in settlement or not, that might have produced the result—many would say, that did produce the result. For instance, in this matter of building cottages, that so much stress is laid on, with the former system of pauper settlement still felt to operate practically, and the fact that cottages will not pay the interest on their cost, both telling as strongly on the owners of estates in fee as on settled estates, and both very influential, it is disingenuous to lay the blame on some other cause, and say nothing about these. Though the majority of estates may be in strict settlement, there are also a large number of estates held in fee. It is a question of easy inquiry, and quite capable of proof, whether the estates in settlement or those held in fee in the kingdom, or in given portions of the kingdom, are in the best condition as to landlords' improvements, cottages, etc. But there is a third class of estates, inquiry into which would be still more instructive, and which, I believe, are very numerous,—those, namely, the bulk of which are in settlement, but of which appreciable portions (one-fourth or one-fifth, perhaps), from one cause or other, as purchase, etc., are held in fee by the tenant for life of the rest. My own property being thus circumstanced, I am the better able to speak of this class. Such estates are very favourable examples :—1. The owner can sell part of the land held in fee to improve the rest. 2. Such parts can be used in providing for younger children. 3. He can improve the parts held in fee to the utmost, and charge the cost, or leave the whole value to younger children. 4. He can borrow money on the best terms for such objects. 5. All the time he has the income of the settled part of the estate to live on, meet jointures or charges, etc. So that if views adverse to settlements were true, the land thus held in fee ought to be a very model of improvement. Yet I will venture to say it is very seldom that such land will be found to be either better or worse managed than the parts of the estate in settlement. To make out proof on the subject, fair and full inquiry, such as I have here suggested, ought to be made. But whilst it is asserted that those who have got no land yet, have a passion for getting it, it is assumed that those who have got it as owners in fee will be ready to sell it for slight cause. There was never a greater mistake. I believe the case of an owner in fee being willing to sell part of his estate in order to improve the rest is excessively rare. The fund from which landlords' improvements ought to be made is the rent. A moderate percentage of the rental applied to this purpose is the proper course. It is the want of will, not the want of power to do this that is the true mischief. Men do not know of, do not feel, its necessity and importance. Often improvements, perhaps from want of management, will not make a fair return. It is a delusion that most tenants are willing to pay a fair interest on landlords' improvements. They are willing enough to ask for them, but many expect not to be charged for them, and on many estates they are done without charge, except perhaps for draining, which pays the tenant double. Sense, knowledge of business and of land, a skilful and trusty agent, the traditions and habits of families, duty, even taste, have a great deal to do with a landlord's making improvements, or not doing so. No doubt there are landlords so wealthy that large improvements are no burden, and others so poor that they are a heavy burden; but so it would be if there were no settlements, and all the minor motives I have alluded to would be equally operative. There is no sort of doubt but that a very large number of settled estates are well managed with due outlay by the tenants for life. The true question is, whether there is any such difference in the condition of estates held in fee, compared with settled estates, as will show a real superiority of one over the other. Upon this, actual inquiry is the only evidence of value. For one, I am not afraid of the result.

The foundation of the views against settlement of land is, that tenants for life are less able and less willing to spend money on improvements than owners in fee. Let us see how far this goes. I will first clear away a point that produces some confusion. What is the true basis of the relation of landlord and tenant? Is it contract, express or implied? or is it a half feudal relation—a partial relic of lord and vassal, with undefined benefits on the one side, and as undefined returns on the other?

It is plain in these days, whenever the question is seriously asked, the answer must be, The relation is one of contract only. Yet the idea that the relation is a half feudal one constantly appears in the minds both of landlords and tenants. It influences men's minds continually. In many districts (and in part in many more) it is the true nature of the relation. Families hold their farms for generations. Rents are fixed, not at the true value of the farm, but with consideration of the person. All sorts of landlord's improvements are made on the same principle, and with little regard to the return they yield to the landlord. This is the true cause of undue expectations by the landlord of a return in the matter of game, and the tenant's vote at elections.

But when such a question as whether tenants for life or owners in fee are the best landlords is to be considered, this semi-feudal idea must be wholly put aside. The relation of landlord and tenant must be treated as one of pure contract, and with all the incidents of a contract which obtains in the case of any other subject-matter.

When, therefore, it is asked whether a tenant for life or owner in fee is more likely to spend money on improvements in the land, it must be understood to be improvement that will make a due return for the outlay, such as a reasonable tenant will be willing to pay interest upon during his term, and such as will pay both landlord and tenant. Less than 5 per cent cannot be considered as a fair return for the outlay on such improvements, which are often buildings more or less perishable. If they will not pay that, they are fancy improvements, which wealthy men with a taste for land improvement, and residing on the estate, may make, but which really proceed from motives nearly or wholly independent of the tenure. Such an improvement as cottage-building may not pay 5 per cent; though even that, by economy of cost, and by adding a larger garden than usual to the cottage, may be made to approach it. The indirect gain from good cottages, in securing better labourers, is, however, large. There is much more than 1s. a week difference between a good labourer and a middling one; a gain in this way of 1s. a week, besides the usual rent, will make a cottage pay well.

Is there any difficulty, therefore, in a tenant for life making improvements that will pay 5 per cent on the outlay? I believe the difficulty is very small—so small as to show that views of settlements hindering outlay on improvements are unsound. The very hypothesis is, that the improvement to be made is a valuable one, paying 5 per cent on the outlay. It is, therefore, clearly right that the tenant who gets the benefit of the improvement should pay 5 per cent on its cost during his term. Good and intelligent tenants will usually be glad to do so. Draining generally pays much more than 5 per cent. Buildings ought to pay that at least. It must be remembered, if a tenant has taken a farm with bad buildings, it is his own fault if he has not taken it at a lower rent than he would have had to pay for a farm with good buildings. All therefore that the tenant for life will have to pay if the occupier pays 5 per cent on the cost of the improvement, is the difference above that rate needful to raise the money. Admit that he cannot afford to pay for the improvement out of the rent, and that he cannot borrow the money and mortgage the land for it, he must then resort to a Land Improvement Company for a loan at a rate to repay principal and interest on a course of several years.

Now, one of the best of these companies, the General Land Drainage and Improvement Company, who have power by Act of Parliament to lend, without investigation of title, and in spite of incumbrances and settlements, will lend a sum of £2000 and upwards for £6 : 0 : 4 per cent for thirty-one years. The charge, therefore, to a tenant for life, if the occupier paid 5 per cent, would be about £20 a year for £2000, £100 a year for £10,000.

That such a charge as this will hinder any tenant for life from making an improvement that he would have made if he had been owner in fee, I do not think any one can contend. Very often the whole expense would be recouped in the course of the term, indirectly if not directly. No doubt there may be chance cases where even this small expense cannot be afforded. But they can be very few, not really influential on the country at large.

When the question is thus brought to figures it is plain enough that, whether settlements are right or wrong, the objections urged against them are unsound. In truth the proof is so simple, one is half-inclined to doubt if it can be as cogent as it really is.

I believe that ignorance on the part of both landlords and tenants—sometimes the one, sometimes the other—the want of true skill and knowledge in dealing with the land, has far more to do with neglect of improvements than any question of the tenure on which the owner holds it. The relation of landlord and tenant is often not looked on as a matter of contract. Often there are unreasonable expectations. Neither landlord nor agent nor tenant thoroughly understand their business, or one of them does not, and past experience of improvements so managed has not shown a profit. No doubt sometimes men who have made money in business buy land and lay out largely in improvements, sometimes without regard to profit, sometimes with a keen business knowledge of what they are doing. Such outlay is not caused by their being owners in fee. Again, residence on the estate has much to do with the making of improvements.

I will end by repeating again that a thorough investigation of circumstances and facts is what is most required in every part of this subject, not *à priori* arguments from what any one thinks likely.

I have a few last words still to say on this subject. I wish to draw attention to Lord Salisbury's speech, on June 21, in the House of Lords, on the Bill for giving tenants for life further powers to charge against their successors the value of improvements made on the estate. Lord Salisbury asserts that, if settlements were abolished, an increase of mortgages, not of sales, would be the result—that owners in fee would never sell part of their land to make improvements. If they wished to raise money for improvements, they would always do it by mortgage. And he asks the very pertinent question, whether land thus in debt would not be as badly or worse off than land in settlement?

Is there not good reason for saying that the idea that owners in fee will sell part of their land in order to improve the rest, is a pure fiction?

Again asking for facts, it may fairly be requested that some instances of owners in fee who have sold part of their land in order to improve the rest may be given. Can they give half a dozen such cases, where draining, for instance (which pays so well and surely), has been thus effected? Can they give any one such case?

If the view adverse to settlements was sound,

France ought to furnish plenty of such cases, since there owners in fee abound. The readiness with which owners in France mortgage their land in order to buy more, even at undue prices, is notorious, and so are the evil consequences of the debts thus incurred; but we have never heard they were willing to sell part of their land to improve the rest, or even to mortgage it for that purpose. Thus everything points to the same conclusion—that other causes, not the fact of the land being held by tenants for life instead of by owners in fee, produce a readiness or unreadiness to spend money on improvements.

It has been said that borrowing money from Land Improvement Companies ends often in a heavy burden without a corresponding return for the outlay. But this is no fault of the mode of raising the money, the fault is in the way in which it has been laid out. If the money had been raised by selling part of the land or by mortgage, and laid out in the same way, the loss would have been just the same.

No doubt much money is badly laid out on what are called improvements in land. The business of landowning is well understood by few. It is very easy to be led into unprofitable or half-profitable improvements, and if money is laid out on these it cannot pay, in whatever way it may have been raised.

The half-feudal idea of the relation between landlord and tenant tends to keep up such unprofitable outlay. Improvements are asked for and expected by tenants without reference to the question of whether they will pay or not. Let the relation be one of fair contract, in which each side shall do its part, and there will be much fewer cases of improvements that do not pay.

But in truth recognising landowning as a business to be managed honestly and fairly like any other business, but still as a business and resting on business principles, will do more to promote all sound land improvements, and will also be a greater money gain to landlords and tenants alike, than most measures that can be devised.

As a class neither landlords nor tenants are usually good men of business, and the world has advanced to that point when, whether they like it or not, and whatever kindly and pleasant connections may thereby be broken, the relations between landlord and tenant must be more and more those of business. It will remove many difficulties. Take, for instance, the game question, in many places so fruitful of ill-will. Looked at as a question of business, who will let the produce of his estate be devoured by such profitless vermin as a multitude of rabbits and hares ?

So with this question of improvements. It is quite right to give tenants for life every additional facility for charging the estate with the value of real improvements. There may be hindrance to a few for want of such power. If the improvement is duly profitable, the remainderman cannot lose by having to pay the charge for a limited number of years.

But the great point is the clear recognition by landlord and steward and tenant that the whole transaction is one of business, and must be made profitable accordingly to all concerned. The larger the sum laid out in profitable improvements, the better for the landlord; the turning point is the profit. If an improvement will not pay the interest on its cost, it is a fancy improvement; that may be very fit for a wealthy man, but is not of public concern. Labourers' cottages, as I have said, are, in one sense, an exception, and the rise of wages is helping to get over even that difficulty. Under a business system, of course, too, there will be much fewer cases of rents 30 per cent below the true value of the land, and of bad farmers injuring the estate. There is no reason why it should be a harsh business system. Thoroughly fair and honest dealing to all, landlords no less than tenants, may well be its motto.

APPENDIX.

I.

LISSELAN, COUNTY CORK.

(From *Agricultural Gazette*, 1880.)

ONE of the many grievances urged against the social system of Ireland is the extent to which landlord absent-eeism is practised. In round numbers, the rental of the country may be set down at £13,000,000 sterling; and of this sum it is estimated that £3,000,000 are annually drained out of the country by absentee landlords. Without offering an opinion on this state of things, we may say that more real property and security exist amongst the tenantry of resident landlords than on the estates of absentee owners. The resident landlord, as a rule, sets an example of sound farming on the land in his own hands, besides affording instruction and encouragement at all times. Nay, many Irish landlords set an example of frugality and thrift to their tenants, which at the present day it would be well to have universal. A remarkable instance of this has come recently under our notice. Mr. Bence Jones's property adjoins the public road from Clonakilty to Bandon, reaching within about half-a-dozen miles of the latter town.

The Home Farm approaches 1000 acres in extent, including some outlying land let to dairymen. From 200 to 220 acres are annually devoted to crops. Sixty acres of roots are grown, which, with the exception of 6 or 7 acres of mangels and a little carrots for the farm horses, are all turnips. The climate is rather cold and the situation too exposed to bring the mangels to perfection. 100 acres of grain, all oats, are produced; 60 acres are annually sown with seeds, part of which is converted into hay in the first season, the ground being subsequently pastured for a number of years. There are besides 20 acres of old irrigated meadow, which, after being cut in the summer, are grazed in autumn. Finally there are about 700 or 800 acres of permanent grass.

It will thus be seen that the rotation is what is known in Ireland as the convertible husbandry system, by which the land, after being cultivated, manured, and cleaned for a few years, is relaid down with fresh and suitable "seeds." There is a judicious admixture of tillage and stock farming, or what is called "mixed" management, which of all others is the best adapted to the circumstances of this country.

By drainage, trenching, subsoiling, clearing of stones, furze, coarse herbage, liming, manuring, and the pursuit of the course of cropping here indicated, Mr. Bence Jones has reclaimed upwards of 400 acres. A good deal of the farm did not, however, require drainage; but the fields have been enlarged and squared fences built, and a vast quantity of planting effected. The land is generally rather light in texture, and some of it rests upon an open subsoil; hence drainage in this case was unnecessary.

Turnips are the crop usually taken after reclamation. In addition to a fair dressing of farmyard dung, 12 cwt. of a mixture of crushed bones, superphosphate, and guano was applied per statute acre. The average acreable yield of roots has been about 30 tons, but in the present season it will not be more than 25 or 26 tons. The high state of the fertility of the soil is attributable to the manner in which the turnips are consumed by sheep-folding. All the turnips are not left on the ground; of every ten drills, six are removed and four allowed to remain alternately. The turnips are pulled, cut into finger bits and supplied in troughs on the field, the machine, troughs, and sheep, being transferred from place to place, according as the ground is vacated. The animals are likewise furnished with an abundance of hay in racks, and a certain quantity of crushed cake and corn. The land, as may be expected, yields a most luxuriant crop of grain in the succeeding season; and is thus enriched for a number of years.

Since the work of reclamation has been in great part accomplished, it has become necessary to break up a considerable amount of the worst grass-producing land with lea oats annually. A fair return is realised with an application of 1 cwt. nitrate of soda and 2 cwt. superphosphate per acre. This year the oats, both of the tillage and lea, has been unusually productive; while 14 cwt. grain has been the average of former years, the results of the cropping of 1879 have been 1 ton of grain and $2\frac{1}{2}$ tons of straw.

The yield of hay this season has been also satisfactory —fully 2 tons per acre; and, notwithstanding the variable character of the weather, it has been well saved, a good deal of energy having been brought to bear in

the operation during a brief spell of sunshine. The
" seeds " are fed by calves in autumn, and in spring by
ewes and lambs, until the middle of April. This plan
is found not to injure the young grasses in the least.

The live stock at Lisselan consist of 100 milch cows,
and twenty-five young springers, eighty weanling calves,
about the same number of young cattle, two stud bulls
(Shorthorn) ; 200 fatting sheep, in addition to cattle
fatting in the stall, 200 breeding ewes, 200 lambs, etc.,
four rams, and eight to ten farm horses.

The cows are half-bred Shorthorns—excellent dairy
cattle, far and away above the average stock of the district—and a few Alderneys to colour the produce. The
springers to replace the old and defective milkers are
annually selected from the most promising of the calves
produced on the place. The animals are pastured in
summer. During the summer six months the yield of
butter in other years averages about 6 lb. weekly per
head, but in the present season it has fallen to about 5
lb. per head per week. Very little butter has hitherto
been produced in winter ; the animals are fed on hay
and straw with a small allowance of turnips—just as
much as maintains the system in a healthy state.

Mr. Jones has commenced butter-making according
to modern improved plans. He has recently erected a
commodious dairy. The milk room is a large, well-
ventilated apartment. The floor is made of concrete,
the walls are constructed of thick, substantial stone
masonry. The roof, which is high, is covered with
slate ; but with a view to the cleanliness of the apartment, as well as to the equalisation of the temperature
in summer and winter, there is a ceiling of timber
immediately underneath the slate. The windows are

furnished with fine wire-gauze screens. The pans employed are the galvanised and common earthenware. The churn is one of the barrel pattern. An American butter-washing and kneading machine, which dispenses with hand manipulation, has lately been added to the stock. Two skimmings have been practised for some time during the past season. The withdrawal of the milk from the churn while the butter is yet in "grains" is commencing to be regarded as of great importance by the more enlightened class of dairy farmers in Ireland.

The first skimming is effected after an interval of twelve hours, and the second in twelve to twenty-four hours subsequently. The most delicious butter is made from the cream of the first skimming. Most of it has been sold in London during the past season, whither it has been sent to private consumers, individual merchants, and large co-operative stores, direct by the producer; and, notwithstanding the low price which for a considerable portion of the year prevailed in all markets, and for the produce of all countries, it fetched from 1s. 1d. to 1s. 4d. per lb., when the market was at its lowest ebb. The butter is mild cured, made up in 2 lb. rolls, and packed off in rectangular boxes constructed after the continental fashion. Butter is now transferred from Bandon to London in twenty-four hours, at a charge of $\frac{1}{2}$d. per lb. The reduction in the tariff was mainly, if not wholly, brought about through the exertions of Mr. Bence Jones. The butter of some of the neighbouring farmers is similarly packed off to London. The cream is churned thrice weekly.

The calves are kept improving from birth. Milk is given for the first three or four months, besides cake, Indian meal, grass, and hay. As soon as the turnips

come in in winter, they are at once accustomed to take
a little. In the following summer there is an abundance
of grass supplemented with artificial food; and roots,
hay, and artificials are supplied *ad lib.*, in the second
winter after which the animals begin to be sold out as
heifer beef. Five cwt. is a common weight at the
age of two years, and the price realised varies from
£14 : 10s. to £18. Although we did not get figures
by which we could estimate the cost of production, we
were assured that this is a most paying system of management, and considering the age and selling prices,
there can, we fancy, be no doubt about it.

The sheep are all Shropshire Downs, with the exception of about fifty lambs bought in annually to supplement the stock produced on the place, the 200 ewes
producing the remainder of the lambs. A little cake
is supplied in troughs on the grass to the ewes before
yeaning, and some mangels are given from the com-
mencement of January. The yeaning season runs from
February to April 1. The fields are well sheltered
with high fences made of stones and earth, and planted
with furze; there are also yeaning sheds constructed
against the fences with hurdles, and covered on the top
with a thick thatch of furze, etc. After dropping, the
ewes get ½ lb. cake per head daily. There is little or
no mortality during the process. Sixty of the most
forward of the progeny are sold fat as yearlings; the
usual price is £3 : 5s., but this year it has fallen to
£2 : 17s. per head. The remainder, save what is required for breeding purposes, are sent out fat at two
years old. Mr. Law has found that it is a peculiarity
of a portion of the Shropshires, that they do not
thrive rapidly until approaching two years of age, when

they put on condition in a wonderfully short space of time. The sheep are fattened by folding, as already described. Plenty of hay is supplied in racks, together with $\frac{1}{2}$ lb. cake each. No ewes are retained for breeding after they have reached the age of four or five years. Sixty draft ewes are fattened out in August and September, and their place supplied by the same number of the most suitable hoggets for breeding. Four rams (Shropshire Downs) are kept—that is one ram for every fifty ewes.

The farm offices, though somewhat elaborate, are rather disconnected. But the land may be apportioned amongst tenants at some future time, and it would not, therefore, answer to have the buildings concentrated in one block. There is a mill worked by a three-quarter shot water-wheel, which economises an enormous amount of labour in sawing timber, which grows on the estate, Mr. Jones being very fond of shedding of all kinds ; there is also an apparatus for grinding corn, and another for crushing bones. The latter are bought up extensively for manuring at £5 per ton.

A large number of labourers are constantly employed on the land, reclaiming, fencing, etc. The farm labour bill alone amounts to £400 per annum. Land which was bought in fee at 5s. or 6s. per acre (some, indeed, we were informed, was purchased long ago at 1d. per acre) would now let freely at from £1 to £2 per acre per annum. The labourers are all furnished with comfortable cottages, and, besides land for potatoes, they receive 9s. per week and upwards, many 12s. We obtained this information from the labourers themselves. The rate of remuneration is excellent for the district, but they are required to work industriously. In summer they must appear in the field, with breakfast taken, at 6 o'clock, with only one stop, at midday, and in winter as soon as the light will permit. A number of mechanics are also constantly employed ; 36 tons of artificial manures, in addition to a large quantity of bones, are annually purchased, and 100 tons of concentrated food for cattle and sheep, besides a large bill for farm seeds, etc.

On the whole, if the yearly outlay on this tract of land were general throughout Ireland, we should be better able to withstand the depression which now prevails. Mr. Bence Jones's system cannot be said to be "high farming," nor yet "low," but probably midway between both, which would seem to be the most judicious, at least for the circumstances of this country. It is proved profitable ; it wears at a glance all the elements of success. It is practical and easy of imitation, but the great drawback to its extensive adoption is the want of capital amongst the tenant-farmer community. This, for years to come, must be the great drawback to our agricultural systems ; and it is well to caution legislators in time against passing any measure which would detach landlord capital from the improvement of the soil.—C. B.

I do not know even the name of the writer of this paper. I was never asked for any information on the subject of it, or knew anything of it till I saw it in the *Agricultural Gazette.* Some unimportant facts are not quite accurately stated, but I judged it best to leave it as it stands, except that I have changed a single word here and there when such a change more exactly expressed the facts.   W. B. J.

II.

DAIRIES AT SHOW OF
ROYAL AGRICULTURAL SOCIETY OF
ENGLAND, 1879.

(Written for Distribution by Co. Cork Agricultural Society.)

I HAVE been asked to write an account of what I saw of the International Dairy at the Kilburn Show. I went there to learn all I could for myself, and with no thought of writing a Report upon it, and so did not examine all parts with the thoroughness that would have been well, had my object been to report. I had seen the dairy of the Aylesbury Company at Notting Hill not long before, and so knew their system. The German and French Dairies I went into much more thoroughly. I spent two long mornings, of over three hours each, at the dairies, and learnt more than many years had before taught me. Dairies in actual work are a new feature at the Shows of the Royal Agricultural Society. French butter averages in the London market 3d. per lb. over English butter. French and Danish salt butter compete in foreign markets, like Rio Janeiro (where Cork butter used to reign supreme), at prices of 2s. to 3s. per lb., prices which are never heard of for Irish butter. It, therefore, could not but be useful to see such butter made by natives of those countries. The system of the North Germans, Danes, Swedes, and Norwegians is nearly the same, and all were represented by Mr. Ahlborn. Of cheese-making I know nothing; I attended only to butter.

Improved Implements.

The chief feature was the use of the Circular Butter-working Machines for squeezing out the buttermilk. It was impossible to see these machines at work without being convinced of their great usefulness. They save much labour, and squeeze out the buttermilk much more thoroughly, leaving the butter much firmer than the hand can do. It is easy with them to make up butter without ever touching it by hand from first to last. In North Germany, Denmark, Sweden, and Norway, their use is almost universal; in America, too, they are common. They are much too dear in price. But there is no trouble in contriving a simple straight form, instead of the circular form, at a very moderate cost within the reach of all, if our machine-makers will condescend to do so. I can say, from trial, that the small hand-machine which only costs a few shillings, answers perfectly for a few cows, though too slow for a large dairy.

The sooner we work our butter by machines in Ireland, instead of by hand, the better it will be for us.

There were many forms of churn, more of the common barrel churn (with small variations in the dashers), than of any other. The Aylesbury Company used barrel churns chiefly; the French dairy had no other. There was an eccentric churn that turned round and up and down at the same time eccentrically; it cost double the price of barrel churns, and seemed to have no particular advantage. There was an American churn that is much praised in the Report of our Secretary of Legation at Washington for this year. In American dairies it is said to be a great improvement. It is simply a long box, without any dashers whatever in it, hung on rockers. The churning is done simply by the cream dashing against the ends of the box as it rocks to and fro. It was tried, and the butter came in forty minutes. It pleased me a good deal, but can be·better judged of from practical trial. It must be very easy to keep clean, and ought to be made cheaply. It was said to answer especially for the plan mentioned hereafter of having the butter in the churn in fine grains, instead of in a lump. The German dairy used the upright Holstein churn, that carried all before it at the competition last year at Bristol. It did its work very well, and was very convenient for taking out the butter without using the hand, after the head and dashers had been lifted out. A small sieve dipped the butter out readily. The judges' report, when published, will enable us to know if last year's opinion in favour of this churn holds good or not. It seemed fitter to be worked by power than by hand. The previous impression on my mind, that there is little gain in one form of churn above another, was not much disturbed by what I saw. I have since ordered of Messrs. M'Kenzie of Cork a barrel churn, with a large opening into it, 15 inches by 8; and the spiggot hole opposite·to the opening for ventilation, as on the whole the best.

Systems of different Countries.
English System.

1. The English system was thoroughly good in substance, not differing from that usual in good private dairies. The cream (as in all the dairies) was quite

sweet, the butter little handled—only, I believe, in
taking it out of the churn; it was washed as usual, put
on the butter-working machine, and the buttermilk
squeezed out, and lifted with wooden trowels in a lump
on the table. The scales had a flat marble top, on which
a boy with trowels rapidly weighed out half-pounds.
These half-pounds he again, with the trowels, rolled on
the table (which, I believe, had a marble slab for its
top), till it formed a cone of 8 or 9 inches high. This
was very dexterously and nicely done. The stamp, to
make it a half-pound pat, was pressed down on the
point of the cone till it became a round pat of equal
thickness throughout. This, again, was turned on its
side upon the slab, the stamp still holding on, and forming a guide for the size as well as a handle to it, so that
it could be again rolled round and round on its side till
the pat was smooth and looked well, the hand never
touching the butter after it took it out of the churn.
It was a very pretty sight to see it done. All the work
of the dairy was done by men and boys. The Manag-
ing Director, Mr. Allender, thinks women are of no use
in a dairy, and that it is much harder to get them to
keep to rules. He advises any one who wants to have a
first-rate dairy to employ young men and boys who have
learnt the business. The butter-working machine used
at this dairy was an American machine. The edges of
the flutings of the roller that presses the butter are
much sharper than those of Ahlborn's German machine.
Ahlborn justifies the roundness of the edges of his
machine by saying that a dairymaid's knuckles are round
and not sharp. But the better opinion seems to be
that the round edges of the roller a little " smear " the
butter, and that the sharper edges are best.

GERMAN, DANISH, SWEDISH, AND NORWEGIAN
SYSTEMS.

2. With one exception, the practical making of the butter at the German, Danish, and Swedish dairies, seemed to me quite perfect.

The churning was done in the upright Holstein churn. Directly the butter came, when it was still in small grains like fine seed, slightly sticking together after the manner of frog spawn, the churning was stopped, so that the butter did not gather in lumps at all; the top of the churn was taken off, and the dasher taken out, the buttermilk drawn off through a sieve to catch any grains of butter, and the sides and top of the churn washed with skim milk to collect the grains of butter sticking to them. The butter was lifted out in a sieve, still in fine grains (I put the point of my knife into the churn, and took out some of the grains; they were a loose small heap of grains lightly touching each other by their outer edges), a few rollings and tossings in the sieve, and the butter was in a lump, the grains having run together. It was thrown out on the table, thence lifted with wooden trowels on the butter-working machine, and a few turns of the roller over it, with one or two more liftings by the trowels, and the work was done. There was no washing at all. The buttermilk was simply squeezed out by the machine. Some think washing lessens the sweet freshness of butter. I doubt it. In Ireland spring water is used. The reason for this practice, of keeping the butter in fine grains, so that the buttermilk can be got rid of with little working, is that the less butter is worked the better

it is. Working, more or less, breaks up the texture.
Thus a finer and fresher quality and appearance are got
with little working, provided all the buttermilk is got
rid of.

Compared with the ordinary way of making up
butter, getting it together in the churn in lumps, which,
of course, enclose much buttermilk, and then working
out the buttermilk with a wooden dish or the dairymaid's knuckles—the saving of labour was very great.
From first to last the hand never touched the butter at
all. The labour used was a minimum, much less than
in the common way of butter-making.

The exception I have mentioned as a defect of this
system is, that the butter was not washed with water at
all. All was trusted to the butter-working machine
squeezing out the buttermilk. I think this is undesir-
able. Spring water can do the butter no harm. The
French system hereafter mentioned, by which Mr.
Jenkins tells us in his article in the last number of the
Journal, the splendid Normandy butter is made, that
sells in Paris for 3s. per lb., and nearly as dear at Rio
Janeiro salted or in tins, is much the same as that I
have just described. By the French system, when the
butter has just come in these fine grains, the buttermilk
is drawn off by the vent-hole through a sieve, the dairymaid holding the spiggot lightly in the vent, so as to
let little butter escape. Spring water is then poured in
and drawn off in the same way after a few turns of the
churn. This is done six or eight times, till the water
comes away quite clear, with no trace of buttermilk.
It is thought in this way, the butter being in fine grains
and no lumps to hold buttermilk in them, the buttermilk is quite washed out. The only object of using

the butter-washing machine then is, to squeeze out any extra water in it, and so make the butter firmer. I have no doubt washing in this way is the best plan for us. If we are still to use barrel churns, as the French do, a small wooden dish or scoop, with holes in the bottom, could easily be contrived to lift the butter out of the churn without handling, or a larger hole to the churn will do it. There is an impression that washing with water hurts the flavour of butter, by washing out the volatile oils, etc., that are in it. I can only doubt if this is so.

The Schwartz system of setting the milk in deep tin pails in iced water, so as to have the cream rise when quite sweet, was shown at this dairy. How to get the iced water is the only difficulty. The water must be below 40 degrees, whilst in Ireland, even in winter, spring water is not below 50 degrees. It answers well in countries where a great heap of snow, covered with earth like mangolds, will last through the summer. So it is common in such Northern countries. There are few places with us where the plan can be used economically. Happily, it is Dr. Voelcker's opinion that skimming the milk, when still quite sweet, will make as good butter. This we can all do, and as sweet milk makes rather more butter than the same quantity of sour milk, it is mere folly not to skim the milk sweet. About Aylesbury they skim the milk after 12 hours for the very best butter, and skim it again after another 12 or 24 hours for less good quality. Each, of course, is churned separately. With the habits of our people, this probably is the best plan for us, namely, to skim the milk sweet after 12 or 24 hours ; let it still stand, and skim it again sour. Send the good butter from the first

x

skimming to London at a good price, and sell the bad in Cork.

There was a very pretty arrangement, something between a table and a bowl, with a hole at the bottom to let water escape, shown at this dairy. It was like half a tree, of lime or some other white close-grained wood, four or five feet long, and hollowed out very gradually to the middle from near the sides, like a bowl; it was four or five inches deep, with no joints or crevices to gather dirt, or be hard to keep clean.

The French System.

3. The French dairymaid used a large barrel churn, for which it was complained the driving gear was too slow. The churning in it, too, was stopped as soon as the butter came, whilst it was in grains. The buttermilk was washed away by repeated waters, as I have described it, and this washing was trusted to, to remove all buttermilk. The butter-working machine was not used; the wooden trowels were used. The butter was lifted out of the churn by hand, and altogether the hand, though not much used, was still more used in making up the butter than was desirable. The whole churning was worked up into a large tall cone, with a good deal of plastering by trowel and hand. One plan the French dairymaid had, which approved itself to me as very good. As soon as the butter was washed, before she took it out of the churn, she half filled the churn with cold water, and let it stand for half an hour to harden the butter. The temperature of cream always rises considerably (some 3 to 5 degrees) in churning. Letting the butter thus stand in cold water must remove this

extra heat, and be good for it. It will be remembered
by many that in Mr. Byrne's excellent Prize Essay on
butter-making last autumn, he advised that in hot
weather, when butter is apt to be soft after churning,
the churn should be filled with cold water, and allowed
to stand, which, he said, would make the butter firm,
a recommendation that was new to many of us. The
French dairymaid goes a step farther, and lets her butter
always stand for half an hour in cold water on the same
principle. As firmness is a point of excellence in butter,
there can be little doubt this practice is right, and one
we ought to follow. Sometimes, I believe, salt is mixed
in the water—enough to salt the butter without putting
any more salt to it. It is said this is a good plan for
fresh and light salted butter.

ANOTHER NEW MACHINE.

An ingenious machine was exhibited, from Sweden
I think, for separating the cream from the milk me-
chanically, viz. by centrifugal action. It was not worked
either day that I was at the Show. It was reported
that the machine had an ugly trick, now and then, of
not only separating the cream, but also of separating
itself—into a hundred pieces, which would have been
awkward amongst the crowd of lookers-on ; besides, the
life of the engineer in charge of that part of the Show
was not insured. Prudently, it was not put to work.
It was worked successfully on a later day, however.
The plan is, that the milk trickles into the machine in
a small stream, and cream and milk trickle out at separate spouts. The milk being heavier than cream, passes
to the outer side of the revolving vessel, whence it

escapes by its spout, whilst the cream, because lighter, draws into the middle to its own spout. The machine requires to be driven at very great speed, so that there are not many dairies where it could be used practically. It is possible, however, in time it may be altered into a more available form for ordinary use. The size of the machine is small and convenient-looking enough. It has since been improved, and is constantly at work at Mr. Tisdale's Holland Park Dairy, Kensington, where it seems to answer his purpose well.

General Impressions.

The general impression left on my mind by the Show was, that (besides the cleanliness and neatness of every part of the dairies and of the dairy servants, whereof the German dairymaid was a capital example, with her smart cap and ribbons, a tidy working apron and bare arms, her sleeves being rolled up to the shoulders that she might work the harder, presenting a sore contrast to many of our dirty dairywomen) there were few new and unusual plans to be learnt by us from Kilburn. The main points that would improve the quality of our butter —(1) The perfect sweetness of the cream used. (2) Perfectly getting rid of the buttermilk by keeping the butter in grains, so that the buttermilk could be washed out, instead of being worked out. (3) Avoiding all touching of the butter by the hand, especially by using the butter-working machines (so as to ensure against any remains of buttermilk, and to improve the firmness of the butter by making it drier).

Moral.

All butter-makers invariably declare their own butter is first-rate; but, to be plain, they do not speak the truth. Making first-rate butter depends on very small details; it is surprising how small. Yet these details make a great difference. Butter may be fairly good, a long way from really bad butter, yet still be far from first-rate. And the difference in price between such butter and first-rate butter is very great. Butter is wanted for the wealthiest consumers in the world, who care much about quality, and very little about price.

(1.) The first leading fact is, that the price to consumers in London is hardly ever less than from 1s. 6d. to 2s. 6d. per lb.; butter bought under 2s. per lb. from respectable shops is very seldom good. This is the principal fact to be borne in mind. It proves that a splendid market is there, of which we do not get the advantage.

(2.) The other main fact is, that the supply of first-rate butter falls very far short of the demand. The difference is made up by secondary butter, washed and made up as well as they can by retailers. Only this Spring I found the family of a friend paying 2s. 4d. per lb. for all their butter; another family, living in one of the best parts of London, had given up eating butter, because their patience was exhausted by getting bad butter at 1s. 10d. per lb., and they thought it extravagant to pay higher. It is believed country towns in a great part of England are even worse supplied. It is quite clear, therefore, there is a demand, at good prices, for all the first-rate butter that can be made. The evil is

the same as with many other kinds of agricultural produce—the consumers pay too much, the producers
receive too little ; while middlemen grow rich.

I can bear witness that respectable retailers in London
and many other places are glad to buy direct from producers at much higher prices than those of Irish markets.

Thus, in Summer I can sell all my butter packed in
French boxes, each holding 12 2-lb. rolls, at 14½d. to
15d. per lb., a very different return from 8d., the price
often of first quality in Cork. When the price is higher
in Cork, I can get a better price also. The retailers
sell it at 2d. per lb. profit. Their customers, who have
once bought it, will take no other from them, and any
delay in its arrival is sorely grumbled at. One retailer
having ordered two boxes the first week, ordered four
the next, and twelve the third. But the butter must
be first-rate, and uniformly good always.

The Irish Butter Markets—Cork Market above all—
are a grievous loss to the country. They are managed
wholly for the gain of the dealers, so that a large profit
may be made off bad butter as well as off good. The
competition in England falls hardest on inferior butter.
In consequence of the great importation of American
butter and of bosh (butterine), Irish farmers are fairly
in a corner. They are competing against inferior produce, that does not cost those who make it half what
Irish produce costs. First-rate butter is subject to no
such competition. There is not enough of it, probably
never will be. Certainly not until the habits of our
people have become the same as the habits of French
and German and Danish dairymaids, which, I fear, is a
far-off time. But our own markets hold out the least
encouragement to good butter, though much encourage-

ment to inferior butter. The whole system of dealing in Cork Market needs to be changed. As was said to me by a great butter-factor, "Cork Market keeps down the price even of good butter by its great mass of middling and inferior butter hanging on the skirts of good butter."

Till the markets are altered, those who make good butter had better seek a market in England for themselves.

When the promised Minister of Agriculture is appointed, it is certain one of the first benefits he will confer on Irish farmers will be the opening and wholly altering Cork Market.

As good butter as any in the world can be made in Ireland. That butter now does not pay us well is partly our own fault in not making first-rate butter, partly that of the middlemen we allow to get rich at our expense in markets like Cork. It is the French dealers who have made the value of French butter, by their influence on producers, and excellent market arrangements.

W. BENCE JONES.

LISSELAN, *July* 20, 1879.

III.

TO MY TENANTS AND THEIR WIVES.

FEBRUARY 1880.

MY FRIENDS—I want you all to understand the plan of making up very light-salted butter in two-lb. rolls, and sending it to London, which I have carried on for over a year, and which has answered and paid me well.

It is quite simple. There is no difficulty about it, except that it is different from the way you are used to.

Either 12 or 18 two-lb. rolls should be packed in each box, which is lined with cheap linen.

The butter must be salted less than light-salted for Cork. You can see the whole thing carried on at the New Dairy at Carrig any day you please, and as often as you please, and the boxes too.

Two things only are necessary to be kept to by those who now make fairly good butter, different from what they now usually do.

1. The milk must be skimmed, both in summer and winter, whilst it is quite sweet. It must not be the least sour. The cream too should be sweet.

2. Every drop of buttermilk must be taken out of the butter.

These are not hard rules to keep to. If they are not strictly kept to, it is useless to send butter to London. Inferior butter in rolls sells worse than inferior butter in firkins.

1. As to skimming the milk sweet. In London they

know the difference of taste between butter made from sweet milk and butter made from sour milk, just as well as you know the difference of taste between milk that is sweet and milk that is sour. You cannot deceive them about it. They will not give the price for butter from sour milk, and it does not travel or keep so well. After the milk has been skimmed sweet for butter to go to London, you may let it stand as much longer as you like, and skim it again and again for a second quality of butter to sell in Cork. Such second quality will be of a lighter colour, and will not keep so well as butter from sweet milk. It is less good.

2. The best way to get out all the buttermilk is to stop churning the moment the butter comes, when it is still in fine grains, like small seeds, and so the buttermilk is not closed up within the lumps. Draw off the buttermilk through a sieve to catch any bits of butter. Pour in spring water, and give 4 or 5 turns of the churn. Draw it off again, and pour in more water, and give a few more turns of the churn, and so on for 6 or 7 times, till the water comes away quite clear and bright. Take out the butter, squeeze out the water, and make it up in rolls of 2 lbs. The butter should not be touched by the hand at all, but with wooden trowels.

This is the whole entire business and secret. It is positively less trouble than the common old-fashioned way. Some of you already partly wash your butter in the churn. But you do not do it thoroughly enough, or stop churning soon enough when it is still in fine grains, or you let the milk stand till it is a little sour. You will see you cannot lose by following these rules.

In the second skimming you get all the butter the milk can possibly yield ; the difference is, the cream from sour milk does injure the first skimming, and the best butter.

There are few who do not keep four cows, these can fill a box of 24 lbs., 12 rolls of two lbs. Those who cannot fill a 24-lb. box, should join with a neighbour, and get some rolls from him. Three or four neighbours had better join in sending their boxes at the same time. The charge for carriage is the same for one box as for two. So it does not answer to send less than two boxes. They should be sent in one name with private marks or numbers, to show to whom each belongs. The charge for carriage to London from Cork for two boxes is just a half-penny per lb. They may go either by Dublin or Milford. Dublin is the best for two boxes, Milford the cheapest for larger lots. It will go by Dublin every evening at 8 p.m., and be delivered in London early the next morning *but one;* butter that goes on Monday evening will be delivered on Wednesday morning. It must be sent for sale to a Butter Factor at the Central Market. I can tell you the names of honest factors who will send back the market price at once. Their charge for selling is another halfpenny per lb. So that the cost of selling in London is one penny per lb., all included. Three boxes hold as much as one firkin, and the boxes cost about the same to make—they ought to cost less. It may be well to add that a thermometer, which can be bought for 2s., is very useful for judging if, in winter, the cream is warm enough to churn. 58 degrees is the right heat for butter to come in proper time.

Any more information you want you can get from me or from Mr. Law, and also you can learn the price we get ourselves each week.

There can be no doubt that in this way you will make a much better price than in Cork Market, if your butter is good. Only remember that it is of no use to send to London any butter not first-rate, and that butter which will go first quality in Cork is not good enough for London market. Even at Clonmell in Tipperary, there are three qualities above Cork seconds. Cork is probably the best market in the world for inferior butter. Any one who wishes to make superior butter, and who has not a good enough dairy, I shall be glad to help to build one. Twopence per lb. above Cork price for butter would put over one million per annum into the pockets of Irish farmers, without one shilling of extra outlay. I get much more than twopence per lb. above Cork price for all my butter. It is wholly your own fault and backwardness if you do not get this price.

The market is there ready, and it will cost you no more to sell in it than it does to sell in Cork. The use of brains and sense is all that is required; and that by cleanliness of vessels which you all know about whether you practise it or not, and keeping to the easy rules I have given you, you should make superior butter.

W. BENCE JONES.

LISSELAN.

IV.

A LETTER TO THE TENANTS OF AGHALUSKY, LISSELAN, AND CLOHEEN.

June 1841.

My Friends—I want to say a few words to you about Green Crops.

Some of you, I know, cannot understand why I am anxious that the tenants should grow green crops. One says, "It is for his honour's amusement:" another, "Because his honour's head is full of English farming, which is not at all suited to poor Irishmen;" while a third finds out, that it is because I want to ruin all the poor farmers, or, at any rate, he is sure they will be ruined if they follow my advice. Now, it is not for my amusement, nor because my head is full of English farming, nor in order that I may ruin poor farmers: it is not for any of these reasons that I wish you to grow clover and turnips; but it is for a reason, which, when I tell it you, you will all allow is a very good reason, but which I think will surprise you a little. It is this. —Because I want farmers to have more manure than they now have. I have now told you the secret;—and can any man in Ireland stand up and say, that if this can be done, it will not be a benefit to every farmer, great or small, rich or poor?

Suppose that I had a great heap of manure in the town of Clonakilty, and that I offered to give 100 butts of it to any tenant who would draw that much home to

his farm, would you not think any man a great fool
who refused so good an offer? But suppose I not only
gave him the manure for nothing, but offered myself to
draw it home for him, and to pay him well for accepting
it, would you not say that a farmer who refused such
an offer must be the greatest fool that ever was born?
In short, you would not believe that any man in Ireland,
let alone Carbery, could be found to refuse such an
offer.

Now, I must tell you plainly, that in neglecting
Green Crops, you are acting just as foolishly as the
man who would refuse the manure, though delivered at
his bahn, and paid for accepting it. And I will now
prove this to you.

Look at the quantity of dung which you are able to
collect in any one year, by the old system, of laying
part of your land out in grazing, feeding your cows and
horses out on this, and giving them in the house only
what little straw and potatoes you can spare. Even by
drawing a great deal of sand to add to it, and gathering
earth and scrapings from old ditches, you still have but
a very small quantity of manure, and this is poor thin
stuff, often more than half of it earth. Now, compare
with this the quantity of good rich manure you would
have, *if you sowed with clover and turnips a moderate quantity of land.* I say, compare the quantity of manure
you could make this way with what you now make.
First, you would be able to keep *more cows.* Secondly,
being kept more in the house, and well fed, they would
make *much more manure* than they now do; and much
richer, as good as that we just spoke of from Clonakilty.
Thirdly, *none of it would be lost,* as it often now is.
There it would be all ready in the bahn;—no trouble of

drawing from Clonakilty. Is not this much the same
as giving you the manure, and drawing it home for
you? And would not the cows fed in this way, and
kept warm in the house in winter, instead of being
exposed in the fields to rain and cold, give very much
more milk, and much richer milk? and would not this
rich milk give more butter than you now get? You
will, besides, be able to keep many cows well, with no
more expense than you now keep a few ill; and would
not this be very like paying you for accepting the
manure from Clonakilty? and do you really think that
a potato garden, manured with this rich manure, would
not pay you better than it does at present? and do you
think you would get a worse wheat crop afterwards?
Now, put all these together, and tell me, if, in advising
you, and showing you how to grow clover and turnips,
and so to increase your manure, I am not doing you an
equal kindness as if I gave you the manure in Clonakilty? Remember, too, that there it is all ready in
your own bahn, just as much as if I drew it home for
you. And if you will in this way get much more
butter, and better crops of potatoes and wheat, will not
these as much put the money into your pockets, as if I
paid you for accepting the manure? And now, if all
this is so, is not what I said true, that you are acting
as foolishly in neglecting it, as the man who would
refuse the manure from Clonakilty, though paid to
accept it? I will leave you to answer the question.

Depend upon it, my friends (for as such I wish to
regard you all), YOU ARE RUINED FOR WANT OF MANURE.
Those who are best off amongst you are not half as
well off as they might be, if they had more manure;
and the poor man, whom I am obliged to put out of his

farm, gets into that state which causes his ruin, only from the want of manure. It is not the loss of a horse, or a cow, or a pig, or of all together, which ruins him; if his land were well manured, the very first crop would enable him to buy a new horse, or cow, or pig; but now his land is worn out for want of manure, and then the first misfortune that comes upon him is his ruin; he has nothing that will enable him to recover it.

The English farmers have a very true saying, that " DUNG IS THE MOTHER OF GOLD." Therefore, if only they can get the dung, they know the gold is sure, sooner or later, to find its way into their pockets, and like wise people, they take care of the mother, for the sake of the benefit, they know, her children will be to them;—they do not expect to have the children, without first having the mother, any more than a man can expect to have a litter of pigs, who has no sow.

But I know many of you have been ready long since to say, " We know quite well the value of manure, and we only wish we had plenty of it; but how are poor people to get it?" There is only one way, unless you have money to go into the towns and buy manure, and that way is, *by feeding cattle on clover and turnips, or other green crops.* The English farmers have another saying which clearly points out this way?—No FOOD NO CATTLE, NO CATTLE NO DUNG, NO DUNG NO CORN, NO CORN NO GOLD." You see it is like building a house;— before you can have sound walls and a safe roof, you must lay the foundations firmly; the food for your cattle is the foundation,—the dung, the corn, and the gold, like the walls and roof, all rest upon this. If you will not lay this foundation, you must not expect the corn or the gold to come steadily in, any more than a man

can expect a safe roof or steady walls, who neglects to
lay a good foundation. I do not think, as some of you
suppose, that all English plans of farming are the best
for Irish farmers, but I am quite sure that the English
farmer is right in thinking, that in order to have his
barn full of corn, and his pocket full of gold, he must
have plenty of dung, and that he cannot have plenty
of dung unless he has plenty of cattle, and that he cannot have plenty of cattle *unless he has food for them;*
and I shall be delighted if any Irish farmer will show
me how his brother farmer in England is wrong in this
calculation. When, therefore, any of you say to me,—
" We know the value of manure ; but how are we poor
farmers to get it ?"—my answer at once is, " By growing
food for cattle,"—that is, clover and turnips. And you
will thus have what I told you at the beginning of this
letter, it was my object you should have, MORE MANURE.

Some people, I know, say,—" These clover and
turnips are the crops to ruin poor farmers." Now,
when next you hear anybody say this, just ask him, if
it will ruin a poor farmer to have more manure ; or if
it will ruin him to have better crops of corn ; and then
ask him to show you some better or cheaper way of
getting manure, than by keeping cattle (except, of
course, buying it, and, in that case, just ask him to give
you the money to do so) ; and then ask him to show you
how to keep cattle, without having food for them ; and
if he cannot answer these questions, or show you how
to do these things, why just set him down for an ignorant meddling fellow, who talks about things of which
he knows nothing ; and do not believe him when he
tells you that clover and turnips will be the ruin of
poor farmers.

To state then once more, as plainly as I can, the
plan I wish you to take up : it is this,—THAT YOU
SHOULD SOW WITH CLOVER AND TURNIPS A REASON-
ABLE PART OF THE LAND THAT YOU NOW LEAVE AS
GRAZING. I do not ask a large quantity, unless hereafter you shall think it most profitable for you to do
so. I say that you will get, at the very least, *double
the weight of food for your cows and horses*, from this
quantity of land if sown with clover and turnips, that
you now get from it as grazing ; and therefore that you
will be able to keep *double the number of cows*, and make
twice the quantity of manure that you now make ; and
that this manure will give you much better crops of
potatoes and wheat and oats, than you now get ; and
thus that you will be much better off. I believe, indeed,
that you will get much more than double the weight of
food from clover and turnips, that you now do from
grazing, and so will have much more than double the
quantity of manure ; but I am contented to take it
that it will only double the weight of food and manure :
—of this I am quite sure; and surely if it only does this,
it will be a great benefit to any farmer.

But some of you will say, " We think clover very
good sowing, but it is the turnips we do not like." I
do not wonder at you liking clover ; it is indeed a
most excellent crop, and admirably suited to your land
and climate. I have never in England seen such fine
clover as I have seen with some of you. The weight
of it you can get from two cuttings, if compared with
the weight of grass you could get from the same field
sown with the best hay-seeds in the country, will be
found very much greater. The clover-seed, besides,
does not cost so much as hay-seed. Nine pounds of

clover-seed will sow an acre, and this at 10d. a pound is 7s. 6d., and the rye-grass 1s. 6d. more—in all 9s. for an acre ; whilst to sow an acre with hay-seeds takes eighteen or twenty firkins, often costing 1s. a firkin— say 18s. an acre, *just double the price of the clover and rye-grass.* I know that by saving your own hay-seeds, you think you get them cheaper, but this is not so really. But another objection to hay-seeds is, that when they are saved from ordinary land, which is not very clean, there are always a great many seeds of weeds amongst them, and these being sown with the hay-seed, grow up and injure the next crop of wheat very much. But clover-seed, on the contrary, has no seeds of weeds amongst it, and grows so thick on the land, that it stifles and kills the weeds which spring up ; and the roots of the clover, when ploughed into the land, serve as a great help of manure for it. It is besides well known, that to have land under good clover for one year, rests it and refreshes it as much as 'f it was three years under poor grass ; so that I have no doubt, but that by growing clover and rye-grass, instead of hay-seed, you will find your land will yield better crops of wheat than it now does. When all these benefits of clover are added together, I really wonder that any farmer will sow any more hay-seed. It is like throwing money (or what in a farmer's eyes should be still worse, manure) into the sea, to do so.

But I must now go on to tell you why I think turnips a more valuable crop for farmers, even than clover, of which you begin to feel the benefit, and which I fully admit is a very valuable crop too. But I say turnips are more valuable.

In the first place, turnips give the farmer food for his cows in winter, *when he has little else for them.* In summer, there is always some grass for the cows, even with the worst farmers; and where a farmer grows clover, his cows are well off during summer, but then what is there for them during winter? You all know what a wretched state cows are in at the end of winter; they can scarcely get a mouthful in the fields; and if it was not for the little dry straw, and potatoes, and chopped furze, they get in the house, they would generally starve. Now dry straw by itself is miserable food for cows, but with turnips it is excellent. Cows fed badly with dry straw, and a little potatoes and chopped furze, give scarcely any milk, and make scarcely any manure, so that for half the year they are *no profit to the farmer,* which is what the farmer cannot afford. But give them turnips and they are profitable through the whole year.

Again, if a farmer has clover enough to keep four cows through the summer and autumn, which he very easily may have, I will thank you to tell me how he is to keep those cows *through the winter.* He must either give them a great many of his potatoes, which would make him money in the spring, or sell at least two of his cows. If he sells two, he *loses the manure of those two cows for near six months—half the year.* He is obliged to sell in November, when everybody knows cows sell very cheap and badly, instead of being able to keep them till May, when the same cows would fetch at least £3 a-head more. If he has no turnips, the two cows he keeps must be out in the fields at least all day; and, cows, when badly fed, do not make half as much manure, nor half as rich, as when well fed;

and this way again the farmer loses both in the quantity and quality of his manure. The cold and wet in the fields, and bad feeding, soon make the cows dry, and thus the farmer again loses in milk and butter; so that when a farmer has no turnips, instead of having the milk and butter and manure of four well-fed cows during the six winter months, he has scarcely any milk and butter, and the manure of only two cows; and he only gets in his yard half their manure, that is to say, he only gets as much manure as one cow would make if always in the house, instead of getting the manure of four cows. *He has, therefore, only one quarter of the manure for his potatoes the next spring, that he would have had if he had sown turnips.* And in fact, he has not so much as one quarter, because, as I said before, there is the greatest difference between the quantity of manure that a well-fed cow and a badly-fed cow will make; and, therefore, I think I am not wrong in saying *that the farmer who grows the most turnips one year, will have the best crop of potatoes the next year*, and of course his wheat crop afterwards will also be better.

The plain fact is, that without turnips or mangel-wurzel, or some crop of that kind as food for cattle in winter, *it is impossible to keep through the winter the same number of cows, that your clover will enable you to keep through the summer, or to make manure enough to keep your land in good heart*, and this is the chief reason why turnips are absolutely necessary for a farmer.

I know it may be said, that he may as well grow potatoes, and give them to his cows, instead of turnips, but there are several reasons why turnips are better. In the first place, a farmer is always tempted to sell his potatoes, instead of giving them to his cows, and then of course he has not the manure for the next year. In the next place, you may grow THREE TIMES *the weight of turnips on an acre, with the same manure, that you can of potatoes.*

I think that any of you who saw my turnip fields last year, will bear witness, that I could not have got one-third part of the weight of potatoes off the same land. Remember it was the poorest and most worn-out part of the farm—judge for yourselves if I could have kept the same number of cows through the winter, if I had planted the same land with potatoes, and even had a good crop of them. By sowing turnips, I have first a good profit from the cows (some of them made as much as £3 a-head profit). Then just see what a heap of manure I got, and all ready on the spot. Calculate for yourselves what it would have cost me to buy that quantity of manure, and then tell me if my turnips have paid me.

Nor did it cost me so much to manure those turnips as some of you suppose. The manure cost me just £3 an acre. But if I had sown the same fields with potatoes, I must have sown forty-eight weights to the acre—the price of which at 5½d. a weight, which I suppose is about what they should be worth in April, would be £1 : 2s. Now the turnip-seed only cost about 2s. per acre, so that I saved £1 in the seed, which, taken from the £3 for manure, leaves only £2 for the cost of my turnips per acre ; because I consider the expense of thinning and weeding them, about equal to the expense of earthing the potatoes. Recollect, that you often put £3 or £4 worth or even more oar-weed on an acre of potatoes, and tell me, if even where a man has to buy manure for his turnips as I did, it is not a cheaper crop to him than his potatoes. The only difference is, he cannot sell them and make money of them, so soon, as he can of his potatoes; but he makes the money just as surely by his cows, and by the quantity of manure he will get for his next year's potatoes and wheat, as I hope to do myself.

Besides this, turnips, if kept clean, do not reduce the land so much as potatoes. They leave more of the goodness of the manure in it; and so you will get a better wheat crop after them than you will after potatoes, as James White of Ballinascarthy did last year.

Nor are my turnips the only good ones in the country. Mr. Shuldham of Dunmanway weighed part of his turnips last year, and found that he had grown more than thirty-two tons weight to the acre—that is above six hundred and forty hundred-weight, or above three thousand four hundred *weights* of twenty-one pounds, and these of the best kind of turnips—Swedes, and many other people have grown as much or more. What do you think of this for food for cattle in winter?

There are two or three objections which I know will be made to what I have said. One man will say, "All this may be true, but how is a poor farmer to get cattle to eat all this clover and turnips?" I answer, in the first place, the cows and horses and pigs (for growing pigs will thrive on clover and turnips), that he now keeps, will eat a great deal more than they now get, if he will give it to them, and what is more, *they will pay for it too.* The cows will give him more milk and butter, the horses will be stronger and do more work, and the pigs will grow and thrive better; *and all will make him a great deal more manure*, which is the grand thing of all.

Next, if he cannot afford to buy another cow or two, he may manage to buy a poor yearling, which some one else has half-starved, or a calf or two, or rear his own calves, or some young pigs, and these, by their improvement *when well fed*, will soon enable him to buy a good cow. In short, let a man get any beast that will make him manure, and he will soon find the improvement in his crops will enable him to buy as many cows as he pleases. Just remember what I paid some of you last year for a little clover—£1 for a quarter of an acre, and for only one cutting. Why, two cuttings of one acre of it, at this price, would, if sold, pay the price of a cow. Only let a man really exert himself, and I will answer for it that he will succeed.

But some one else will say, that " they manure their land well with sand and oar-weed and earth, which is as good as having all this dung." This I wholly deny. When a man has manured his land well with dung, sand and oar-weed are excellent as additional manures, but *by themselves* they are not nearly so good as people think, and will not give good crops. As to putting on earth, it is only robbing one part of the field for the sake of another part : you gain nothing by it, unless where you throw down an old ditch, or something of that sort.

The chief objection, however, is, " We cannot spare the dung for the turnips, we want it for the potatoes." Now, no doubt, the potatoes will be the better of all the dung you can give them ; and I allow that in giving part of it to the turnips, you will, *for that year*, lose in the potatoes ; but then the next year, YOU WILL GAIN THREE TIMES OVER WHAT YOU LOST THE YEAR BEFORE. The manure you will have, by feeding your cattle in the

house on the turnips through the winter, will be many
times more than what you lost in order to grow those
turnips; and of course when you give this to your next
year's potato gardens, it will more than make up for
what you lost. It is, in fact, *as if you put some of your
manure out at interest.* You could not think a man had
made a bad bargain, who lent £1 in May, to receive
£3 back that day year; yet this is really what you
are doing by sparing some of your manure for turnips
one year in order to have more manure the next; the
only difference is, that the manure will pay you back
more than £3 for £1; and there is no fear of your
debtor running away. There is an old saying, "Those
that do not play cannot win." If you will not spare
something one year, it is impossible that you should be
better off the next. If you really know the value of
manure, you will not grudge a little loss at first, in
order so much to profit afterwards.

But I think I can hear another man objecting against
clover and turnips, "Sure but we get great trouble by
them." Now, any man who says this, really does not
deserve to have a farm at all. Can you grow any crop—
potatoes, wheat, or any other—without trouble? Would
it not be a pleasant thing if we had only to sit still,
and every kind of crop was to grow of itself? You can
get nothing in this world without trouble; and no one
but an idle lazy fellow, would make this objection.
The real question is, not whether you will get trouble
by them, but *whether they will pay you for your trouble.*
I have no doubt but that they will do so, especially if
your wives make the butter, and you employ your
children in cutting the clover, and in hoeing and thinning and pulling the turnips and in feeding the cows.

The children will then be a real benefit to you, instead of a burthen, as they too often now are.

And so I have now come round to what I began this letter with speaking about, the great value of manure ; and my firm belief that it is because you have not enough manure, you are not better off. It is the case with tenants in most parts of Ireland. I have, as you know, made myself acquainted with the circumstances of all of you, and with the state of your different farms. It is my clear opinion, that more manure is what you all chiefly want. I have myself seen a gentleman's property in another part of Ireland, upon which the tenants were, a few years ago, much worse off than you are, and with farms much smaller than yours ; by following the plan I have advised you, namely, by sowing clover and turnips, *they are now a great deal more comfortably off than you are ;*—many of them paying their rent (and it is a high rent) only by the butter which their clover and turnips enable them to make, and so having all their wheat and potatoes for themselves. Mind, this is Irish farming, not English. Now I wish you to be as comfortable as that gentleman's tenants. I have done all that I can do to lead you to it : will you do your part, by taking the advice and assistance that is offered you for your good, or not ? It is not because you can manage now to pay your rent, that you will always be able to do so. Depend upon it, bad times will come : we have had them before, and you know how hard it was then to get on ; you may be sure they will come again. Indeed, by God's appointment, times are always changing : sometimes bad, sometimes good. If you will exert yourselves, you may now, while times are good, so prosper, as far less to be injured by the bad times ; but it must be by honest industry, taking the means of improvement which are offered you, and which others have found for their benefit.

I cannot bring this letter to an end, without showing you the result of what I have advised, by the fortunes of two farmers in the county of ——.

Timothy Hennessy and Patrick O'Brien were neighbours. Each had a farm of about twenty acres.

A little before the time I am speaking of, Tim had taken his farm, having some cows and other stock of his own, and bearing the character of a decent man ; so that his landlord thought he would make a good tenant, and was glad to give him the farm. Tim, however, farmed on the old plan ; he set his potatoes and his wheat, and sowed a few firkins of hay-seeds with his wheat, and so kept a good part of his land always for grazing, as bawn-field, upon which, with the help of a quarter or half an acre of furze-brake, he just managed to keep two cows and his horse. In summer his cows did pretty well ; it is true he got very little manure from them, because they were obliged to be out in the field grazing, both by day and night. Nor did they give nearly as much milk or butter, as they would have done, if they had been better fed ; still there was some grass for them, and they gave some milk. But in winter, poor beasts! they had a hard life of it. They were always out in the field all day, as they must be there to try and get a bellyful ; and often, for the same reason, they were out all night also ; and you might hear them stand lowing in the fields, from cold and hunger. Of course they gave scarce any milk at this time ; the cold and rain, and want of food, often quite dried them up. However, Tim did the best he could : he kept them in

at night, when he had any straw or furze for them, and
they got what praties he could spare ; though he always
sorely grudged these last, as he knew praties would
fetch a fine price in April. But often, with his best
management, he was obliged to sell one of the cows in
the middle of winter, when cows bore a bad price—not
more than £4 or £5—instead of keeping her till the
spring, when she would have calved, or been near calving, and would have brought £8 at the least ; and even
when he did succeed in keeping them both through the
winter, they were always in the spring very weak and
poor, looking more like ghosts of dead cows than real
living ones. Their calves, besides, were weak and
sickly ; and the cows being so reduced, did not after
calving give nearly so much milk as Tim had expected.
But the worst of the business is yet to come ; for Tim
was able to keep his stock so little in the house, and
had so little to give them to eat, that though he
gathered up all the dung dropped in fields, still he had
but a small quantity of manure for his potatoes, and
was always obliged to make shift with scrapings from
his ditches, and mixing earth and sand. For the first
few years of his being in the farm, Tim drew a good
deal of sand ; and, by buying oar-weed, he managed to
get a tolerable potato crop. To be sure, his wheat, after
the potatoes, was very moderate, still he consoled himself with thinking that there were few of the neighbours
who were much better off ; and he often reasoned with
himself, that his father and his grandfather had farmed
in the same way as he did ; and as it happened,
that the first few years he had the farm, times were
good, and wheat and oats, and pigs and butter, fetched
a good price, Tim, by tilling his old bawn-fields, and

working the best of his ground, managed to pay his rent, and keep his head above water. Still, somehow, he could not conceal from himself that his crops every year got worse, and his land was more and more reduced. When he was obliged to sell his cow in the autumn or winter, in consequence of not having food for her, he found it more and more difficult to buy another in her place, till at last he was obliged to content himself with only one cow, and of course found himself the next season with still less manure for his garden ; and though by the help of ditch-scrapings and earth, he planted the same number of acres of potatoes, yet no one but himself was surprised that part of them were hardly worth digging. Tim was not a man to give way to trifles, he still struggled manfully, sowed every bit of land he could with wheat, let several acres of bawn-field to cottagers and labourers for gardens, though part of it had only been in grazing one or two years; and, in short, did his very best to recover himself.

That winter, however, he had the misfortune to lose a fine fat pig, to which he had trusted to pay a good part of his summer's rent. His landlord, however, as he had before been tolerably regular, gave him time for his rent, and Tim hoped by his wheat and the rent of his gardens to make it all up after harvest; but alas ! the bad times had come—wheat, which for several years before had been 30s. a barrel, and sometimes more, now fell to 18s. or 20s. per barrel ; and oats fell as much. Butter and pigs, to be sure, did not fall so much, but Tim had been unfortunate with his pigs, and of course his one cow could not give him much butter, especially now that he had so much tillage, and of course so little and weak grazing for her. The summer, too, in Ireland turned out wet and cold, and the wheat did not fill well; there was but a small produce from it, though before harvest it looked pretty well; and this, with the great fall of price, quite prevented him from doing what he had expected. But another gale was now due, and Tim's heart began to misgive him, that he should be unable to recover himself; he began to grow careless and indifferent; and to give up struggling as he formerly had done. He must sell his cow. Even this way, he was only able to pay one half-year's rent, but he again got time for the rest, though every one plainly saw that he had no means of meeting the gale, which would be coming due the next summer. Tim and his family saw this too; and though they still hoped something might be done for them, yet never in their lives had they passed such a miserable winter. They had no heart for anything, and to add to their troubles, their potatoes (I told you before some of them were not worth digging) ran short, and they were obliged to buy for the family, and so spent the little money they had been gathering against the rent.

But let us turn from this painful picture to Tim's neighbour Pat. What has he been doing all this time? Pat had been farming on quite a different plan. Just before Tim took his farm, Pat's father had died, and his landlord had given Pat the farm. Pat's father had left him much in the same circumstances as Tim was in, but then he had left a good sum of money as fortunes to his two sisters. Pat knew he must one day pay this, and it weighed him down very much. Just upon his father's death, his landlord had been advising his tenants to sow clover and turnips, as a means of improving their condition, and had told them a good deal of the great profits tenants in other parts of Ireland had made in this way. He had, indeed, made it a condition, when he gave Pat the farm, that he should grow these crops ; and as Pat had no reason to think that his landlord would advise him for his hurt, he resolved to try this new plan, although, to say the truth, his old father had, before his death, spoken against it ; and besides it vexed him much to be laughed at by his neighbours for his pains.

He began with only a couple of acres of clover, and half an acre of turnips ; and though the first year the turnips were not very good, yet they were a great help to his two cows (for he, too, had like his neighbour Tim, at first, but two cows). The cows gave him more milk through the winter than they had ever done before, and he made something by the butter. Besides, as he was very careful to follow the advice of keeping them as much as possible in the house, he certainly had much more manure than he had ever had before. In the spring, his clover came on ; but on cutting it, he soon found that even though he gave it to his horse as well as to his cows, there would be more of it than they could eat. He, therefore, made a cock of hay of part of the first cutting, and resolved to rear the calves his cows had given him, which would help to eat the second cutting, and still further increase his manure. This year, too, he prepared his land better for turnips, by breaking it early in the winter ; and the turnips of the former year having increased his stock of manure, he was able to allow a larger share of it to the turnips of this year. His crop was accordingly excellent—far beyond what he had expected ; and now the laugh began to be on his side, and instead of his neighbours laughing at him, Pat began to laugh at them. He had, in the spring, sown a still larger quantity of clover, and knowing that this would, the next summer, require more cattle to eat it, he made up his mind in the autumn to buy another cow in calf, when they were very cheap, and accordingly he sold his cock of hay, and with the money and a little more he added to it, at the fair of ——, he bought a cow for £4 : 10s., which one of his neighbours was obliged to sell, having nothing to feed her with through the winter. Though Pat's turnips were good, still he was hard pressed to keep the three cows and two calves through the winter, but what with straw, and furze, and turnips, and a few potatoes, he did manage it ; and in the spring he found himself with such a heap of manure, as had never been seen on the farm before, and this he did not fail to increase with all the sand and earth he could draw. I need hardly tell you the effect of this—his potato crop was better than ever ; the wheat after it was also very good, the grain fine and full—so that not only did it produce well, but he also got the best price. His cows being well fed, gave much more milk and butter than they ever had done before—in short, all prospered with him. I will not stop to tell you how he got on during several years after ; it is enough to say, that every year he made more and more manure, and his wheat and potatoes by means of this still improved. By rearing his calves, and buying another cow or two, when other people for want of food found themselves obliged to sell, he increased his stock so much, as to find that his butter alone went near to pay his rent. While other farmers' wives and children were doing nothing, and only putting their husbands and fathers to expense in supporting them,

his wife was making him money by her butter, and even
his young children of six or seven years old were gain-
fully employed, cutting clover and attending to the
cows, and thinning and weeding the turnips, in summer,
and pulling his turnips and cutting and cleaning them,
in winter. When the cows were out in the field, as
they always were for two hours every day, the children
watched them. A happier family could not be found
in the county ; a pleasanter sight you could not see than
those honest people with their industrious children. The
children took the greatest delight in their employment,
and instead of being ill-mannered, and idle, and dis-
obedient to their parents, and a burthen to them, they
were of great use and benefit to them. Well, things
went on in this way during the good times ; and when
the bad times, which we saw breaking poor Tim, came
upon Pat, how did he get on ? Sure enough the bad
times did come, and Pat's wheat and potatoes were not
nearly so good as they had been, nor did he get the
price for them he had done. Still, even in that wet
summer, his land being in good heart, his wheat filled
better than his neighbours' ; and what was bad for his
wheat and potatoes, did no hurt to his clover and
turnips. As I told you, even when wheat and oats
were so low, butter and pigs bore a good price ; and
now Pat found the advantage of being able to pay his
rent with his butter.—Of course he did not, during these
bad times, put so much money into his pocket from his
wheat and potatoes, but his butter and pigs always paid
his rent and more, and so he was in no fear of losing
his farm. Indeed, had he lost it, there was not a
gentleman in the country but would have been glad to
have given him the best farm on his estate. Pat, too,

had his misfortunes. One year he lost a horse, and another year his finest cow got choked by a turnip and died; but these things, which we have seen helped to ruin his neighbour Tim, though, of course, they vexed Pat much, and were a great loss to him, yet did not seriously injure him — his land, as I have said, being in good heart, the very first crop set him all right again.

Ten years after the time, when my story begins, the bad times had passed away, and all thanked God that the good times had come again. But what a difference it found in the situation of the two neighbours. It found poor Tim without a farm, living in the neighbouring town of ——, doubting whether he should go to America, or what he should do with himself—his family nearly starving about him. It found Pat one of the most comfortable farmers in the country, having paid his sisters their fortunes — not owing a sixpence to any man, and with money in his pocket; just on the point of getting another farm, still larger than his old one.

A gentleman who had been out of this country for some years, but who had known Pat formerly, one day asked him the question,—"How it was his circumstances had so improved?" His answer was a very short one : "SIR, UNDER GOD'S BLESSING, I OWE IT ALL TO HAVING FOLLOWED MY LANDLORD'S ADVICE, IN GROWING CLOVER AND TURNIPS."

That you may all be in Pat's circumstances, this time ten years, is the object and hearty wish of

Your sincere friend,

WILLIAM BENCE JONES.

AGHALUSKY.

Z

I have added this letter to show the very primitive state farming was in the bypast of Ireland, when I began improving, and long before the famine.

W. B. J.

December 1880.

THE END.

Printed by R. & R. CLARK, *Edinburgh.*

BEDFORD STREET, STRAND, LONDON, W.C.
December, 1879.

MACMILLAN & CO.'S CATALOGUE of Works in the Departments of History, Biography, Travels, Critical and Literary Essays, Politics, Political and Social Economy, Law, etc.; and Works connected with Language.

HISTORY, BIOGRAPHY, TRAVELS, &c.

Albemarle.—FIFTY YEARS OF MY LIFE. By GEORGE THOMAS, Earl of Albemarle. With Steel Portrait of the first Earl of Albemarle, engraved by JEENS. Third and Cheaper Edition. Crown 8vo. 7s. 6d.

" *The book is one of the most amusing of its class. . . . These reminiscences have the charm and flavour of personal experience, and they bring us into direct contact with the persons they describe.*"—EDINBURGH REVIEW.

Anderson.—MANDALAY TO MOMIEN; a Narrative of the Two Expeditions to Western China, of 1868 and 1875, under Colonel E. B. Sladen and Colonel Horace Browne. By Dr. ANDERSON, F.R.S.E., Medical and Scientific Officer to the Expeditions. With numerous Maps and Illustrations. 8vo. 21s.

"*A pleasant, useful, carefully-written, and important work.*"—ATHENÆUM.

Appleton.—Works by T. G. APPLETON :—

A NILE JOURNAL. Illustrated by EUGENE BENSON. Crown 8vo. 6s.

SYRIAN SUNSHINE. Crown 8vo. 6s.

Arnold (M.)—ESSAYS IN CRITICISM. By MATTHEW ARNOLD. New Edition, Revised and Enlarged. Crown 8vo. 9s.

Arnold (W. T.)—THE ROMAN SYSTEM OF PROVINCIAL ADMINISTRATION TO THE ACCESSION OF CONSTANTINE THE GREAT. Being the Arnold Prize Essay for 1879. By W. T. Arnold, B.A. Crown 8vo. 6s.

15.000.12.79.   A

Atkinson.—AN ART TOUR TO NORTHERN CAPITALS OF EUROPE, including Descriptions of the Towns, the Museums, and other Art Treasures of Copenhagen, Christiania, Stockholm, Abo, Helsingfors, Wiborg, St. Petersburg, Moscow, and Kief. By J. BEAVINGTON ATKINSON. 8vo. 12s.

Bailey.—THE SUCCESSION TO THE ENGLISH CROWN. A Historical Sketch. By A. BAILEY, M.A., Barrister-at-Law. Crown 8vo. 7s. 6d.

Baker (Sir Samuel W.)—Works by Sir SAMUEL BAKER, Pacha, M.A., F.R.S., F.R.G.S. :—

CYPRUS AS I SAW IT IN 1879. With Frontispiece. 8vo. 12s. 6d.

ISMAILIA : A Narrative of the Expedition to Central Africa for the Suppression of the Slave Trade, organised by Ismail, Khedive of Egypt. With Portraits, Map, and fifty full-page Illustrations by ZWECKER and DURAND. New and Cheaper Edition. With New Preface. Crown 8vo. 6s.

"A book which will be read with very great interest."—TIMES. *"Well written and full of remarkable adventures."*—PALL MALL GAZETTE. *"Adds another thrilling chapter to the history of African adventure."*—DAILY NEWS. *"Reads more like a romance. . . . incomparably more entertaining than books of African travel usually are."*—MORNING POST.

THE ALBERT N'YANZA Great Basin of the Nile, and Exploration of the Nile Sources. Fifth Edition. Maps and Illustrations. Crown 8vo. 6s.

" Charmingly written;" says the SPECTATOR, *"full, as might be expected, of incident, and free from that wearisome reiteration of useless facts which is the drawback to almost all books of African travel."*

THE NILE TRIBUTARIES OF ABYSSINIA, and the Sword Hunters of the Hamran Arabs. With Maps and Illustrations. Sixth Edition. Crown 8vo. 6s.

The TIMES *says : "It adds much to our information respecting Egyptian Abyssinia and the different races that spread over it. It contains, moreover, some notable instances of English daring and enterprising skill ; it abounds in animated tales of exploits dear to the heart of the British sportsman ; and it will attract even the least studious reader, as the author tells a story well, and can describe nature with uncommon power."*

Bancroft.—THE HISTORY OF THE UNITED STATES OF AMERICA, FROM THE DISCOVERY OF THE CONTINENT. By GEORGE BANCROFT. New and thoroughly Revised Edition. Six Vols. Crown 8vo. 54s

Barker (Lady).—Works by LADY BARKER :—

A YEAR'S HOUSEKEEPING IN SOUTH AFRICA. With Illustrations. New and Cheaper Edition. Crown 8vo. 6s.

"*We have to thank Lady Barker for a very amusing book, over which we have spent many a delightful hour, and of which we will not take leave without alluding to the ineffably droll illustrations which add so very much to the enjoyment of her clear and sparkling descriptions.*"—MORNING POST.

Beesly.—STORIES FROM THE HISTORY OF ROME. By Mrs. BEESLY. Extra fcap. 8vo. 2s. 6d.

"*A little book for which every cultivated and intelligent mother will be grateful for.*"—EXAMINER.

Bismarck—IN THE FRANCO-GERMAN WAR. An Authorized Translation from the German of Dr. MORITZ BUSCH. Two Vols. Crown 8vo. 18s.

The TIMES *says* :—"*The publication of Bismarck's after-dinner talk, whether discreet or not, will be of priceless biographical value, and Englishmen, at least, will not be disposed to quarrel with Dr. Busch for giving a picture as true to life as Boswell's 'Johnson' of the foremost practical genius that Germany has produced since Frederick the Great.*"

Blackburne.—BIOGRAPHY OF THE RIGHT HON. FRANCIS BLACKBURNE, Late Lord Chancellor of Ireland. Chiefly in connexion with his Public and Political Career. By his Son, EDWARD BLACKBURNE, Q.C. With Portrait Engraved by JEENS. 8vo. 12s.

Blanford (W. T.)—GEOLOGY AND ZOOLOGY OF ABYSSINIA. By W. T. BLANFORD. 8vo. 21s.

Brontë.—CHARLOTTE BRONTË. A Monograph. By T. WEMYSS REID. With Illustrations. Third Edition. Crown 8vo. 6s.

Brooke.—THE RAJA OF SARAWAK: an Account of Sir James Brooke, K.C.B., LL.D. Given chiefly through Letters or Journals. By GERTRUDE L. JACOB. With Portrait and Maps. Two Vols. 8vo. 25s.

Bryce.—Works by JAMES BRYCE, D.C.L., Regius Professor of Civil Law, Oxford :—

THE HOLY ROMAN EMPIRE. Sixth Edition, Revised and Enlarged. Crown 8vo. 7s. 6d.

"*It exactly supplies a want: it affords a key to much which men read of in their books as isolated facts, but of which they have hitherto had no connected exposition set before them.*"—SATURDAY REVIEW.

Bryce.—*continued.*

TRANSCAUCASIA AND ARARAT: being Notes of a Vacation Tour in the Autumn of 1876. With an Illustration and Map. Third Edition. Crown 8vo. 9s.

"*Mr. Bryce has written a lively and at the same time an instructive description of the tour he made last year in and about the Caucasus. When so well-informed a jurist travels into regions seldom visited, and even walks up a mountain so rarely scaled as Ararat, he is justified in thinking that the impressions he brings home are worthy of being communicated to the world at large, especially when a terrible war is casting a lurid glow over the countries he has lately surveyed.*"—ATHENÆUM.

Burgoyne. — POLITICAL AND MILITARY EPISODES DURING THE FIRST HALF OF THE REIGN OF GEORGE III. Derived from the Life and Correspondence of the Right Hon. J. Burgoyne, Lieut.-General in his Majesty's Army, and M.P. for Preston. By E. B. DE FONBLANQUE. With Portrait, Heliotype Plate, and Maps. 8vo. 16s.

Burke.—EDMUND BURKE, a Historical Study.   By JOHN MORLEY, B.A., Oxon. Crown 8vo. 7s. 6d.

Burrows.—WORTHIES OF ALL SOULS : Four Centuries of English History. Illustrated from the College Archives. By MONTAGU BURROWS, Chichele Professor of Modern History at Oxford, Fellow of All Souls. 8vo. 14s.

"*A most amusing as well as a most instructive book.*—GUARDIAN.

Cameron.—OUR FUTURE HIGHWAY. By V. LOVETT CAMERON, C.B., Commander R.N. With Illustrations. 2 vols. Crown 8vo.   [*Shortly.*

Campbell.—LOG-LETTERS FROM THE "CHALLENGER." By Lord GEORGE CAMPBELL. With Map. Fifth and cheaper Edition. Crown 8vo. 6s.

"*A delightful book, which we heartily commend to the general reader.*" —SATURDAY REVIEW.

"*We do not hesitate to say that anything so fresh, so picturesque, so generally delightful, as these log-letters has not appeared among books o travel for a long time.*"—EXAMINER.

Campbell.—MY CIRCULAR NOTES : Extracts from Journals ; Letters sent Home ; Geological and other Notes, written while Travelling Westwards round the World, from July 6th, 1874, to July 6th, 1875. By J. F. CAMPBELL, Author of "Frost and Fire." Cheaper Issue. Crown 8vo. 6s.

Campbell.—TURKS AND GREEKS. Notes of a recent Excursion. By the Hon. DUDLEY CAMPBELL, M.A. With Coloured Map. Crown 8vo. 3s. 6d.

Carpenter.—LIFE AND WORK OF MARY CARPENTER By the Rev. J. E. CARPENTER. With Portrait engraved by JEENS. Crown 8vo. *[Shortly.*

Carstares.—WILLIAM CARSTARES : a Character and Career of the Revolutionary Epoch (1649—1715). By ROBERT STORY, Minister of Rosneath. 8vo. 12s.

Chatterton : A BIOGRAPHICAL STUDY. By DANIEL WILSON, LL.D., Professor of History and English Literature in University College, Toronto. Crown 8vo. 6s. 6d.

Chatterton : A STORY OF THE YEAR 1770. By Professor MASSON, LL.D. Crown 8vo. 5s.

Clark.—MEMORIALS FROM JOURNALS AND LETTERS OF SAMUEL CLARK, M.A., formerly Principal of the National Society's Training College, Battersea. Edited with Introduction by his WIFE. With Portrait. Crown 8vo. 7s. 6d.

Clifford (W. K.)—LECTURES AND ESSAYS. Edited by LESLIE STEPHEN and FREDERICK POLLOCK, with Introduction by F. POLLOCK. Two Portraits. 2 vols. 8vo. 25s.
    The TIMES *of October 22, 1879, says :—" Many a friend of the author on first taking up these volumes and remembering his versatile genius and his keen enjoyment of all realms of intellectual activity must have trembled lest they should be found to consist of fragmentary pieces of work, too disconnected to do justice to his powers of consecutive reasoning and too varied to have any effect as a whole. Fortunately those fears are groundless . . . . It is not only in subject that the various papers are closely related. There is also a singular consistency of view and of method throughout . . . . It is in the social and metaphysical subjects that the richness of his intellect shows itself most forcibly in the variety and originality of the ideas which he presents to us. To appreciate this variety, it is necessary to read the book itself, for it treats, in some form or other, of nearly all the subjects of deepest interest in this age of questioning."*

Combe.—THE LIFE OF GEORGE COMBE, Author of "The Constitution of Man." By CHARLES GIBBON. With Three Portraits engraved by JEENS. Two Vols. 8vo. 32s.
    " A graphic and interesting account of the long life and indefatigable labours of a very remarkable man."—SCOTSMAN.

Cooper.—ATHENÆ CANTABRIGIENSES. By CHARLES HENRY COOPER, F.S.A., and THOMPSON COOPER, F.S.A. Vol. I. 8vo., 1500—85, 18s.; Vol. II., 1586—1609, 18s.

Correggio.—ANTONIO ALLEGRI DA CORREGGIO. From the German of Dr. JULIUS MEYER, Director of the Royal Gallery, Berlin. Edited, with an Introduction, by Mrs. HEATON. Containing Twenty Woodbury-type Illustrations. Royal 8vo. Cloth elegant. 31s. 6d.

Cox (G. V.)—RECOLLECTIONS OF OXFORD. By G. V. COX, M.A., New College, late Esquire Bedel and Coroner in the University of Oxford. *Cheaper Edition.* Crown 8vo. 6s.

Cunynghame (Sir A. T.)—MY COMMAND IN SOUTH AFRICA, 1874—78. Comprising Experiences of Travel in the Colonies of South Africa and the Independent States. By Sir ARTHUR THURLOW CUNYNGHAME, G.C.B., then Lieutenant-Governor and Commander of the Forces in South Africa. Third Edition. 8vo. 12s. 6d.

The TIMES *says :—"It is a volume of great interest, ... full of incidents which vividly illustrate the condition of the Colonies and the character and habits of the natives. . . . . It contains valuable illustrations of Cape warfare, and at the present moment it cannot fail to command wide-spread attention."*

"Daily News."—THE DAILY NEWS' CORRESPONDENCE of the War between Germany and France, 1870—1. Edited with Notes and Comments. New Edition. Complete in One Volume. With Maps and Plans. Crown 8vo. 6s.

THE DAILY NEWS' CORRESPONDENCE of the War between Russia and Turkey, to the fall of Kars. Including the letters of Mr. Archibald Forbes, Mr. J. E. McGahan, and other Special Correspondents in Europe and Asia. Second Edition, enlarged. Cheaper Edition. Crown 8vo. 6s.

FROM THE FALL OF KARS TO THE CONCLUSION OF PEACE. Cheaper Edition. Crown 8vo. 6s.

Davidson.—THE LIFE OF A SCOTTISH PROBATIONER; being a Memoir of Thomas Davidson, with his Poems and Letters. By JAMES BROWN, Minister of St. James's Street Church, Paisley. Second Edition, revised and enlarged, with Portrait. Crown 8vo. 7s. 6d.

Deas.—THE RIVER CLYDE. An Historical Description of the Rise and Progress of the Harbour of Glasgow, and of the Improvement of the River from Glasgow to Port Glasgow. By J. DEAS, M. Inst. C.E. 8vo. 10s. 6d.

Denison.—A HISTORY OF CAVALRY FROM THE EAR-
LIEST TIMES. With Lessons for the Future. By Lieut.-Col.
GEORGE DENISON, Commanding the Governor-General's Body
Guard, Canada, Author of "Modern Cavalry." With Maps and
Plans. 8vo. 18s.

Dilke.—GREATER BRITAIN. A Record of Travel in English-
speaking Countries during 1866-7. (America, Australia, India.
By Sir CHARLES WENTWORTH DILKE, M.P. Sixth Edition·
Crown 8vo. 6s.
"*Many of the subjects discussed in these pages,*" *says the* DAILY NEWS,
"*are of the widest interest, and such as no man who cares for the future
of his race and of the world can afford to treat with indifference.*"

Doyle.—HISTORY OF AMERICA. By J. A. DOYLE. With
Maps. 18mo. 4s. 6d.
"*Mr. Doyle's style is clear and simple, his facts are accurately stated,
and his book is meritoriously free from prejudice on questions where
partisanship runs high amongst us.*"—SATURDAY REVIEW.

Drummond of Hawthornden : THE STORY OF HIS
LIFE AND WRITINGS. By PROFESSOR MASSON. With Portrait and Vignette engraved by C. H. JEENS. Crown 8vo. 10s. 6d.

Duff.—Works by M. E. GRANT-DUFF, M.P., late Under Secretary
of State for India :—

NOTES OF AN INDIAN JOURNEY. With Map. 8vo. 10s. 6d.

MISCELLANIES POLITICAL AND LITERARY. 8vo. 10s. 6d.

Eadie.—LIFE OF JOHN EADIE, D.D., LL.D. By JAMES
BROWN, D.D., Author of "The Life of a Scottish Probationer."
With Portrait. Second Edition. Crown 8vo. 7s. 6d.
"*An ably written and characteristic biography.*"—TIMES.

Elliott.—LIFE OF HENRY VENN ELLIOTT, of Brighton.
By JOSIAH BATEMAN, M.A. With Portrait, engraved by JEENS.
Extra fcap. 8vo. Third and Cheaper Edition. 6s.

Elze.—ESSAYS ON SHAKESPEARE. By Dr. KARL ELZE.
Translated with the Author's sanction by L. DORA SCHMITZ.
8vo. 12s.

English Men of Letters. Edited by JOHN MORLEY. A
Series of Short Books to tell people what is best worth knowing
as to the Life, Character, and Works of some of the great
English Writers. In crown 8vo. Price 2s. 6d. each.

English Men of Letters.—*continued.*

I. DR. JOHNSON. By Leslie Stephen.

"*The new series opens well with Mr. Leslie Stephen's sketch of Dr. Johnson. It could hardly have been done better; and it will convey to the readers for whom it is intended a juster estimate of Johnson than either of the two essays of Lord Macaulay*"—Pall Mall Gazette.

II. SIR WALTER SCOTT. By R. H. Hutton.

"*The tone of the volume is excellent throughout.*"—Athenæum.

"*We could not wish for a more suggestive introduction to Scott and his poems and novels.*"—Examiner.

III. GIBBON. By J. C. Morison.

"*As a clear, thoughtful, and attractive record of the life and works of the greatest among the world's historians, it deserves the highest praise.*"—Examiner.

IV. SHELLEY. By J. A. Symonds.

"*The lovers of this great poet are to be congratulated on having at their command so fresh, clear, and intelligent a presentment of the subject, written by a man of adequate and wide culture.*"—Athenæum.

V. HUME. By Professor Huxley.

"*It may fairly be said that no one now living could have expounded Hume with more sympathy or with equal perspicuity.*"—Athenæum.

VI. GOLDSMITH. By William Black.

"*Mr. Black brings a fine sympathy and taste to bear in his criticism of Goldsmith's writings as well as in his sketch of the incidents of his life.*" Athenæum.

VII. DEFOE. By W. Minto.

"*Mr. Minto's book is careful and accurate in all that is stated, and faithful in all that it suggests. It will repay reading more than once.*" Athenæum.

VIII. BURNS. By Principal Shairp, Professor of Poetry in the University of Oxford.

"*It is impossible to desire fairer criticism than Principal Shairp's on Burns's poetry . . . . None of the series has given a truer estimate either of character or of genius than this little volume . . . . and all who read it will be thoroughly grateful to the author for this monument to the genius of Scotland's greatest poet.*"—Spectator.

IX. SPENSER. By the Very Rev. the Dean of St. Paul's.

"*Dr. Church is master of his subject, and writes always with good taste.*"—Academy.

X. THACKERAY. By Anthony Trollope.

"*Mr. Trollope's sketch is excellently adapted to fufil the purpose of the series in which it appears.*"—Athenæum.

XI. BURKE. By John Morley.

"*Perhaps the best criticism yet published on the life and character of*

English Men of Letters.—*continued.*

Burke is contained in Mr. Morley's compendious biography. His style is vigorous and polished, and both his political and personal judgment, and his literary criticisms are just, generous, subtle, and in a high degree interesting."—SATURDAY REVIEW.

MILTON. By MARK PATTISON.   [*Just ready.*]
HAWTHORNE. By HENRY JAMES.
SOUTHEY. By Professor DOWDEN.
CHAUCER. By Professor WARD.
COWPER. By GOLDWIN SMITH.   [*In preparation.*]
BUNYAN. By J. A. FROUDE.
WORDSWORTH. By F. W. H. MYERS.

Others in preparation.

Eton College, History of. By H. C. MAXWELL LYTE,
M.A. With numerous Illustrations by Professor DELAMOTTE, Coloured Plates, and a Steel Portrait of the Founder, engraved by C. H. JEENS. New and cheaper Issue, with Corrections. Medium 8vo. Cloth elegant. 21*s.*

" *We are at length presented with a work on England's greatest public school, worthy of the subject of which it treats. . . . A really valuable and authentic history of Eton College.*"—GUARDIAN.

European History, Narrated in a Series of Historical
Selections from the best Authorities. Edited and arranged by E. M. SEWELL and C. M. YONGE. First Series, crown 8vo. 6*s.* ; Second Series, 1088–1228, crown 8vo. 6*s.* Third Edition.

" *We know of scarcely anything,*" says *the* GUARDIAN, *of this volume,* "*which is so likely to raise to a higher level the average standard of English education.*"

Faraday.—MICHAEL FARADAY. By J. H. GLADSTONE,
Ph.D., F.R.S. Second Edition, with Portrait engraved by JEENS from a photograph by J. WATKINS. Crown 8vo. 4*s.* 6*d.* PORTRAIT. Artist's Proof. 5*s.*

Forbes.—LIFE AND LETTERS OF JAMES DAVID
FORBES, F.R.S., late Principal of the United College in the University of St. Andrews. By J. C. SHAIRP, LL.D., Principal of the United College in the University of St. Andrews ; P. G. TAIT, M.A., Professor of Natural Philosophy in the University of Edinburgh ; and A. ADAMS-REILLY, F.R.G.S. 8vo. with Portraits, Map, and Illustrations, 16*s.*

Freeman.—Works by EDWARD A. FREEMAN, D.C.L., LL.D. :—
HISTORICAL ESSAYS. Third Edition. 8vo. 10*s.* 6*d.*

CONTENTS :—*I. "The Mythical and Romantic Elements in Early English History;" II. "The Continuity of English History;" III. "The Relations between the Crowns of England and Scotland;" IV.*

Freeman—*continued.*

" *St. Thomas of Canterbury and his Biographers;*" *V.* "*The Reign of Edward the Third:*" *VI.* "*The Holy Roman Empire;*" *VII.* "*The Franks and the Gauls;*" *VIII.* "*The Early Sieges of Paris;*" *IX.* "*Frederick the First, King of Italy;*" *X.* "*The Emperor Frederick the Second:*" *XI.* "*Charles the Bold;*" *XII.* "*Presidential Government.*

HISTORICAL ESSAYS. SECOND SERIES. 8vo. 10s. 6d.
The principal Essays are:—"*Ancient Greece and Mediæval Italy:*" "*Mr. Gladstone's Homer and the Homeric Ages:*" "*The Historians of Athens:*" "*The Athenian Democracy:*" "*Alexander the Great:*" "*Greece during the Macedonian Period:*" "*Mommsen's History of Rome:*" "*Lucius Cornelius Sulla:*" "*The Flavian Cæsars.*"

HISTORICAL ESSAYS. Third Series. 8vo. 12s.
CONTENTS :—"*First Impressions of Rome.*" "*The Illyrian Emperors and their Land.*" "*Augusta Treverorum.*" "*The Goths at Ravenna.*" "*Race and Language.*" "*The Byzantine Empire.*" "*First Impressions of Athens.*" "*Mediæval and Modern Greece.*" "*The Southern Slaves.*" "*Sicilian Cycles.*" "*The Normans at Palermo.*"

COMPARATIVE POLITICS.—Lectures at the Royal Institution. To which is added the "Unity of History," the Rede Lecture at Cambridge, 1872. 8vo. 14s.

THE HISTORY AND CONQUESTS OF THE SARACENS. Six Lectures. Third Edition, with New Preface. Crown 8vo. 3s. 6d.

HISTORICAL AND ARCHITECTURAL SKETCHES: chiefly Italian. With Illustrations by the Author. Crown 8vo. 10s. 6d.

HISTORY OF FEDERAL GOVERNMENT, from the Foundation of the Achaian League to the Disruption of the United States. Vol. I. General Introduction. History of the Greek Federations. 8vo. 21s.

OLD ENGLISH HISTORY. With *Five Coloured Maps.* Fourth Edition. Extra fcap. 8vo., half-bound. 6s.
" *The book indeed is full of instruction and interest to students of all ages, and he must be a well-informed man indeed who will not rise from its perusal with clearer and more accurate ideas of a too much neglected portion of English history.*"—SPECTATOR.

HISTORY OF THE CATHEDRAL CHURCH OF WELLS, as illustrating the History of the Cathedral Churches of the Old Foundation. Crown 8vo. 3s. 6d.
" *The history assumes in Mr. Freeman's hands a significance, and, we may add, a practical value as suggestive of what a cathedral ought to be, which make it well worthy of mention.*"—SPECTATOR.

Freeman—*continued.*

THE GROWTH OF THE ENGLISH CONSTITUTION FROM THE EARLIEST TIMES. Crown 8vo. 5*s.* Third Edition, revised.

GENERAL SKETCH OF EUROPEAN HISTORY. Being Vol. I. of a Historical Course for Schools edited by E. A. FREEMAN. New Edition, enlarged with Maps, Chronological Table, Index, &c. 18mo. 3*s.* 6*d.*

"*It supplies the great want of a good foundation for historical teaching. The scheme is an excellent one, and this instalment has been accepted in a way that promises much for the volumes that are yet to appear.*"—EDUCATIONAL TIMES.

THE OTTOMAN POWER IN EUROPE : its Nature, its Growth, and its Decline. With Three Coloured Maps. Crown 8vo. 7*s.* 6*d.*

Galileo.—THE PRIVATE LIFE OF GALILEO. Compiled principally from his Correspondence and that of his eldest daughter, Sister Maria Celeste, Nun in the Franciscan Convent of S. Matthew in Arcetri. With Portrait. Crown 8vo. 7*s.* 6*d.*

Geddes.—THE PROBLEM OF THE HOMERIC POEMS. By W. D. GEDDES, LL. D., Professor of Greek in the University of Aberdeen. 8vo. 14*s.*

Gladstone—Works by the Right Hon. W. E. GLADSTONE, M.P.:—
JUVENTUS MUNDI. The Gods and Men of the Heroic Age. Crown 8vo. cloth. With Map. 10*s.* 6*d.* Second Edition.

"*Seldom,*" *says the* ATHENÆUM, "*out of the great poems themselves, have these Divinities looked so majestic and respectable. To read these brilliant details is like standing on the Olympian threshold and gazing at the ineffable brightness within.*"

HOMERIC SYNCHRONISM. An inquiry into the Time and Place of Homer. Crown 8vo. 6*s.*

"*It is impossible not to admire the immense range of thought and inquiry which the author has displayed.*"—BRITISH QUARTERLY REVIEW.

Goethe and Mendelssohn (1821—1831). Translated from the German of Dr. KARL MENDELSSOHN, Son of the Composer, by M. E. VON GLEHN. From the Private Diaries and Home Letters of Mendelssohn, with Poems and Letters of Goethe never before printed. Also with two New and Original Portraits, Facsimiles, and Appendix of Twenty Letters hitherto unpublished. Crown 8vo. 5*s.* Second Edition, enlarged.

" . . . *Every page is full of interest, not merely to the musician, but to the general reader. The book is a very charming one, on a topic of deep and lasting interest.*"—STANDARD.

Goldsmid.—TELEGRAPH AND TRAVEL. A Narrative of the Formation and Development of Telegraphic Communication between England and India, under the orders of Her Majesty's Government, with incidental Notices of the Countries traversed by the Lines. By Colonel Sir FREDERIC GOLDSMID, C.B., K.C.S.I., late Director of the Government Indo-European Telegraph. With numerous Illustrations and Maps. 8vo. 21s.

" *The merit of the work is a total absence of exaggeration, which does not, however, preclude a vividness and vigour of style not always characteristic of similar narratives.*"—STANDARD.

Gordon.—LAST LETTERS FROM EGYPT, to which are added Letters from the Cape. By LADY DUFF GORDON. With a Memoir by her Daughter, Mrs. Ross, and Portrait engraved by JEENS. Second Edition. Crown 8vo. 9s.

" *The intending tourist who wishes to acquaint himself with the country he is about to visit, stands embarrassed amidst the riches presented for his choice, and in the end probably rests contented with the sober usefulness of Murray. He will not, however, if he is well advised, grudge a place in his portmanteau to this book.*"—TIMES.

Gray.—CHINA. A History of the Laws, Manners, and Customs of the People. By the VENERABLE JOHN HENRY GRAY. LL.D., Archdeacon of Hong Kong, formerly H.B.M. Consular Chaplain at Canton. Edited by W. Gow Gregor. With 150 Full-page Illustrations, being Facsimiles of Drawings by a Chinese Artist. 2 Vols. Demy 8vo. 32s.

" *Its pages contain the most truthful and vivid picture of Chinese life which has ever been published.*"—ATHENÆUM.

" *The only elaborate and valuable book we have had for many years treating generally of the people of the Celestial Empire.*"—ACADEMY.

Green.—Works by JOHN RICHARD GREEN :—

HISTORY OF THE ENGLISH PEOPLE. Vol. I.—Early England—Foreign Kings—The Charter—The Parliament. With 8 Coloured Maps. 8vo. 16s. Vol. II.—The Monarchy, 1461—1540 ; the Restoration, 1540—1603. 8vo. 16s. Vol. III. —Puritan England, 1603—1660 ; the Revolution, 1660—1688. With 4 Maps. 8vo. 16s. [*Vol. IV. in the press.*

" *Mr. Green has done a work which probably no one but himself could have done. He has read and assimilated the results of all the labours of students during the last half century in the field of English history, and has given them a fresh meaning by his own independent study. He has fused together by the force of sympathetic imagination all that he has so*

Green.—*continued.*

collected, and has given us a vivid and forcible sketch of the march of English history. His book, both in its aims and its accomplishments, rises far beyond any of a similar kind, and it will give the colouring to the popular view to English history for some time to come."—EXAMINER.

A SHORT HISTORY OF THE ENGLISH PEOPLE. With Coloured Maps, Genealogical Tables, and Chronological Annals. Crown 8vo. 8s. 6d. Sixty-third Thousand.

" To say that Mr. Green's book is better than those which have preceded it, would be to convey a very inadequate impression of its merits. It stands alone as the one general history of the country, for the sake of which all others, if young and old are wise, will be speedily and surely set aside."

STRAY STUDIES FROM ENGLAND AND ITALY. Crown 8vo. 8s. 6d. Containing : Lambeth and the Archbishops—The Florence of Dante—Venice and Rome—Early History of Oxford —The District Visitor—Capri—Hotels in the Clouds—Sketches in Sunshine, &c.

" One and all of the papers are eminently readable."—ATHENÆUM.

Guest.—LECTURES ON THE HISTORY OF ENGLAND. By M. J. GUEST. With Maps. Crown 8vo. 6s.

" The book is pleasant reading, it is full of information, much of it is valuable, most of it is correct, told in a gossipy and intelligible way."— ATHENÆUM.

Hamerton.—Works by P. G. HAMERTON :—

THE INTELLECTUAL LIFE. With a Portrait of Leonardo da Vinci, etched by LEOPOLD FLAMENG. Second Edition. Crown 10s. 6d. 8vo.

" We have read the whole book with great pleasure, and we can recommend it strongly to all who can appreciate grave reflections on a very important subject, excellently illustrated from the resources of a mind stored with much reading and much keen observation of real life."— SATURDAY REVIEW.

THOUGHTS ABOUT ART. New Edition, revised, with an Introduction. Crown 8vo. 8s. 6d.

" A manual of sound and thorough criticism on art."—STANDARD.

Hill.—THE RECORDER OF BIRMINGHAM. A Memoir of Matthew Davenport Hill, with Selections from his Correspondence. By his Daughters ROSAMOND and FLORENCE DAVENPORT-HILL. With Portrait engraved by C. H. JEENS. 8vo. 16s.

Hill.—WHAT WE SAW IN AUSTRALIA. By ROSAMOND and FLORENCE HILL. Crown 8vo. 10s. 6d.

"*May be recommended as an interesting and truthful picture of the condition of those lands which are so distant and yet so much like home.*"—SATURDAY REVIEW.

Hodgson.—MEMOIR OF REV. FRANCIS HODGSON, B.D., Scholar, Poet, and Divine. By his Son, the Rev. JAMES T. HODGSON, M.A. Containing numerous Letters from Lord Byron and others. With Portrait engraved by JEENS. Two Vols. Crown 8vo. 18s.

"*A book that has added so much of a healthy nature to our knowledge of Byron, and that contains so rich a store of delightful correspondence.*"—ATHENÆUM.

Hole.—A GENEALOGICAL STEMMA OF THE KINGS OF ENGLAND AND FRANCE. By the Rev. C. HOLE, M.A., Trinity College, Cambridge. On Sheet, 1s.

A BRIEF BIOGRAPHICAL DICTIONARY. Compiled and Arranged by the Rev. CHARLES HOLE, M.A. Second Edition. 18mo. 4s. 6d.

Hooker and Ball.—MAROCCO AND THE GREAT ATLAS: Journal of a Tour in. By Sir JOSEPH D. HOOKER, K.C.S.I., C.B., F.R.S., &c., and JOHN BALL, F.R.S. With an Appendix, including a Sketch of the Geology of Marocco, by G. MAW, F.L.S., F.G.S. With Illustrations and Map. 8vo. 21s.

"*It is long since any more interesting book of travels has issued from our press.*"—SATURDAY REVIEW. "*This is, without doubt, one of the most interesting and valuable books of travel published for many years.*"—SPECTATOR.

Hozier (H. M.)—Works by CAPTAIN HENRY M. HOZIER, late Assistant Military Secretary to Lord Napier of Magdala :—

THE SEVEN WEEKS' WAR; Its Antecedents and Incidents. *New and Cheaper Edition.* With New Preface, Maps, and Plans. Crown 8vo. 6s.

THE INVASIONS OF ENGLAND : a History of the Past, with Lessons for the Future. Two Vols. 8vo. 28s.

Hübner.—A RAMBLE ROUND THE WORLD IN 1871. By M. LE BARON HÜBNER, formerly Ambassador and Minister. Translated by LADY HERBERT. New and Cheaper Edition. With numerous Illustrations. Crown 8vo. 6s.

"*It is difficult to do ample justice to this pleasant narrative of travel .... it does not contain a single dull paragraph.*"—MORNING POST.

Hughes.—Works by THOMAS HUGHES, Q.C., Author of "Tom Brown's School Days."

ALFRED THE GREAT. New Edition. Crown 8vo. 6s.

MEMOIR OF A BROTHER. With Portrait of GEORGE HUGHES, after WATTS. Engraved by JEENS. Crown 8vo. 5s. Sixth Edition.

" *The boy who can read this book without deriving from it some additional impulse towards honourable, manly, and independent conduct, has no good stuff in him.*"—DAILY NEWS.

Hunt.—HISTORY OF ITALY. By the Rev. W. HUNT, M.A. Being the Fourth Volume of the Historical Course for Schools. Edited by EDWARD A. FREEMAN, D.C.L. 18mo. 3s.

" *Mr. Hunt gives us a most compact but very readable little book, containing in small compass a very complete outline of a complicated and perplexing subject. It is a book which may be safely recommended to others besides schoolboys.*"—JOHN BULL.

Irving.—THE ANNALS OF OUR TIME. A Diurnal of Events, Social and Political, Home and Foreign, from the Accession of Queen Victoria to the Peace of Versailles. By JOSEPH IRVING. *Fourth Edition.* 8vo. half-bound. 16s.

ANNALS OF OUR TIME. Supplement. From Feb. 28, 1871, to March 19, 1874. 8vo. 4s. 6d.

ANNALS OF OUR TIME. Second Supplement. From March, 1874, to the Occupation of Cyprus. 8vo. 4s. 6d.

" *We have before us a trusty and ready guide to the events of the past thirty years, available equally for the statesman, the politician, the public writer, and the general reader.*"—TIMES.

James.—Works by HENRY JAMES, Jun. FRENCH POETS AND NOVELISTS. Crown 8vo. 8s. 6d.

CONTENTS:—*Alfred de Musset : Théophile Gautier ; Baudelaire ; Honoré de Balzac ; George Sand ; The Two Ampères ; Turgenieff, &c.*

Johnson's Lives of the Poets.—The Six Chief Lives—Milton, Dryden, Swift, Addison, Pope, Gray. With Macaulay's "Life of Johnson." Edited, with Preface, by MATTHEW ARNOLD. Crown 8vo. 6s.

Killen.—ECCLESIASTICAL HISTORY OF IRELAND, from the Earliest Date to the Present Time. By W. D. KILLEN, D.D., President of Assembly's College, Belfast, and Professor of Ecclesiastical History. Two Vols. 8vo. 25s.

" *Those who have the leisure will do well to read these two volumes. They are full of interest, and are the result of great research. . . . We have no hesitation in recommending the work to all who wish to improve their acquaintance with Irish history."*—SPECTATOR.

Kingsley (Charles).—Works by the Rev. CHARLES KINGSLEY, M.A., Rector of Eversley and Canon of Westminster. (For other Works by the same Author, *see* THEOLOGICAL and BELLES LETTRES Catalogues.)

ON THE ANCIEN RÉGIME as it existed on the Continent before the FRENCH REVOLUTION. Three Lectures delivered at the Royal Institution. Crown 8vo. 6*s.*

AT LAST: A CHRISTMAS in the WEST INDIES. With nearly Fifty Illustrations. Sixth Edition. Crown 8vo. 6*s.*
Mr. Kingsley's dream of forty years was at last fulfilled, when he started on a Christmas expedition to the West Indies, for the purpose of becoming personally acquainted with the scenes which he has so vividly described in " Westward Ho !" These two volumes are the journal of his voyage. Records of natural history, sketches of tropical landscape, chapters on education, views of society, all find their place. " We can only say that Mr. Kingsley's account of a ' Christmas in the West Indies' is in every way worthy to be classed among his happiest productions."—STANDARD.

THE ROMAN AND THE TEUTON. A Series of Lectures delivered before the University of Cambridge. New and Cheaper Edition, with Preface by Professor MAX MÜLLER. Crown 8vo. 6*s.*

PLAYS AND PURITANS, and other Historical Essays. With Portrait of Sir WALTER RALEIGH. New Edition. Crown 8vo. 6*s.*
In addition to the Essay mentioned in the title, this volume contains other two—one on " Sir Walter Raleigh and his Time," and one on Froude's " History of England."

Kingsley (Henry).—TALES OF OLD TRAVEL. Re-narrated by HENRY KINGSLEY, F.R.G.S. With *Eight Illustrations* by HUARD. Fifth Edition. Crown 8vo. 5*s.*
" We know no better book for those who want knowledge or seek to refresh it. As for the ' sensational,' most novels are tame compared with these narratives."—ATHENÆUM.

Lang.—CYPRUS: Its History, its Present Resources and Future Prospects. By R. HAMILTON LANG, late H.M. Consul for the Island of Cyprus. With Two Illustrations and Four Maps. 8vo. 14*s.*
" The fair and impartial account of her past and present to be found in these pages has an undoubted claim on the attention of all intelligent readers."—MORNING POST.

Laocoon.—Translated from the Text of Lessing, with Preface and Notes by the Right Hon. SIR ROBERT J. PHILLIMORE, D.C.L. With Photographs. 8vo. 12s.

Leonardo da Vinci and his Works.—Consisting of a Life of Leonardo Da Vinci, by MRS. CHARLES W. HEATON, Author of "Albrecht Dürer of Nürnberg," &c., an Essay on his Scientific and Literary Works by CHARLES CHRISTOPHER BLACK, M.A., and an account of his more important Paintings and Drawings. Illustrated with Permanent Photographs. Royal 8vo, cloth, extra gilt. 31s. 6d.

Liechtenstein.—HOLLAND HOUSE. By Princess MARIE LIECHTENSTEIN. With Five Steel Engravings by C. H. JEENS, after Paintings by WATTS and other celebrated Artists, and numerous Illustrations drawn by Professor P. H. DELAMOTTE, and engraved on Wood by J. D. COOPER, W. PALMER, and JEWITT & Co. Third and Cheaper Edition. Medium 8vo. cloth elegant. 16s.

Also, an Edition containing, in addition to the above, about 40 Illustrations by the Woodbury-type process, and India Proofs of the Steel Engravings. Two vols. medium 4to. half morocco elegant. 4l. 4s.

Lloyd.—THE AGE OF PERICLES. A History of the Arts and Politics of Greece from the Persian to the Peloponnesian War. By W. WATKISS LLOYD. Two Vols. 8vo. 21s.

" *No such account of Greek art of the best period has yet been brought together in an English work. . . . . Mr. Lloyd has produced a book of unusual excellence and interest.*"—PALL MALL GAZETTE.

Loch Etive and the Sons of Uisnach.—With Illustrations. 8vo. 14s.

" *Not only have we Loch Etive of the present time brought before us in colours as true as they are vivid, but stirring scenes which happened on the borders of the beautiful lake in semi-mythical times are conjured up with singular skill. Nowhere else do we remember to have met with such a well-written account of the invasion of Scotland by the Irish.*"—GLOBE.

Loftie.—A RIDE IN EGYPT FROM SIOOT TO LUXOR, IN 1879 ; with Notes on the Present State and Ancient History of the Nile Valley, and some account of the various ways of making the voyage out and home. By the Rev. W. J. LOFTIE. With Illustrations. Crown 8vo. 10s. 6d.

" *We prophesy that Mr. Loftie's little book will accompany many travellers on the Nile in the coming winters.*"—TIMES.

Lubbock. — ADDRESSES, POLITICAL AND EDUCA-
TIONAL. By Sir JOHN LUBBOCK, Bart., M.P., D.C.L.,
F.R.S. 8vo. 8s. 6d.

Macdonell.—FRANCE SINCE THE FIRST EMPIRE. By
JAMES MACDONELL. Edited with Preface by his Wife. Crown
8vo. [*Shortly.*

Macarthur.—HISTORY OF SCOTLAND, By MARGARET
MACARTHUR. Being the Third Volume of the Historical Course
for Schools, Edited by EDWARD A. FREEMAN, D.C.L. Second
Edition. 18mo. 2s.

"*It is an excellent summary, unimpeachable as to facts, and putting
them in the clearest and most impartial light attainable.*"—GUARDIAN.
"*No previous History of Scotland of the same bulk is anything like so
trustworthy, or deserves to be so extensively used as a text-book.*"—GLOBE.

Macmillan (Rev. Hugh).—For other Works by same Author,
see THEOLOGICAL and SCIENTIFIC CATALOGUES.

HOLIDAYS ON HIGH LANDS ; or, Rambles and Incidents in
search of Alpine Plants. Second Edition, revised and enlarged.
Globe 8vo. cloth. 6s.

"*Botanical knowledge is blended with a love of nature, a pious en-
thusiasm, and a rich felicity of diction not to be met with in any works
of kindred character, if we except those of Hugh Miller.*"—TELEGRAPH.

Macready.—MACREADY'S REMINISCENCES AND SE-
LECTIONS FROM HIS DIARIES AND LETTERS. Edited
by Sir F. POLLOCK, Bart., one of his Executors. With Four
Portraits engraved by JEENS. New and Cheaper Edition. Crown
8vo. 7s. 6d.

"*As a careful and for the most part just estimate of the stage during
a very brilliant period, the attraction of these volumes can scarcely be
surpassed. . . . . Readers who have no special interest in theatrical
matters, but enjoy miscellaneous gossip, will be allured from page to page,
attracted by familiar names and by observations upon popular actors and
authors.*"—SPECTATOR.

Mahaffy.—Works by the Rev. J. P. MAHAFFY, M.A., Fellow of
Trinity College, Dublin :—

SOCIAL LIFE IN GREECE FROM HOMER TO MENAN-
DER. Third Edition, revised and enlarged, with a new chapter
on Greek Art. Crown 8vo. 9s.

"*It should be in the hands of all who desire thoroughly to understand
and to enjoy Greek literature, and to get an intelligent idea of the old Greek
life, political, social, and religious.*"—GUARDIAN.

Mahaffy.—*continued.*

RAMBLES AND STUDIES IN GREECE. With Illustrations. Crown 8vo. 10s. 6d. New and enlarged Edition, with Map and Illustrations.

"*A singularly instructive and agreeable volume.*"—ATHEN.EUM.

"Maori."—SPORT AND WORK ON THE NEPAUL FRONTIER; or, Twelve Years' Sporting Reminiscences of an Indigo Planter. By "MAORI." With Illustrations. 8vo. 14s.

"*Every day's adventures, with all the joys and perils of the chase, are told as only a keen and cunning sportsman can tell them.*"—STANDARD.

Margary.—THE JOURNEY OF AUGUSTUS RAYMOND MARGARY FROM SHANGHAE TO BHAMO AND BACK TO MANWYNE. From his Journals and Letters, with a brief Biographical Preface, a concluding chapter by Sir RUTHERFORD ALCOCK, K.C.B., and a Steel Portrait engraved by JEENS, and Map. 8vo. 10s. 6d.

"*There is a manliness, a cheerful spirit, an inherent vigour which was never overcome by sickness or debility, a tact which conquered the prejudices of a strange and suspicious population, a quiet self-reliance, always combined with deep religious feeling, unalloyed by either priggishness, cant, or superstition, that ought to commend this volume to readers sitting quietly at home who feel any pride in the high estimation accorded to men of their race at Yarkand or at Khiva, in the heart of Africa, or on the shores of Lake Seri-kul.*"—SATURDAY REVIEW.

Markham.—NORTHWARD HO! By Captain ALBERT H. MARKHAM, R.N., Author of "The Great Frozen Sea," &c. Including a Narrative of Captain Phipps's Expedition, by a Midshipman. With Illustrations. Crown 8vo. 10s. 6d.

"*Captain Markham's interesting volume has the advantage of being written by a man who is practically conversant with the subject.*"—PALL MALL GAZETTE.

Martin.—THE HISTORY OF LLOYD'S, AND OF MARINE INSURANCE IN GREAT BRITAIN. With an Appendix containing Statistics relating to Marine Insurance. By FREDERICK MARTIN, Author of "The Statesman's Year Book." 8vo. 14s.

Martineau.—BIOGRAPHICAL SKETCHES, 1852—1875. By HARRIET MARTINEAU. With Additional Sketches, and Autobiographical Sketch. Fifth Edition. Crown 8vo. 6s.

Masson (David).—For other Works by same Author, *see* PHILOSOPHICAL and BELLES LETTRES CATALOGUES.

B 2

Masson (David).—*continued.*

CHATTERTON : A Story of the Year 1770   By DAVID MASSON, LL.D., Professor of Rhetoric and English Literature in the University of Edinburgh.   Crown 8vo   5s.

THE THREE DEVILS : Luther's, Goethe's, and Milton's ; and other Essays.   Crown 8vo.   5s.

WORDSWORTH, SHELLEY, AND KEATS ;   and other Essays.   Crown 8vo.   5s.

Mathews.—LIFE OF CHARLES J. MATHEWS, Chiefly Autobiographical.   With Selections from his Correspondence and Speeches.   Edited by CHARLES DICKENS.

" *One of the pleasantest and most readable books of the season.   From first to last these two volumes are alive with the inimitable artist and comedian. . . . The whole book is full of life, vigour, and wit, and even through some of the gloomy episodes of volume two, will repay most careful study.   So complete, so varied a picture of a man's life is rarely to be met with.*"—STANDARD.

Maurice.—THE FRIENDSHIP OF BOOKS ; AND OTHER LECTURES.   By the REV. F. D. MAURICE.   Edited with Preface, by THOMAS HUGHES, Q.C.   Crown 8vo.   10s. 6d.

Mayor (J. E. B.)—WORKS edited by JOHN E. B. MAYOR, M.A., Kennedy Professor of Latin at Cambridge :—

CAMBRIDGE IN THE SEVENTEENTH CENTURY.   Part II Autobiography of Matthew Robinson.   Fcap. 8vo.   5s. 6d.

LIFE OF BISHOP BEDELL.   By his SON.   Fcap. 8vo.   3s. 6d.

Melbourne.—MEMOIRS OF THE RT. HON. WILLIAM. SECOND VISCOUNT MELBOURNE.   By W. M. TORRENS, M.P.   With Portrait after Sir. T. Lawrence.   Second Edition. 2 Vols.   8vo.   32s.

" *As might be expected, he has produced a book which will command and reward attention.   It contains a great deal of valuable matter and a great deal of animated, elegant writing.*"—QUARTERLY REVIEW.

Mendelssohn.—LETTERS AND RECOLLECTIONS.   By FERDINAND HILLER.   Translated by M. E. VON GLEHN.   With Portrait from a Drawing by KARL MÜLLER, never before published.   Second Edition.   Crown 8vo.   7s. 6d.

" *This is a very interesting addition to our knowledge of the great German composer.   It reveals him to us under a new light, as the warmhearted comrade, the musician whose soul was in his work, and the homeloving, domestic man.*"—STANDARD.

Merewether.—BY SEA AND BY LAND. Being a Trip through Egypt, India, Ceylon, Australia, New Zealand, and America—all Round the World. By HENRY ALWORTH MERE-WETHER, one of Her Majesty's Counsel. Crown 8vo. 8s. 6d.

Michael Angelo Buonarotti ; Sculptor, Painter, Architect. The Story of his Life and Labours. By C. C. BLACK, M.A. Illustrated by 20 Permanent Photographs. Royal 8vo. cloth elegant, 31s. 6d.

" The story of Michael Angelo's life remains interesting whatever be the manner of telling it, and supported as it is by this beautiful series of photographs, the volume must take rank among the most splendid of Christmas books, fitted to serve and to outlive the season."—PALL MALL GAZETTE.

Michelet.—A SUMMARY OF MODERN HISTORY. Translated from the French of M. MICHELET, and continued to the present time by M. C. M. SIMPSON. Globe 8vo. 4s. 6d.

Milton.—LIFE OF JOHN MILTON. Narrated in connection with the Political, Ecclesiastical, and Literary History of his Time. By DAVID MASSON, M.A., LL.D., Professor of Rhetoric and English Literature in the University of Edinburgh. With Portraits. Vol. I. 18s. Vol. II., 1638—1643. 8vo. 16s. Vol. III. 1643—1649. 8vo. 18s. Vols. IV. and V. 1649—1660. 32s. Vol. VI. concluding the work in the press.

This work is not only a Biography, but also a continuous Political, Ecclesiastical, and Literary History of England through Milton's whole time.

Mitford (A. B.)—TALES OF OLD JAPAN. By A. B. MITFORD, Second Secretary to the British Legation in Japan. With upwards of 30 Illustrations, drawn and cut on Wood by Japanese Artists. New and Cheaper Edition. Crown 8vo. 6s.

" These very original volumes will always be interesting as memorials of a most exceptional society, while regarded simply as tales, they are sparkling, sensational, and dramatic."—PALL MALL GAZETTE.

Monteiro.—ANGOLA AND THE RIVER CONGO. By JOACHIM MONTEIRO. With numerous Illustrations from Sketches taken on the spot, and a Map. Two Vols. crown 8vo. 21s.

Morison.—THE LIFE AND TIMES OF SAINT BERNARD, Abbot of Clairvaux. By JAMES COTTER MORISON, M.A. New Edition. Crown 8vo. 6s.

Moseley.—NOTES BY A NATURALIST ON THE CHAL-LENGER : being an Account of various Observations made during the Voyage of H.M.S. *Challenger*, Round the World, in 1872–76. By H. N. MOSELEY, F.R.S., Member of the Scientific Staff of the *Challenger*. 8vo. with Maps, Coloured Plates, and Woodcuts. 21s.

"*This is certainly the most interesting and suggestive book, descriptive of a naturalist's travels, which has been published since Mr. Darwin's 'Journal of Researches' appeared, more than forty years ago.*"—NATURE. "*We cannot point to any book of travels in our day more vivid in its powers of description, more varied in its subject matter, or more attractive to every educated reader.*"—SATURDAY REVIEW.

Murray.—ROUND ABOUT FRANCE. By E. C. GRENVILLE MURRAY. Crown 8vo. 7s. 6d.

"*These short essays are a perfect mine of information as to the present condition and future prospects of political parties in France. . . . It is at once extremely interesting and exceptionally instructive on a subject on which few English people are well informed.*"—SCOTSMAN.

Napier.—MACVEY NAPIER'S SELECTED CORRE-SPONDENCE. Edited by his Son, MACVEY NAPIER. 8vo. 14s.

The TIMES says :—"*It is replete with useful material for the biographers of many distinguished writers of the generation which is passing away. Since reading it we understand several noteworthy men, and Brougham in particular, far better than we did before.*" "*It would be useless to attempt within our present limits to give any adequate idea of the abundance of interesting passages which meet us in the letters of Macaulay, Brougham, Carlyle, Jeffrey, Senior, and many other well-known writers. Especially piquant are Jeffrey's periodical criticisms on the contents of the Review which he had formerly edited.*"—PALL MALL GAZETTE.

Napoleon.—THE HISTORY OF NAPOLEON I. By P. LANFREY. A Translation with the sanction of the Author. 4 vols. 8vo. Vols. I. II. and III. price 12s. each. Vol. IV. 6s.

The PALL MALL GAZETTE says it is "*one of the most striking pieces of historical composition of which France has to boast,*" and the SATURDAY REVIEW calls it "*an excellent translation of a work on every ground deserving to be translated. It is unquestionably and immeasurably the best that has been produced. It is in fact the only work to which we can turn for an accurate and trustworthy narrative of that extraordinary career. . . . The book is the best and indeed the only trustworthy history of Napoleon which has been written.*"

Nichol.—TABLES OF EUROPEAN LITERATURE AND HISTORY, A.D. 200—1876. By J. NICHOL, LL.D., Professor of English Language and Literature, Glasgow. 4to. 6s. 6d.

TABLES OF ANCIENT LITERATURE AND HISTORY, B.C. 1500—A.D. 200. By the same Author. 4to. 4s. 6d.

Nordenskiöld's Arctic Voyages, 1858-79. — With
Maps and numerous Illustrations.   8vo.   16s.
"*A volume of great interest and much scientific value.*"—NATURE.

Oliphant (Mrs.).—THE MAKERS OF FLORENCE : Dante
Giotto, Savonarola, and their City.   By Mrs. OLIPHANT.   With
numerous Illustrations from drawings by Professor DELAMOTTE,
and portrait of Savonarola, engraved by JEENS.   Second Edition.
Medium 8vo.   Cloth extra.   21s.
" *We are grateful to Mrs. Oliphant for her eloquent and beautiful
sketches of Dante, Fra Angelico, and Savonarola.   They are picturesque,
full of life, and rich in detail, and they are charmingly illustrated by the
art of the engraver.*"—SPECTATOR.

Oliphant.—THE DUKE AND THE SCHOLAR ; and other
Essays.   By T. L. KINGTON OLIPHANT.   8vo.   7s. 6d.
" *This volume contains one of the most beautiful biographical essays we
have seen since Macaulay's days.*"—STANDARD.

Otte.—SCANDINAVIAN HISTORY.   By E. C. OTTE.   With
Maps.   Extra fcap. 8vo.   6s.

Owens College Essays and Addresses.—By PRO-
FESSORS AND LECTURERS OF OWENS COLLEGE, MANCHESTER.
Published in Commemoration of the Opening of the New College
Buildings, October 7th, 1873.   8vo.   14s.

Palgrave (R. F. D.)—THE HOUSE OF COMMONS ;
Illustrations of its History and Practice.   By REGINALD F. D.
PALGRAVE, Clerk Assistant of the House of Commons.   New
and Revised Edition.   Crown 8vo.   2s. 6d.

Palgrave (Sir F.)—HISTORY OF NORMANDY AND
OF ENGLAND.   By Sir FRANCIS PALGRAVE, Deputy Keeper
of Her Majesty's Public Records.   Completing the History to the
Death of William Rufus.   4 Vols. 8vo.   4l. 4s.

Palgrave (W. G.)—A NARRATIVE OF A YEAR'S
JOURNEY THROUGH CENTRAL AND EASTERN
ARABIA, 1862-3.   By WILLIAM GIFFORD PALGRAVE, late of
the Eighth Regiment Bombay N. I.   Sixth Edition.   With Maps,
Plans, and Portrait of Author, engraved on steel by Jeens.   Crown
8vo.   6s.
" *He has not only written one of the best books on the Arabs and one
of the best books on Arabia, but he has done so in a manner that must
command the respect no less than the admiration of his fellow-country-
men.*"—FORTNIGHTLY REVIEW.

Palgrave.—*continued.*

ESSAYS ON EASTERN QUESTIONS. By W. GIFFORD
PALGRAVE. 8vo. 10s. 6d.

"*These essays are full of anecdote and interest. The book is decidedly
a valuable addition to the stock of literature on which men must
base their opinion of the difficult social and political problems suggested by the designs of Russia, the capacity of Mahometans for
sovereignty, and the good government and retention of India.*"—
SATURDAY REVIEW.

DUTCH GUIANA. With Maps and Plans. 8vo. 9s.

"*His pages are nearly exhaustive as far as facts and statistics go,
while they are lightened by graphic social sketches as well as sparkling
descriptions of scenery.*"—SATURDAY REVIEW.

Patteson.—LIFE AND LETTERS OF JOHN COLERIDGE
PATTESON, D. D., Missionary Bishop of the Melanesian Islands.
By CHARLOTTE M. YONGE, Author of "The Heir of Redclyffe."
With Portraits after RICHMOND and from Photograph, engraved by
JEENS. With Map. Fifth Edition. Two Vols. Crown 8vo. 12s.

"*Miss Yonge's work is in one respect a model biography. It is made
up almost entirely of Patteson's own letters. Aware that he had left his
home once and for all, his correspondence took the form of a diary, and
as we read on we come to know the man, and to love him almost as if we
had seen him.*"—ATHENÆUM. "*Such a life, with its grand lessons of
unselfishness, is a blessing and an honour to the age in which it is lived ;
the biography cannot be studied without pleasure and profit, and indeed
we should think little of the man who did not rise from the study of it
better and wiser. Neither the Church nor the nation which produces
such sons need ever despair of its future.*"—SATURDAY REVIEW.

Pauli.—PICTURES OF OLD ENGLAND. By Dr. REINHOLD
PAULI. Translated, with the approval of the Author, by E. C.
OTTE. Cheaper Edition. Crown 8vo. 6s.

Payne.—A HISTORY OF EUROPEAN COLONIES. By
E. J. PAYNE, M.A. With Maps. 18mo. 4s. 6d.

The TIMES says :—"*We have seldom met with a historian capable of
forming a more comprehensive, far-seeing, and unprejudiced estimate of
events and peoples, and we can commend this little work as one certain to
prove of the highest interest to all thoughtful readers.*"

Persia.—EASTERN PERSIA. An Account of the Journeys of
the Persian Boundary Commission, 1870-1-2.—Vol. I. The Geography, with Narratives by Majors ST. JOHN, LOVETT, and EUAN
SMITH, and an Introduction by Major-General Sir FREDERIC
GOLDSMID, C.B., K.C.S.I., British Commissioner and Arbitrator.

With Maps and Illustrations.—Vol. II. The Zoology and Geology. By W. T. BLANFORD, A.R.S.M., F.R.S. With Coloured Illustrations. Two Vols. 8vo. 42*s.*

"*The volumes largely increase our store of information about countries with which Englishmen ought to be familiar. . . . . They throw into the shade all that hitherto has appeared in our tongue respecting the local features of Persia, its scenery, its resources, even its social condition. They contain also abundant evidence of English endurance, daring, and spirit.*"*--*TIMES.

Prichard.—THE ADMINISTRATION OF INDIA. From 1859 to 1868. The First Ten Years of Administration under the Crown. By I. T. PRICHARD, Barrister-at-Law. Two Vols. Demy 8vo. With Map. 21*s.*

Raphael.—RAPHAEL OF URBINO AND HIS FATHER GIOVANNI SANTI. By J. D. PASSAVANT, formerly Director of the Museum at Frankfort. With Twenty Permanent Photographs. Royal 8vo. Handsomely bound. 31*s.* 6*d.*

The SATURDAY REVIEW *says of them, " We have seen not a few elegant specimens of Mr. Woodbury's new process, but we have seen none that equal these."*

Reynolds.—SIR JOSHUA REYNOLDS AS A PORTRAIT PAINTER. AN ESSAY. By J. CHURTON COLLINS, B.A. Balliol College, Oxford. Illustrated by a Series of Portraits of distinguished Beauties of the Court of George III. ; reproduced in Autotype from Proof Impressions of the celebrated Engravings, by VALENTINE GREEN, THOMAS WATSON, F. R. SMITH, E. FISHER, and others. Folio half-morocco. £5 5*s.*

Rogers (James E. Thorold).—HISTORICAL GLEAN-INGS : A Series of Sketches. Montague, Walpole, Adam Smith, Cobbett. By Prof. ROGERS. Crown 8vo. 4*s.* 6*d.* Second Series. Wiklif, Laud, Wilkes, and Horne Tooke. Crown 8vo. 6*s.*

Routledge.—CHAPTERS IN THE HISTORY OF POPULAR PROGRESS IN ENGLAND, chiefly in Relation to the Freedom of the Press and Trial by Jury, 1660—1820. With application to later years. By J. ROUTLEDGE. 8vo. 16*s.*

" *The volume abounds in facts and information, almost always useful and often curious.*"—TIMES.

Rumford.—COUNT RUMFORD'S COMPLETE WORKS, with Memoir, and Notices of his Daughter. By GEORGE ELLIS. Five Vols. 8vo. 4*l.* 14*s.* 6*d.*

Seeley (Professor).—LECTURES AND ESSAYS. By
J. R. SEELEY, M.A. Professor of Modern History in the
University of Cambridge. 8vo. 10s. 6d.
CONTENTS :—*Roman Imperialism :* 1. *The Great Roman Revolu-
tion ;* 2. *The Proximate Cause of the Fall of the Roman Empire ;
The Later Empire.* — *Milton's Political Opinions* — *Milton's Poetry
—Elementary Principles in Art—Liberal Education in Universities
— English in Schools — The Church as a Teacher of Morality — The
Teaching of Politics : an Inaugural Lecture delivered at Cambridge.*

Shelburne.—LIFE OF WILLIAM, EARL OF SHELBURNE,
AFTERWARDS FIRST MARQUIS OF LANSDOWNE.
With Extracts from his Papers and Correspondence. By Lord
EDMOND FITZMAURICE. In Three Vols. 8vo. Vol. I. 1737—
1766, 12s. ; Vol. II. 1766—1776, 12s. ; Vol. III. 1776—1805. 16s.
"*Lord Edmond Fitzmaurice has succeeded in placing before us a
wealth of new matter, which, while casting valuable and much-needed
light on several obscure passages in the political history of a hundred
years ago, has enabled us for the first time to form a clear and consistent
idea of his ancestor.*"—SPECTATOR.

Sime.—HISTORY OF GERMANY. By JAMES SIME, M.A.
18mo. 3s. Being Vol. V. of the Historical Course for Schools:
Edited by EDWARD A. FREEMAN, D.C.L.
" *This is a remarkably clear and impressive History of Germany.*"—
STANDARD.

Squier.—PERU : INCIDENTS OF TRAVEL AND EX-
PLORATION IN THE LAND OF THE INCAS. By E. G.
SQUIER, M.A., F.S.A., late U.S. Commissioner to Peru. With
300 Illustrations. Second Edition. 8vo. 21s.
The TIMES *says :*—" *No more solid and trustworthy contribution has
been made to an accurate knowledge of what are among the most wonderful
ruins in the world. The work is really what its title implies. While of
the greatest importance as a contribution to Peruvian archæology, it is also a
thoroughly entertaining and instructive narrative of travel. Not the least
important feature must be considered the numerous well executed illustrations.*"

Strangford.—EGYPTIAN SHRINES AND SYRIAN SEPUL-
CHRES, including a Visit to Palmyra. By EMILY A. BEAUFORT
(Viscountess Strangford), Author of " The Eastern Shores of
the Adriatic." New Edition. Crown 8vo. 7s. 6d.

Tait.—AN ANALYSIS OF ENGLISH HISTORY, based upon
Green's " Short History of the English People." By C. W. A.
TAIT, M.A., Assistant Master, Clifton College. Crown 8vo.
3s. 6d.

Tait.—CATHARINE AND CRAUFURD TAIT, WIFE AND
SON OF ARCHIBALD CAMPBELL, ARCHBISHOP OF
CANTERBURY : a Memoir, Edited, at the request of the Arch-
bishop, by the Rev. W. BENHAM, B.D., Vicar of Margate, and
One of the Six Preachers of Canterbury Cathedral. With Two
Portraits engraved by JEENS. Crown 8vo. 12*s*. 6*d*.

" *The volume can scarcely fail to be read widely and with deep interest.
. . . It is difficult to put it down when once taken in hand, still more
difficult to get through it without emotion. . . . We commend the volume
to those who knew Catharine and Craufurd Tait as one which will bring
back to their minds recollections of their characters as true as the recollections of the faces brought back by the two excellent portraits which adorn
the book ; while to those who knew them not, we commend it as containing
the record of two noble Christian lives, which it will be a pleasure to
them to contemplate and an advantage to emulate.*"—TIMES.

Thomas.—THE LIFE OF JOHN THOMAS, Surgeon of the
"Earl of Oxford" East Indiaman, and First Baptist Missionary to
Bengal. By C. B. LEWIS, Baptist Missionary.   8vo.   10*s*. 6*d*.

Thompson.—HISTORY OF ENGLAND.   By EDITH THOMP-
SON. Being Vol. II. of the Historical Course for Schools, Edited
by EDWARD A. FREEMAN, D.C.L.   New Edition, revised and
enlarged, with Maps.   18mo.   2*s*. 6*d*.

" *Freedom from prejudice, simplicity of style, and accuracy of statement, are the characteristics of this volume.   It is a trustworthy text-book,
and likely to be generally serviceable in schools.*"—PALL MALL GAZETTE.
" *In its great accuracy and correctness of detail it stands far ahead of the
general run of school manuals.   Its arrangement, too, is clear, and its
style simple and straightforward.*"—SATURDAY REVIEW.

Todhunter.—THE   CONFLICT   OF   STUDIES ;   AND
OTHER ESSAYS ON SUBJECTS CONNECTED WITH
EDUCATION. By ISAAC TODHUNTER, M.A., F.R.S., late
Fellow and Principal Mathematical Lecturer of St. John's College,
Cambridge.   8vo.   10*s*. 6*d*.

Trench (Archbishop).—For other Works by the same Author,
see THEOLOGICAL and BELLES- LETTRES CATALOGUES, and
page 30 of this Catalogue.

GUSTAVUS ADOLPHUS IN GERMANY, and other Lectures
on the Thirty Years' War.   Second Edition, revised and enlarged.
Fcap. 8vo.   4*s*. '

PLUTARCH, HIS LIFE, HIS LIVES, AND HIS MORALS.
Five Lectures.   Second Edition, enlarged.   Fcap. 8vo.   3*s*. 6*d*.

LECTURES ON MEDIEVAL CHURCH HISTORY.   Being
the substance of Lectures delivered in Queen's College, London.
Second Edition, revised.   8vo.   12*s*.

Trench (Maria).—THE LIFE OF ST. TERESA. By MARIA TRENCH. With Portrait engraved by JEENS. Crown 8vo, cloth extra. 8s. 6d.

" *A book of rare interest.*"—JOHN BULL.

Trench (Mrs. R.)—REMAINS OF THE LATE MRS. RICHARD TRENCH. Being Selections from her Journals, Letters, and other Papers. Edited by ARCHBISHOP TRENCH. New and Cheaper Issue, with Portrait. 8vo. 6s.

Trollope.—A HISTORY OF THE COMMONWEALTH OF FLORENCE FROM THE EARLIEST INDEPENDENCE OF THE COMMUNE TO THE FALL OF THE REPUBLIC IN 1831. By T. ADOLPHUS TROLLOPE. 4 Vols. 8vo. Half morocco. 21s.

Uppingham by the Sea.—A NARRATIVE OF THE YEAR AT BORTH. By J. H. S. Crown 8vo. 3s. 6d.

Victor Emmanuel II., First King of Italy.—HIS LIFE. By G. S. GODKIN. 2 vols., crown 8vo. 16s.

" *An extremely clear and interesting history of one of the most important changes of later times.*"—EXAMINER.

Wallace.—THE MALAY ARCHIPELAGO : the Land of the Orang Utan and the Bird of Paradise. By ALFRED RUSSEL WALLACE. A Narrative of Travel with Studies of Man and Nature. With Maps and numerous Illustrations. Sixth Edition. Crown 8vo. 7s. 6d.

" *The result is a vivid picture of tropical life, which may be read with unflagging interest, and a sufficient account of his scientific conclusions to stimulate our appetite without wearying us by detail. In short, we may safely say that we have never read a more agreeable book of its kind.*"— SATURDAY REVIEW.

Ward.—A HISTORY OF ENGLISH DRAMATIC LITERA-TURE TO THE DEATH OF QUEEN ANNE. By A. W. WARD, M.A., Professor of History and English Literature in Owens College, Manchester. Two Vols. 8vo. 32s.

" *As full of interest as of information. To students of dramatic literature invaluable, and may be equally recommended to readers for mere pastime.*"—PALL MALL GAZETTE.

Ward (J.)—EXPERIENCES OF A DIPLOMATIST. Being recollections of Germany founded on Diaries kept during the years 1840—1870. By JOHN WARD, C.B., late H.M. Minister-Resident to the Hanse Towns. 8vo. 10s. 6d.

Waterton (C.)—WANDERINGS IN SOUTH AMERICA, THE NORTH-WEST OF THE UNITED STATES, AND THE ANTILLES IN 1812, 1816, 1820, and 1824. With Original Instructions for the perfect Preservation of Birds, etc., for Cabinets of Natural History. By CHARLES WATERTON. New Edition, edited with Biographical Introduction and Explanatory Index by the Rev. J. G. WOOD, M.A. With 100 Illustrations. Cheaper Edition. Crown 8vo. 6s.

Wedgwood.—JOHN WESLEY AND THE EVANGELICAL REACTION of the Eighteenth Century. By JULIA WEDGWOOD. Crown 8vo. 8s. 6d.

Whewell.—WILLIAM WHEWELL, D.D., late Master of Trinity College, Cambridge. An Account of his Writings, with Selections from his Literary and Scientific Correspondence. By I. TODHUNTER, M.A., F.R.S. Two Vols. 8vo. 25s.

White.—THE NATURAL HISTORY AND ANTIQUITIES OF SELBORNE. By GILBERT WHITE. Edited, with Memoir and Notes, by FRANK BUCKLAND, A Chapter on Antiquities by LORD SELBORNE, Map, &c., and numerous Illustrations by P. H. DELAMOTTE. Royal 8vo. Cloth, extra gilt. Cheaper Issue. 21s.

Also a Large Paper Edition, containing, in addition to the above, upwards of Thirty Woodburytype Illustrations from Drawings by Prof. DELAMOTTE. Two Vols. 4to. Half morocco, elegant. 4l. 4s.

"*Mr. Delamotte's charming illustrations are a worthy decoration of so dainty a book. They bring Selborne before us, and really help us to understand why White's love for his native place never grew cold.*"— TIMES.

Wilson.—A MEMOIR OF GEORGE WILSON, M.D., F.R.S.E., Regius Professor of Technology in the University of Edinburgh. By his SISTER. New Edition. Crown 8vo. 6s.

Wilson (Daniel, LL.D.)—Works by DANIEL WILSON, LL.D., Professor of History and English Literature in University College, Toronto :—

PREHISTORIC ANNALS OF SCOTLAND. New Edition, with numerous Illustrations. Two Vols. demy 8vo. 36s.

"*One of the most interesting, learned, and elegant works we have seen for a long time.*"—WESTMINSTER REVIEW.

PREHISTORIC MAN : Researches into the Origin of Civilization in the Old and New World. New Edition, revised and enlarged throughout, with numerous Illustrations and two Coloured Plates. Two Vols. 8vo. 36s.

Wilson.—*continued.*

"*A valuable work pleasantly written and well worthy of attention both by students and general readers.*"—ACADEMY.

CHATTERTON : A Biographical Study.   By DANIEL WILSON, LL. D., Professor of History and English Literature in University College, Toronto.   Crown 8vo.   6*s*. 6*d*.

Yonge (Charlotte M.)—Works by CHARLOTTE M. YONGE, Author of "The Heir of Redclyffe," &c., &c. :—

A PARALLEL HISTORY OF FRANCE AND ENGLAND : consisting of Outlines and Dates.   Oblong 4to.   3*s*. 6*d*.

CAMEOS FROM ENGLISH HISTORY.   From Rollo to Edward II.   Extra fcap. 8vo.   Third Edition.   5*s*.

SECOND SERIES, THE WARS IN FRANCE.   Extra fcap. 8vo.   Third Edition.   5*s*.

THIRD SERIES, THE WARS OF THE ROSES.   Extra fcap. 8vo.   5*s*.

"*Instead of dry details,*" *says the* NONCONFORMIST, "*we have living pictures, faithful, vivid, and striking.*"

FOURTH SERIES.   Reformation Times.   Extra fcap. 8vo.   5*s*.

HISTORY OF FRANCE.   Maps.   18mo.   3*s*. 6*d*.
[*Historical Course for Schools.*

POLITICS, POLITICAL AND SOCIAL ECONOMY, LAW, AND KINDRED SUBJECTS.

Anglo-Saxon Law.—ESSAYS IN. Contents : Law Courts —Land and Family Laws and Legal Procedure generally. With Select cases. Medium 8vo. 18s.

Arnold.—THE ROMAN SYSTEM OF PROVINCIAL ADMIN-ISTRATION TO THE ACCESSION OF CONSTANTINE THE GREAT. Being the Arnold Prize Essay for 1879. By W. T. Arnold, B.A. Crown 8vo. 6s.

Ball.—THE STUDENT'S GUIDE TO THE BAR. By WALTER W. BALL, M.A., of the Inner Temple, Barrister-at-Law. Crown 8vo. 2s. 6d.
" *The student will here find a clear statement of the several steps by which the degree of barrister is obtained, and also useful advice about the advantages of a prolonged course of 'reading in Chambers.'"*— ACADEMY.

Bernard.—FOUR LECTURES ON SUBJECTS CONNECTED WITH DIPLOMACY. By MONTAGUE BERNARD, M.A., Chichele Professor of International Law and Diplomacy, Oxford. 8vo. 9s.
"*Singularly interesting lectures, so able, clear, and attractive."*—SPEC-TATOR.

Bright (John, M.P.)—Works by the Right Hon. JOHN BRIGHT, M.P.
SPEECHES ON QUESTIONS OF PUBLIC POLICY. Edited by Professor THOROLD ROGERS. Author's Popular Edition. Globe 8vo. 3s. 6d.
" *Mr. Bright's speeches will always deserve to be studied, as an apprenticeship to popular and parliamentary oratory ; they will form materials for the history of our time, and many brilliant passages, perhaps some entire speeches, will really become a part of the living litera-ture of England."*—DAILY NEWS.

LIBRARY EDITION. Two Vols. 8vo. With Portrait. 25s.

PUBLIC ADDRESSES. Edited by J. THOROLD ROGERS. 8vo. 14s.

Bucknill.—HABITUAL DRUNKENNESS AND INSANE DRUNKARDS. By J. C. Bucknill, M.D., F.R.S., late Lord Chancellor's Visitor of Lunatics. Crown 8vo. 2s. 6d.

Cairnes.—Works by J. E. Cairnes, M.A., Emeritus Professor of Political Economy in University College, London.

ESSAYS IN POLITICAL ECONOMY, THEORETICAL and APPLIED. By J. E. Cairnes, M.A., Professor of Political Economy in University College, London. 8vo. 10s. 6d.

POLITICAL ESSAYS. 8vo. 10s. 6d.

SOME LEADING PRINCIPLES OF POLITICAL ECONOMY NEWLY EXPOUNDED. 8vo. 14s.

CONTENTS :—*Part I. Value. Part II. Labour and Capital. Part III. International Trade.*

" *A work which is perhaps the most valuable contribution to the science made since the publication, a quarter of a century since, of Mr. Mill's 'Principles of Political Economy.'*"—DAILY NEWS.

THE CHARACTER AND LOGICAL METHOD OF POLITICAL ECONOMY. New Edition, enlarged. 8vo. 7s. 6d.

" *These lectures are admirably fitted to correct the slipshod generalizations which pass current as the science of Political Economy.*"—TIMES.

Cobden (Richard).—SPEECHES ON QUESTIONS OF PUBLIC POLICY. By Richard Cobden. Edited by the Right Hon. John Bright, M.P., and J. E. Thorold Rogers. Popular Edition. 8vo. 3s. 6d.

Fawcett.—Works by Henry Fawcett, M.A., M.P., Fellow of Trinity Hall, and Professor of Political Economy in the University of Cambridge :—

THE ECONOMIC POSITION OF THE BRITISH LABOURER. Extra fcap. 8vo. 5s.

MANUAL OF POLITICAL ECONOMY. Fifth Edition, with New Chapters on the Depreciation of Silver, etc. Crown 8vo. 12s.

The DAILY NEWS *says:* "*It forms one of the best introductions to the principles of the science, and to its practical applications in the problems of modern, and especially of English, government and society.*"

PAUPERISM : ITS CAUSES AND REMEDIES. Crown 8vo. 5s. 6d.

The ATHENÆUM *calls the work* "*a repertory of interesting and well digested information.*"

SPEECHES ON SOME CURRENT POLITICAL QUESTIONS. 8vo. 10s. 6d.

" *They will help to educate, not perhaps, parties, but the educators of parties.*"—DAILY NEWS.

Fawcett.—*continued.*

FREE TRADE AND PROTECTION: an Inquiry into the Causes which have retarded the general adoption of Free Trade since its introduction into England. Third Edition. 8vo. 7s. 6d.

"*No greater service can be rendered to the cause of Free Trade than a clear explanation of the principles on which Free Trade rests. Professor Fawcett has done this in the volume before us with all his habitual clearness of thought and expression.*"—ECONOMIST.

ESSAYS ON POLITICAL AND SOCIAL SUBJECTS. By PROFESSOR FAWCETT, M.P., and MILLICENT GARRETT FAWCETT. 8vo. 10s. 6d.

"*They will all repay the perusal of the thinking reader.*"—DAILY NEWS.

Fawcett (Mrs.)—Works by MILLICENT GARRETT FAWCETT.

POLITICAL ECONOMY FOR BEGINNERS. WITH QUESTIONS. New Edition. 18mo. 2s. 6d.

The DAILY NEWS *calls it* "*clear, compact, and comprehensive;*" *and the* SPECTATOR *says,* "*Mrs. Fawcett's treatise is perfectly suited to its purpose.*"

TALES IN POLITICAL ECONOMY. Crown 8vo. 3s.

"*The idea is a good one, and it is quite wonderful what a mass of economic teaching the author manages to compress into a small space...The true doctrines of International Trade, Currency, and the ratio between Production and Population, are set before us and illustrated in a masterly manner.*"—ATHENÆUM.

Freeman (E. A.), M.A., D.C.L.—COMPARATIVE POLITICS. Lectures at the Royal Institution, to which is added "The Unity of History," being the Rede Lecture delivered at Cambridge in 1872. 8vo. 14s.

"*We find in Mr. Freeman's new volume the same sound, careful, comprehensive qualities which have long ago raised him to so high a place amongst historical writers. For historical discipline, then, as well as historical information, Mr. Freeman's book is full of value.*"—PALL MALL GAZETTE.

Goschen.—REPORTS AND SPEECHES ON LOCAL TAXATION. By GEORGE J. GOSCHEN, M.P. Royal 8vo. 5s.

"*The volume contains a vast mass of information of the highest value.*"—ATHENÆUM.

Guide to the Unprotected, in Every Day Matters Relating to Property and Income. By a BANKER'S DAUGHTER. Fourth Edition, Revised. Extra fcap. 8vo. 3s. 6d.

c

"Many an unprotected female will bless the head which planned and the hand which compiled this admirable little manual. . . . This book was very much wanted, and it could not have been better done."— MORNING STAR.

Hamilton.—MONEY AND VALUE: an Inquiry into the Means and Ends of Economic Production, with an Appendix on the Depreciation of Silver and Indian Currency. By ROWLAND HAMILTON. 8vo. 12s.

" The subject is here dealt with in a luminous style, and by presenting it from a new point of view in connection with the nature and functions of money, a genuine service has been rendered to commercial science."— BRITISH QUARTERLY REVIEW.

Harwood.—DISESTABLISHMENT: a Defence of the Principle of a National Church. By GEORGE HARWOOD, M.A. 8vo. 12s.

Hill.—OUR COMMON LAND; and other Short Essays. By OCTAVIA HILL. Extra fcap. 8vo. 3s. 6d.
CONTENTS:—*Our Common Land. District Visiting. A More Excellent Way of Charity. A Word on Good Citizenship. Open Spaces. Effectual Charity. The Future of our Commons.*

Historicus.—LETTERS ON SOME QUESTIONS OF INTERNATIONAL LAW. Reprinted from the *Times*, with considerable Additions. 8vo. 7s. 6d. Also, ADDITIONAL LETTERS. 8vo. 2s. 6d.

Holland.—THE TREATY RELATIONS OF RUSSIA AND TURKEY FROM 1774 TO 1853. A Lecture delivered at Oxford, April 1877. By T. E. HOLLAND, D.C.L., Professor of International Law and Diplomacy, Oxford. Crown 8vo. 2s.

Hughes (Thos.)—THE OLD CHURCH: WHAT SHALL WE DO WITH IT? By THOMAS HUGHES, Q.C. Crown 8vo. 6s.

Jevons.—Works by W. STANLEY JEVONS, M.A., Professor of Political Economy in University College, London. (For other Works by the same Author, *see* EDUCATIONAL and PHILOSOPHICAL CATALOGUES.)

THE THEORY OF POLITICAL ECONOMY. Second Edition, revised, with new Preface and Appendices. 8vo. 10s. 6d.
"Professor Jevons has done invaluable service by courageously claiming political economy to be strictly a branch of Applied Mathematics."—WESTMINSTER REVIEW.

PRIMER OF POLITICAL ECONOMY. 18mo. 1s.

Laveleye. — PRIMITIVE PROPERTY. By EMILE DE LAVELEYE. Translated by G. R. L. MARRIOTT, LL.B., with an Introduction by T. E. CLIFFE LESLIE, LL.B. 8vo. 12*s.*

" It is almost impossible to over-estimate the value of the well-digested knowledge which it contains ; it is one of the most learned books that have been contributed to the historical department of the literature of economic science."—ATHENÆUM.

Leading Cases done into English. By an APPRENTICE OF LINCOLN'S INN. Third Edition. Crown 8vo. 2*s.* 6*d.*

" Here is a rare treat for the lovers of quaint conceits, who in reading this charming little book will find enjoyment in the varied metre and graphic language in which the several tales are told, no less than in the accurate and pithy rendering of some of our most familiar 'Leading Cases.' "—SATURDAY REVIEW.

Lubbock.—ADDRESSES, POLITICAL AND EDUCA-TIONAL. By Sir JOHN LUBBOCK, Bart., M.P., &c., &c. 8vo, pp. 209. 8*s.* 6*d.*

The ten speeches given are (1) on the Imperial Policy of Great Britain, (2) on the Bank Act of 1844, (3) on the Present System of Public School Education, 1876, (4) on the Present System of Elementary Education, (5) on the Income Tax, (6) on the National Debt, (7) on the Declaration of Paris, (8) on Marine Insurances, (9) on the Preservation of Ancient Monuments, and (10) on Egypt.

Macdonell.—THE LAND QUESTION, WITH SPECIAL REFERENCE TO ENGLAND AND SCOTLAND. By JOHN MACDONELL, Barrister-at-Law. 8vo. 10*s.* 6*d.*

Marshall.—THE ECONOMICS OF INDUSTRY. By A. MARSHALL, M.A., Principal of University College, Bristol, and MARY PALEY MARSHALL, late Lecturer at Newnham Hall, Cambridge. Extra fcap. 8vo. 2*s.* 6*d.*

Martin.—THE STATESMAN'S YEAR-BOOK: A Statistical and Historical Annual of the States of the Civilized World, for the year 1880. By FREDERICK MARTIN. Seventeenth Annual Publication. Revised after Official Returns. Crown 8vo. 10*s.* 6*d.*

The Statesman's Year-Book is the only work in the English language which furnishes a clear and concise account of the actual condition of all the States of Europe, the civilized countries of America, Asia, and Africa, and the British Colonies and Dependencies in all parts of the world. The new issue of the work has been revised and corrected, on the basis of official reports received direct from the heads of the leading Govern-ments of the world, in reply to letters sent to them by the Editor. Through the valuable assistance thus given, it has been possible to collect an amount of information, political, statistical, and commercial, of the latest date, and of unimpeachable trustworthiness, such as no publication of the same kind has ever been able to furnish. "*As indispensable as Bradshaw.*"— TIMES.

Monahan.—THE METHOD OF LAW: an Essay on the Statement and Arrangement of the Legal Standard of Conduct. By J. H. MONAHAN, Q.C. Crown 8vo. 6s.

"*Will be found valuable by careful law students who have felt the importance of gaining clear ideas regarding the relations between the parts of the complex organism they have to study.*"—BRITISH QUARTERLY REVIEW.

Paterson.—THE LIBERTY OF THE SUBJECT AND THE LAWS OF ENGLAND RELATING TO THE SECURITY OF THE PERSON. Commentaries on. By JAMES PATERSON, M.A., Barrister at Law, sometime Commissioner for English and Irish Fisheries, etc. Cheaper issue. Two Vols. Crown 8vo. 21s.

"*Two or three hours' dipping into these volumes, not to say reading them through, will give legislators and stump orators a knowledge of the liberty of a citizen of their country, in its principles, its fulness, and its modification, such as they probably in nine cases out of ten never had before.*" —SCOTSMAN.

Phillimore.—PRIVATE LAW AMONG THE ROMANS, from the Pandects. By JOHN GEORGE PHILLIMORE, Q.C. 8vo. 16s.

Rogers.—COBDEN AND POLITICAL OPINION. By J. E. THOROLD ROGERS. 8vo. 10s. 6d.

"*Will be found most useful by politicians of every school, as it forms a sort of handbook to Cobden's teaching.*"—ATHENÆUM.

Stephen (C. E.)—THE SERVICE OF THE POOR; Being an Inquiry into the Reasons for and against the Establishment of Religious Sisterhoods for Charitable Purposes. By CAROLINE EMILIA STEPHEN. Crown 8vo. 6s. 6d.

"*The ablest advocate of a better line of work in this direction that we have ever seen.*"—EXAMINER.

Stephen.—Works by Sir JAMES F. STEPHEN, K.C.S.I., Q.C.

A DIGEST OF THE LAW OF EVIDENCE. Third Edition with New Preface. Crown 8vo. 6s.

A DIGEST OF THE CRIMINAL LAW. (Crimes and Punishments.) 8vo. 16s.

"*We feel sure that any person of ordinary intelligence who had never looked into a law-book in his life might, by a few days' careful study of*

Stephen.—*continued.*

this volume, obtain a more accurate understanding of the criminal law, a more perfect conception of its different bearings, a more thorough and intelligent insight into its snares and pitfalls, than an ordinary practitioner can boast of after years of study of the ordinary text-books and practical experience of the Courts unassisted by any competent guide."—SATURDAY REVIEW.

A GENERAL VIEW OF THE CRIMINAL LAW OF ENG-LAND. Two Vols. Crown 8vo.   [*New edition in the press.*

Stubbs.—VILLAGE POLITICS. Addresses and Sermons on the Labour Question. By C. W. STUBBS, M.A., Vicar of Granborough, Bucks. Extra fcap. 8vo.   3s. 6d.

Thornton.—Works by W. T. THORNTON, C.B., Secretary for Public Works in the India Office :—

ON LABOUR : Its Wrongful Claims and Rightful Dues ; Its Actual Present and Possible Future. Second Edition, revised, 8vo. 14s.

A PLEA FOR PEASANT PROPRIETORS : With the Outlines of a Plan for their Establishment in Ireland. New Edition, revised. Crown 8vo. 7s. 6d.

INDIAN PUBLIC WORKS AND COGNATE INDIAN TOPICS. With Map of Indian Railways. Crown 8vo. 8s. 6d.

Walker.—Works by F. A. WALKER, M.A., Ph.D., Professor of Political Economy and History, Yale College :—

THE WAGES QUESTION. A Treatise on Wages and the Wages Class. 8vo. 14s.

MONEY. 8vo. 16s.

" *It is painstaking, laborious, and states the question in a clear and very intelligible form. . . . The volume possesses a great value as a sort of encyclopædia of knowledge on the subject.*"—ECONOMIST.

MONEY IN ITS RELATIONS TO TRADE AND INDUSTRY. Crown 8vo.   [*Shortly.*

Work about the Five Dials. With an Introductory Note by THOMAS CARLYLE. Crown 8vo. 6s.

" *A book which abounds with wise and practical suggestions.*"—PALL MALL GAZETTE.

WORKS CONNECTED WITH THE SCIENCE OR THE HISTORY OF LANGUAGE.

Abbott.—A SHAKESPERIAN GRAMMAR : An Attempt to illustrate some of the Differences between Elizabethan and Modern English. By the Rev. E. A. ABBOTT, D.D., Head Master of the City of London School. New and Enlarged Edition. Extra fcap. 8vo. 6s.

"*Valuable not only as an aid to the critical study of Shakespeare, but as tending to familiarize the reader with Elizabethan English in general.*"—ATHENÆUM.

Breymann.—A FRENCH GRAMMAR BASED ON PHILO-LOGICAL PRINCIPLES. By HERMANN BREYMANN, Ph.D., Professor of Philology in the University of Munich late Lecturer on French Language and Literature at Owens College, Manchester. Extra fcap. 8vo. 4s. 6d.

Ellis.—PRACTICAL HINTS ON THE QUANTITATIVE PRONUNCIATION OF LATIN, FOR THE USE OF CLASSICAL TEACHERS AND LINGUISTS. By A. J. ELLIS, B.A., F.R.S., &c. Extra fcap. 8vo. 4s. 6d.

Fleay.—A SHAKESPEARE MANUAL. By the Rev. F. G. FLEAY, M.A., Head Master of Skipton Grammar School. Extra fcap. 8vo. 4s. 6d,

Goodwin.—Works by W. W. GOODWIN, Professor of Greek Literature in Harvard University.

SYNTAX OF THE GREEK MOODS AND TENSES. New Edition. Crown 8vo. 6s. 6d.

AN ELEMENTARY GREEK GRAMMAR. Crown 8vo. 6s.

"*It is the best Greek Grammar of its size in the English language.*"—ATHENÆUM.

Hadley.—ESSAYS PHILOLOGICAL AND CRITICAL. Selected from the Papers of JAMES HADLEY, LL.D., Professor of Greek in Yale College, &c. 8vo. 16s.

Hales.—LONGER ENGLISH POEMS. With Notes, Philological and Explanatory, and an Introduction on the Teaching of English. Chiefly for use in Schools. Edited by J. W. HALES, M.A., Professor of English Literature at King's College, London, &c. &c. Fifth Edition. Extra fcap. 8vo. 4s. 6d.

Helfenstein (James).—A COMPARATIVE GRAMMAR OF THE TEUTONIC LANGUAGES : Being at the same time a Historical Grammar of the English Language, and comprising Gothic, Anglo-Saxon, Early English, Modern English, Icelandic (Old Norse), Danish, Swedish, Old High German, Middle High German, Modern German, Old Saxon, Old Frisian, and Dutch. By JAMES HELFENSTEIN, Ph.D. 8vo. 18s.

Masson (Gustave).—A COMPENDIOUS DICTIONARY OF THE FRENCH LANGUAGE (French-English and English-French). Followed by a List of the Principal Diverging Derivations, and preceded by Chronological and Historical Tables. By GUSTAVE MASSON, Assistant-Master and Librarian, Harrow School. Fourth Edition. Crown 8vo. Half-bound. 6s.

"*A book which any student, whatever may be the degree of his advancement in the language, would do well to have on the table close at hand while he is reading.*"—SATURDAY REVIEW.

Mayor.—A BIBLIOGRAPHICAL CLUE TO LATIN LITERATURE. Edited after Dr. E. HUBNER. With large Additions by JOHN E. B. MAYOR, M.A., Professor of Latin in the University of Cambridge. Crown 8vo. 6s. 6d.

"*An extremely useful volume that should be in the hands of all scholars.*"—ATHENÆUM.

Morris.—Works by the Rev. RICHARD MORRIS, LL.D., Member of the Council of the Philol. Soc., Lecturer on English Language and Literature in King's College School, Editor of "Specimens of Early English," etc., etc. :—

HISTORICAL OUTLINES OF ENGLISH ACCIDENCE, comprising Chapters on the History and Development of the Language, and on Word-formation. Sixth Edition. Fcap. 8vo. 6s.

ELEMENTARY LESSONS IN HISTORICAL ENGLISH GRAMMAR, containing Accidence and Word-formation. Third Edition. 18mo. 2s. 6d.

Oliphant.—THE OLD AND MIDDLE ENGLISH. By T. L. KINGTON OLIPHANT, M.A., of Balliol College, Oxford. A New Edition, revised and greatly enlarged, of "The Sources of Standard English." Extra fcap. 8vo. 9s.

"*Mr. Oliphant's book is to our mind, one of the ablest and most scholarly contributions to our standard English we have seen for many years.*"—SCHOOL BOARD CHRONICLE. "*The book comes nearer to a history of the English language than anything we have seen since such a history could be written, without confusion and contradictions.*"—SATURDAY REVIEW.

Peile (John, M.A.)—AN INTRODUCTION TO GREEK AND LATIN ETYMOLOGY. By JOHN PEILE, M.A., Fellow and Tutor of Christ's College, Cambridge. Third and revised Edition. Crown 8vo. 10s. 6d.

"The book may be accepted as a very valuable contribution to the science of language."—SATURDAY REVIEW.

Philology.—THE JOURNAL OF SACRED AND CLASSICAL PHILOLOGY. Four Vols. 8vo. 12s. 6d. each.

THE JOURNAL OF PHILOLOGY. New Series. Edited by JOHN E. B. MAYOR, M.A., and W. ALDIS WRIGHT, M.A. 4s. 6d. (Half-yearly.)

Roby (H. J.)—A GRAMMAR OF THE LATIN LANGUAGE, FROM PLAUTUS TO SUETONIUS. By HENRY JOHN ROBY, M.A., late Fellow of St. John's College, Cambridge. In Two Parts. Second Edition. Part I. containing :—Book I. Sounds. Book II. Inflexions. Book III. Word Formation. Appendices. Crown 8vo. 8s. 6d. Part II.—Syntax, Prepositions, &c. Crown 8vo. 10s. 6d.

"The book is marked by the clear and practical insight of a master in his art. It is a book which would do honour to any country."—ATHENÆUM. *"Brings before the student in a methodical form the best results of modern philology bearing on the Latin language."*—SCOTSMAN.

Schmidt.—THE RYTHMIC AND METRIC OF THE CLASSICAL LANGUAGES. To which are added, the Lyric Parts of the "Medea" of Euripides and the "Antigone" of Sophocles; with Rhythmical Scheme and Commentary. By Dr. J. H. SCHMIDT. Translated from the German by J. W. WHITE, D.D. 8vo. 10s. 6d.

Taylor.—Works by the Rev. ISAAC TAYLOR, M.A.:—

ETRUSCAN RESEARCHES. With Woodcuts. 8vo. 14s.

The TIMES *says :*—*" The learning and industry displayed in this volume deserve the most cordial recognition. The ultimate verdict of science we shall not attempt to anticipate ; but we can safely say this, that it is a learned book which the unlearned can enjoy, and that in the descriptions of the tomb-builders, as well as in the marvellous coincidences and unexpected analogies brought together by the author, readers of every grade may take delight as well as philosophers and scholars."*

WORDS AND PLACES ; or, Etymological Illustrations of History, Ethnology, and Geography. By the Rev. ISAAC TAYLOR. Third Edition, revised and compressed. With Maps. Globe 8vo. 6s.

GREEKS AND GOTHS : a Study on the Runes. 8vo. 9s.

Trench.—Works by R. CHENEVIX TRENCH, D.D., Archbishop of Dublin. (For other Works by the same Author, *see* THEOLOGICAL CATALOGUE.)

SYNONYMS OF THE NEW TESTAMENT. Eighth Edition, enlarged. 8vo, cloth. 12*s.*

"He is," the ATHENÆUM *says, "a guide in this department of knowledge to whom his readers may entrust themselves with confidence."*

ON THE STUDY OF WORDS. Lectures Addressed (originally) to the Pupils at the Diocesan Training School, Winchester. Seventeenth Edition, enlarged. Fcap. 8vo. 5*s.*

ENGLISH PAST AND PRESENT. Tenth Edition, revised and improved. Fcap. 8vo. 5*s.*

A SELECT GLOSSARY OF ENGLISH WORDS USED FORMERLY IN SENSES DIFFERENT FROM THEIR PRESENT. Fifth Edition, enlarged. Fcap. 8vo. 5*s.*

Vincent and Dickson.—A HANDBOOK TO MODERN GREEK. By EDGAR VINCENT and T. G. DICKSON. Extra fcap. 8vo. 5*s.*

Whitney.—A COMPENDIOUS GERMAN GRAMMAR. By W. D. WHITNEY, Professor of Sanskrit and Instructor in Modern Languages in Yale College. Crown 8vo. 6*s.*

" After careful examination we are inclined to pronounce it the best grammar of modern language we have ever seen."—SCOTSMAN.

Whitney and Edgren.—A COMPENDIOUS GERMAN AND ENGLISH DICTIONARY, with Notation of Correspondences and Brief Etymologies. By Professor W. D. WHITNEY, assisted by A. H. EDGREN. Crown 8vo. 7*s.* 6*d.*

The GERMAN-ENGLISH Part may be had separately. Price 5*s.*

Yonge.—HISTORY OF CHRISTIAN NAMES. By CHARLOTTE M. YONGE, Author of "The Heir of Redclyffe." Cheaper Edition. Two Vols. Crown 8vo. 12*s.*

ENGLISH MEN OF LETTERS.

Edited by JOHN MORLEY.

A Series of Short Books to tell people what is best worth knowing to the Life, Character, and Works of some of the great English Writers.

ENGLISH MEN OF LETTERS.—JOHNSON. By LESLIE STEPHEN.

"The new series opens well with Mr. Leslie Stephen's sketch of Dr. Johnson. It could hardly have been done better, and it will convey to the readers for whom it is intended a juster estimate of Johnson than either of the two essays of Lord Macaulay."—*Pall Mall Gazette*

ENGLISH MEN OF LETTERS.—SCOTT. By R. H. HUTTON.

"The tone of the volume is excellect throughout."—*Athenæum.*

"We could not wish for a more suggestive introduction to Scott and his poems and novels."—*Examiner*.

ENGLISH MEN OF LETTERS.—GIBBON. By J. C. MORISON.

"As a clear, thoughtful, and attractive record of the life and works of the greatest among the world's historians, it deserves the highest praise."—*Examiner*.

ENGLISH MEN OF LETTERS.—SHELLEY. By J. A. SYMONDS.

"The lovers of this great poet are to be congratulated on having at their command so fresh, clear, and intelligent a presentment of the subject, written by a man of adequate and wide culture."—*Athenæum.*

ENGLISH MEN OF LETTERS.—HUME. By Professor HUXLEY.

"It may fairly be said that no one now living could have expounded Hume with more sympathy or with equal perspicuity."—*Athenæum.*

ENGLISH MEN OF LETTERS. —GOLDSMITH. By WILLIAM BLACK.

"Mr. Black brings a fine sympathy and taste to bear in his criticism of Goldsmith's writings, as well as in his sketch of the incidents of his life."—*Athenæum.*

ENGLISH MEN OF LETTERS.—DEFOE. By W. MINTO.

"Mr. Minto's book is careful and accurate in all that is stated, and faithful in all that it suggests. It will repay reading more than once."—*Athenæum.*

ENGLISH MEN OF LETTERS—*Continued.*

ENGLISH MEN OF LETTERS.—BURNS. By Principal SHAIRP, Professor of Poetry in the University of Oxford.

" It is impossible to desire fairer criticism than Principal Shairp's on Burns's poetry. . . . . None of the series has given a truer estimate either of character or of genius than this little volume. . . . and all who read it will be thoroughly grateful to the author for this monument to the genius of Scotland's greatest poet."—*Spectator.*

ENGLISH MEN OF LETTERS.—SPENSER. By the Very Rev. the DEAN OF ST. PAUL'S.

" Dr. Church is master of his subject, and writes always with good taste."—*Academy.*

ENGLISH MEN OF LETTERS.—THACKERAY. By ANTHONY TROLLOPE.

" Mr. Trollope's sketch is exceedingly adapted to fulfil the purpose of the series in which it appears."—*Athenæum.*

ENGLISH MEN OF LETTERS. — BURKE. By JOHN MORLEY.

" Perhaps the best criticism yet published on the life and character of Burke is contained in Mr. Morley's compendious biography. His style is vigorous and polished, and both his political and personal judgment and his literary criticisms are just, generous, subtle, and in a high degree interesting."—*Saturday Review.*

Just ready.

MILTON. By MARK PATTISON.

In preparation.

HAWTHORNE. By HENRY JAMES.

SOUTHEY. By Professor DOWDEN.

CHAUCER. By Professor WARD.

COWPER. By GOLDWIN SMITH.

BUNYAN. By J. A. FROUDE.

WORDSWORTH. By F. W. H. MYERS.

Others in preparation.

MACMILLAN AND CO., LONDON

LONDON:

R. CLAY, SONS, AND TAYLOR, PRINTERS,

BREAD STREET HILL.

www.ingramcontent.com/pod-product-compliance
Lightning Source LLC
Chambersburg PA
CBHW022256280326
41932CB00010B/884